Imperial Subjects as
Global Citizens

Asia World

Series editor: Mark Selden

This series charts the frontiers of Asia in global perspective. Central to its concerns are Asian interactions—political, economic, social, cultural, and historical—that are transnational and global, that cross and redefine borders and networks, including those of nation, region, ethnicity, gender, technology, and demography. It looks to multiple methodologies to chart the dynamics of a region that has been the home to major civilizations and is central to global processes of war, peace, and development in the new millennium.

Titles in the Series

Imperial Subjects as Global Citizens

Nationalism, Internationalism, and Education in Japan

Mark Lincicome

LEXINGTON BOOKS

A division of
ROWMAN & LITTLEFIELD PUBLISHERS, INC.
Lanham • Boulder • New York • Toronto • Plymouth, UK

LEXINGTON BOOKS

A division of Rowman & Littlefield Publishers, Inc.
A wholly owned subsidary of The Rowman & Littlefield Publishing Group, Inc.
4501 Forbes Boulevard, Suite 200
Lanham, MD 20706

Estover Road
Plymouth PL6 7PY
United Kingdom

British Library Cataloguing in Publication Information Available

Library of Congress Cataloging-in-Publication Data

Lincicome, Mark Elwood, 1953–
  Imperial subjects as global citizens: nationalism, internationalism, and education in
Japan / Mark Lincicome.
      p. cm. — (AsiaWorld)
  Includes bibliographical references and index.
  ISBN-13: 978-0-7391-3113-8 (cloth: alk. paper)
  ISBN-10: 0-7391-3113-3 (cloth: alk. paper)
  ISBN-13: 978-0-7391-3114-5 (pbk.: alk. paper)
  ISBN-10: 0-7391-3114-1 (pbk.: alk. paper)
  ISBN-13: 978-0-7391-3115-2 (e-book)
  ISBN-10: 0-7391-3115-X (e-book)
  1. Education and state—Japan. 2. Nationalism and education—Japan. 3. International
education—Japan. I. Title.
  LC94.J3L56 2009
  379.52—dc22

                                                         2008044671

Printed in the United States of America

⊗™ The paper used in this publication meets the minimum requirements of American
National Standard for Information Sciences—Permanence of Paper for Printed Library
Materials, ANSI/NISO Z39.48–1992.

For Mayumi

Contents

Acknowledgments

Having spent the past seventeen years working at a small liberal arts college in the United States, where heavy teaching and service responsibilities constantly vie with scholarly research for a faculty member's time, this book project has taken a good deal longer to complete than I anticipated. Without the support and assistance of numerous individuals and institutions along the way, the manuscript would still be languishing somewhere in my "current projects" file drawer.

Recognizing that faculty teaching and scholarship go hand in hand, the College of the Holy Cross helped to make this book possible by providing a two-semester research leave in 2001–2002, a two-semester sabbatical leave in 2006–2007, and research funds courtesy of an Arthur J. O'Leary Faculty Award. Complimenting this financial assistance was the moral support I received from my colleagues in the Department of History.

Additional funding to conduct research in Japan was provided through generous grants from the Social Science Research Council, the Japan Foundation, and the Fulbright Scholar Program, which is administered in Tokyo by the United States-Japan Educational Commission.

In Japan, two scholars deserve special thanks for rendering various forms of assistance whenever I asked for it. Nakano Akira, Professor Emeritus at Chuo University, took an early interest in my research, directed me to relevant historical documents, and shared with me his own prolific writings on the Taishō-era liberal education (*jiyū kyōiku*) movement and on educational reformers like Sawayanagi Masatarō and Shimonaka Yasaburō. Long-time friend Igarashi Akio managed, on several occasions, to persuade his institution, Rikkyō University, to grant me visiting faculty status—complete with on-campus housing and library privileges—and invited me to present my research to multi-national audiences of scholars who gathered at Rikkyō for

ix

workshops held under the auspices of Igarashi's ambitious Asian Studies Frontier Research Project.

In addition to the staff members at the Rikkyō University Library, I am indebted to their counterparts at the following institutions in Japan: Tokyo University, including the Faculty of Education and the Meiji Shinbun Zasshi Bunko; Chūō University; Waseda University; the National Institute for Educational Policy Research; Tōsho Bunko; and the Seijō Gakuen Kyōiku Kenkyūjo, especially Ms. Iwami Hisako. For permission to reprint photographs of their archived materials I wish to thank: the National Institute for Educational Policy Research; Meiji Shinbun Zasshi Bunko; Seijō Gakuen Kyōiku Kenkyūjo; and the Heibonsha Publishing Company, especially Shimonaka Mito, Executive Editor and granddaughter of Heibonsha's founder, Shimonaka Yasaburō.

Mark Selden read the entire manuscript with a practiced eye and offered many suggestions to improve both form and content. Susan McEachern, Senior Editor at Rowman and Littlefield, and Patrick Dillon, former Acquisitions Editor at Lexington Books, were early supporters of the publication project, while Patrick's successor, Michael Sisskin, has patiently guided me through the process.

Last, but not least, thanks are due to friends and family members who coaxed me to "keep plugging away" during the on-again, off-again writing phase. Fellow Asianists Mark Caprio, Alexis Dudden and Douglas Howland helped me get off to a good start by offering encouragement and good humor during our overlapping residence at Rikkyō. Back at home in the US, my wife Mayumi patiently advised me on questions concerning Japanese-to-English translation, and proofread the entire manuscript. Any errors that remain are my responsibility.

This book is dedicated to Mayumi, whose battle against cancer two years ago, and whose subsequent determination to return to a "normal life" under abnormal circumstances, has been a source of inspiration to family and friends alike.

August 25, 2008
Worcester, Massachusetts

Note on Japanese Names and Terms

Japanese personal names appear in the customary order, family name first, except for persons of Japanese ancestry whose names commonly appear in the reverse order, e.g., Akira Iriye, Kyoko Inoue. Macrons have been eliminated from proper nouns and other terms that usually appear in English without them, e.g., Tokyo, Kyoto.

Introduction

By February 1999, patience had worn thin at the Hiroshima Prefecture Board of Education. Nearly a decade had passed since Japan's Ministry of Education (MOE)[1] mandated that schools fly the Hinomaru flag and sing the Kimigayo anthem at all official ceremonies. Yet, with the end of the school year rapidly approaching, Hiroshima officials faced the likelihood that some primary and secondary school teachers would continue to boycott the MOE's directive during the upcoming graduation exercises, following the lead of the local branch of the Japan Teachers Union (Nihon Kyōshokuin Kumiai, or Nikkyōso; hereafter JTU).[2] Whereas the MOE contends that the flag and the anthem help to instill a healthy sense of national pride and patriotism in Japanese youth, the union has long argued that they remain potent symbols of the militarism and imperialism that propelled Japan into a disastrous war in the 1930s and a humiliating defeat by 1945. From the union's perspective, the MOE's unilateral order to reinstate these symbols in the schools is not simply another in a long series of attempts to expand its authority over Japanese education. It is also seen as another assault upon the democratic, pacifist spirit of the postwar constitution by conservative politicians, bureaucrats, and right-wing groups determined to steer the nation back toward militarism.[3]

Opposition between the MOE and the JTU has been a regular feature of Japanese education since the union was established in 1947, so it is unlikely that either the media or the public would have been surprised by the boycott or by the board of education's directive on February 23, ordering all school principals in the prefecture to comply with the MOE's longstanding regulation. Even veteran observers were shocked, however, when the principal at one high school took his own life five days later; just one day before his school was to conduct its commencement exercises. The story received national media coverage and caused a public outcry. The local union objected that the national media unfairly blamed his suicide upon its refusal to compromise on the issue of the flag and the anthem, and it scrambled to garner public support for its position over the next several months.[4] After all, it was the MOE that, in 1991, began to discipline principals of schools that resisted this directive, creating an untenable situation in which principals "would be punished by their superiors if they did not comply with the regulations, but they would meet with resistance and disruption [from teachers] if they did."[5] However, the damage to the local union's cause had already been done. Riding the initial wave of government- and media-orchestrated public disgust at the union, conservative members of the Japanese Diet wasted no time in passing legislation that granted legal recognition to the Hinomaru and Kimigayo as the country's "national" flag and anthem, respectively.[6]

The tragedy surrounding this incident (which, depending upon one's point of view, includes not only the fate of the hapless school principal but the Diet's opportunistic legal maneuver, as well) is made even more poignant by the irony accompanying it. For, according to one account at least, this sequence of events can be traced back to one man's successful crusade to instill a "healthy" (*kenzen*) nationalism in Japanese schools and society. That man was Nakasone Yasuhiro, during his tenure as prime minister (1982–1987).[7]

Nakasone's bid to promote his healthy nationalism was part of a broader campaign to reform Japanese education, which began in 1984 with a highly publicized political maneuver that was nearly unprecedented in the postwar history of Japanese education. For the first time since the Allied Occupation, he established—with parliamentary approval—an Ad Hoc Council on Education (Rinji Kyōiku Shingikai) under the prime minister's direct control, in an attempt to circumvent the notoriously conservative MOE. During the next three years, the Council—composed of representatives from business and industry, organized labor, and all levels of the educational system—carried out its mandate to review existing government policies and educational practices and make recommendations for their reform, although not without interference by the Ministry, and even by certain politicians in Nakasone's own Liberal Democratic Party. Its findings, published in a series of four reports between 1985 and 1987, attracted considerable publicity at the time, inasmuch as they were supposed to outline a broad program of educational reform that would prepare Japan to face the challenges of the twenty-first century.

The composition and deliberations of the Ad Hoc Council, the content of its reports and recommendations, its impact upon the concurrent education reform campaign involving the MOE and other interest groups, and the outcome of that campaign have all been analyzed in various books and periodicals by Japanese and non-Japanese scholars alike, most of them published shortly after the committee concluded its work. The verdict, in all cases, depends upon which of these studies one chooses to believe. The first and most widely read English-language monograph, by Leonard Schoppa, appeared in 1991. Schoppa's aim was not to contribute to knowledge of Japanese education, per se. Rather, he approached this reform campaign as a case study of the policy-making process in Japan; or, to be more precise, as a glaring example of "immobilism" by a government known for its earlier policy successes in sectors ranging from industry and trade to environmental protection and defense.[8]

Schoppa's characterization of Japan's education reform process as immobilist has not gone unchallenged. At least two subsequent monographs claim that the campaign launched by the government in the 1980s achieved tangible results in the 1990s. Marie Roesgaard contends that the dearth of new education laws passed by the Japanese Diet in the wake of the Ad Hoc Council's deliberations is not an accurate measure of its impact. Rather, it is the MOE that has guided and sustained the implementation phase by unilaterally issuing administrative guidelines. "Seen in this light the educational system is in fact undergoing a lot of change and though Diet politics may be static, the Ministry of Education policies are quite active."[9] Christopher Hood parts company with both authors, declaring that Nakasone himself "has set the trajectory and policy agenda for the future. . . . For Nakasone did manage to influence the education reform debate, the reforms were not a failure, and those involved in the education reform debate are not totally divided on the direction for future changes."[10]

Hood looks beyond the policymaking process itself to examine the impact of the ensuing reforms upon educational content and practice, as do a small number of journal articles and individual book chapters published in English.[11] However, the most extensive treatment of this facet of the reform movement has come from Japanese scholars and critics, some of whom write from a "progressive" or "leftist" ideological orientation. These writers assail Nakasone and the members of the Ad Hoc Council on Education for pushing an educational agenda that is nationalistic, militaristic, capitalistic, and elitist. Typical of this group is Horio Teruhisa, who charges that the Council members

> have sought to dramatically alter the meaning of "Japan's modernization," to shift the focus of attention from a program designed to help Japan "catch up with the West" to one which will make it possible for the nation to finally overcome and surpass the West. Shifting the focus of attention in this manner certainly serves to place even greater emphasis upon the cultivation of those elites who will be responsible for leading the Japanese into the forefront of the post-industrialized world, because it is only these elites, the argument goes, who will be able to manage society's needs for new and ever greater amounts of

information. . . . Thus it must be remembered that the various debates on school reform which seek to "liberalize" or "diversify" education are in reality little more than attempts to streamline the cultivation of elites as the cornerstone of our nation's educational system.[12]

Having spent their professional careers railing against what they see as bureaucratic assaults by the MOE upon postwar Japan's hard-won democratic principles of equality of educational opportunity, respect for the individual, intellectual freedom, local control of schools, and teacher autonomy, they tend to take a similar view of the work of Nakasone's Ad Hoc Council, in spite of the documented disagreements between the Council and the MOE over various reform proposals. Occasionally, this has prompted them to advocate positions that may seem paradoxical. For example, as indicated by Horio's remarks, they oppose the Council's calls to "liberalize" (*jiyūka*) the process through which middle school graduates apply for admission to high school (which is not compulsory in Japan) and to diversify the types of high schools available to students, fearing that these innovations will encourage academic tracking, emphasize vocational training and careerism over "whole-person" education, and promote elitism and social inequality.[13]

Of course, the Ad Hoc Council on Education also has its share of Japanese supporters, including its erstwhile rival, the MOE. Not surprisingly, however, the MOE devotes more space and plaudits in its publications to its own role in devising and implementing specific policies based upon the Council's recommendations, rather than dwelling on the work of the Council itself.[14]

Collectively, these monographs, articles, and reports offer a wealth of information, insights, and contrasting opinions regarding the 1980s education reform campaign. Nevertheless, by applying a different methodology and asking a different set of questions, there is still more to be learned from this event about the interplay of ideology, politics and power in Japanese education. Accordingly, for reasons that are explained below, this study adopts an approach that is narrower than its predecessors in one respect, yet broader in another. It is narrower because rather than undertake a comprehensive examination of the entire reform agenda, it concentrates on the issue that prompted Nakasone's call for a healthy nationalism and the MOE's order to reintroduce the symbols of Japanese nationalism in the schools. It is broader because rather than concentrate exclusively upon the 1980s reform proposals and ensuing policy pronouncements, it incorporates a much longer historical perspective, ranging from the late nineteenth century to the new millennium.

COPING WITH INTERNATIONALIZATION

Among the eight major issues that the Ad Hoc Council on Education identified for special consideration, one of the few that reportedly achieved a broad consensus among its own membership, and even won support among rival policymakers, was "coping with internationalization" (*kokusaika e no taiō*).[15] Beyond this circle of elite policymakers, however, consensus dissipated as other interest groups began to debate the meaning, purpose, and pedagogical implications of coping with internationalization through the Council's strategy for "internationalizing education" (*kyōiku no kokusaika*). Some progressive intellectuals viewed the council's initiative to internationalize Japanese education as another battle in a long-running ideological struggle waged by reactionary conservatives. Others, including some local education officials, university administrators, and school principals, were less concerned about ideology than about how to interpret and respond to the resulting policy directives without undermining the status quo. And among teachers and students, especially those caught in the grind of preparing for high school and college entrance examinations, many were ambivalent about the goals of this internationalization movement and skeptical about its prospects for success.

As the phrase "coping with internationalization" suggests, the Ad Hoc Council's recommendations for internationalizing Japanese education were made in response to a process of fundamental economic and cultural change that was understood to be well underway in Japan. Through education this process could, it was hoped, be brought under greater control and directed toward specific goals. Hence, the movement to internationalize Japanese education has involved forming and disseminating an ideology that, if successful, would result in the identification of a commonly accepted set of values, goals, social practices and social relations. But, as Michael Apple explains, the process of ideological production and reproduction that takes place through education does not go uncontested. The school is not merely an agent through which the ruling classes unilaterally impose a dominant ideology, and thus maintain the state's hegemony over the governed. Rather, the school, like the state itself, is a site where different classes or interest groups regularly engage in ideological struggles over meaning, values, and principles. Dominant ideologies are thus products of compromise. "By integrating varied ideological elements from differing and often contending groups around its [the state's] own unifying principles, consensus can be gained and the sense that practices based on these hegemonic principles actually help these contending groups can be maintained."[16]

Nakasone clearly recognized the ideological dimensions of this campaign and willingly led the crusade. According to Hood, Nakasone's "healthy" (*kenzen*) or "justifiable" (*tadashii*) nationalism was a deliberate attempt to reconcile nationalism and internationalism, in contrast to the state-centered "*kokkashugi* type of nationalism" that is blamed for the intensification of Japanese militarism and imperialism during the 1930s and early 1940s.[17] However, Nakasone's critics have rejected this claim and accompanying reform initiatives, as the events in Hiroshima in 1999 demonstrate. They see little difference between the MOE's assertion of authority in 1990 over the use of the Hinomaru and Kimigayo in the schools, and its systematic assertion of authority over school rituals, curricula and textbooks, teacher training and conduct, and most every other facet of Japanese education throughout the period when *kokkashugi* was prevalent. Even the principal's suicide in Hiroshima conjures up associations with the past: a poignant reminder that the excesses of *kokkashugi* also created martyrs among an earlier generation of school principals, who were idolized for sacrificing their lives in vain attempts to rescue the Emperor's portrait or the sacred copy of the Imperial Rescript on Education from school buildings besieged by fires or earthquakes.[18] Yamashina Saburō also evokes historical precedent to mount a sweeping condemnation of Nakasone's educational reform initiative: drawing ominous parallels between the formation of Nakasone's Ad Hoc Council and the creation of an Ad Hoc Conference on Education (Rinji Kyōiku Kaigi) by Prime Minister Terauchi Masatake and his cabinet in 1917, whose policy recommendations Yamashina and other Japanese scholars blame for the systematic militarization of Japanese schools beginning in the 1920s.[19]

Resistance to government measures like this one does not mean that opponents such as the teachers unions or progressive academicians reject the notion of internationalizing Japanese education, per se. Rather, it signals their rejection of Nakasone's "healthy nationalism," which they regard as the antithesis of genuine internationalization: in their words, it is *kokusuika* (Japanism) masquerading as *kokusaika* (internationalism).[20] In order to counter this ideological and political offensive, they advocate what they insist is a different definition of internationalization: consisting of radically different aims, and a radically different program of educational reforms to achieve those aims.

COPING WITH HISTORY

From these examples it is clear that history frequently informs this ideological and political debate over nationalism, internationalization, and education reform in Japan. But just how well informed about Japanese history are the various parties to this debate?

According to Hood, what distinguishes Nakasone's healthy nationalism from the *kokkashugi* variety that has been implicated in the Asia-Pacific War is the former's conciliatory posture toward internationalism. To illustrate this attribute of healthy nationalism Hood quotes from a 1987 tract by Nakasone, published by his Liberal Democratic Party, titled *My Political Philosophy*:

> It is important that we unite in peace and culture around the Emperor, that we contribute culturally, politically, and economically to the rest of the world, that we join together with other nations in seriously considering these issues, and that we share our prosperity with the rest of the global community. Yet we cannot do any of this unless we are also confident of our own identity. A nationalism that endeavors to foster self-identity in this sense is a completely justifiable nationalism. And we must teach this through education.[21]

However, closer examination of Japanese history reveals that Nakasone's commitment "to reconcile nationalism and internationalism," in and of itself, does not distinguish his healthy nationalism from *kokkashugi* and its proponents earlier in the century. Apart from his provocative decision to resume official visits to Yasukuni Shrine for the first time since 1945, where he and members of his cabinet worshipped the 2,466,000 *kami* (spirits) of those "who made [the] ultimate sacrifice for their nation since 1853 during national crises such as the Boshin War, the Seinan War, the Sino-Japanese and Russo-Japanese wars, World War I, the Manchurian Incident, the China Incident and the Greater East Asian War (World War II),"[22] Nakasone's declaration of the need to "contribute culturally, politically, and economically to the rest of the world" as proud and confident Japanese, united around the Emperor, echoes sentiments expressed by members of an earlier generation of politicians, business leaders, intellectuals, and educators. Prominent among them was Ōkuma Shigenobu: influential member of the early Meiji government, founder of Waseda University, founder and president of the powerful Kenseikai political party, two-time prime minister, and a founding member of the League of Nations Association of Japan. During his second term as prime minister (1914–1916), which saw Japan expand its military, seize German-held territories in China and the South Pacific during the Great War, and present China with the so-called Twenty-One Demands, Ōkuma found time to pen an essay on "Our National Mission," which appeared in a collection published in English under the title, *Japan's Message to America: A Symposium of Representative Japanese on Japan and American-Japanese Relations*. Ōkuma assures his American readers that

> The Japan of today is no longer the Japan of Japan, but the Japan of the world. What is, then, the mission of the new Japan? It is to make a large contribu-

tion to human progress by playing an active part in the great drama of world politics. To put it in a more concrete way, it is Japan's mission to harmonize Eastern and Western civilizations in order to help bring about the unification of the world.[23]

Nor do the similarities end there. Like Nakasone, Ōkuma views national culture as the source of Japan's future contributions to the world. "The true difference of mankind," he explains, "is neither in the color of the skin nor in the frame of the body, but is, if any, in the degree of culture itself. It is this difference that distinguishes winner and loser in the struggle for existence. A nation, like an individual, must always endeavor to make up its own defects by adopting the merits of another, and to display its strong points at the same time." Specifically, it is Japan's unique talent for borrowing, and improving upon, the best features of foreign cultures that defines its mission. "We Japanese, standing at a point where the Eastern and Western civilizations meet, are given facilities to serve as interpreters of the Orient, and to represent the former before the Occidentals. Therefore, to harmonize the East and West and contribute to the unification of the world, is an ideal part to be played by Japan."[24]

If culture is key to reconciling nationalism and internationalism, then so, too, is education: the principal agent of national culture in the era of the modern nation-state.[25] Nakasone understood this connection when he wrote that teaching "a nationalism that endeavors to foster self-identity" through education is a prerequisite for Japan to contribute to the world. So did his Ad Hoc Council on Education, when it presented its policy recommendations for internationalizing Japanese education. And so did Ōkuma's contemporaries some sixty years earlier. Inspired by signs of a new world order emerging from the ashes of the Great War in Europe—wherein a commitment to disarmament, multilateral diplomacy, and peaceful economic competition would replace unilateral arms buildups, secret bilateral agreements, and colonial conquest—a group of reform-minded educators launched Japan's first "international education movement" (*kokusai kyōiku undō*) in the early 1920s, including the establishment of an International Education Association (Kokusai Kyōiku Kyōkai). While the differences between this event and the 1980s campaign by the Ad Hoc Council to internationalize Japanese education cannot be denied, neither can their uncanny similarities. More than six decades before Nakasone's Ad Hoc Council convened its first meeting, this group of interwar reformers had reached a similar conclusion about the need to reorient Japanese education so that education could, in turn, reorient the nation to the challenges and opportunities attending this new world order. They also set about inventing much of the terminology and debating many of the same issues that would resurface in the 1980s. Issues such as the future of international relations between rival states; the future of relations between the individual, society, and the state in the face of growing popular demands—both at home and abroad—for more individual freedom and a more equitable distribution of political and economic power; the future of Japanese nationalism and its relationship to internationalism; and, last but not least, the practical educational reforms necessary to promote and sustain these new arrangements among the Japanese people.

More surprising, perhaps, than the existence of these remarkable historical parallels, is the fact that they have gone practically unnoticed and unmentioned in the literature and speeches emanating from the 1980s reform movement. Just as Ōkuma's description of Japan's unique culture is indebted to the development of a new field of historical study that Stefan Tanaka refers to as *tōyōshi* (lit., Oriental history),[26] history has also been an important ally for both proponents and critics of the government-orchestrated movement to reform Japanese education during and after the 1980s. Needless to say, however, their interpretations of the historical record, and the lessons they derive from it, differ considerably. The Ad Hoc Council described its mission as nothing less than completing the third great educational reform in modern Japanese history that was prematurely launched by the MOE's Central Council on Education (Chūō Kyōiku Shingikai) in 1970.

According to this account,[27] the first reform was launched in 1872 on the heels of the Meiji Restoration with the promulgation of the nation's first universal, compulsory education law. The resulting educational system, which survived until the end of the Asia-Pacific War, was designed to serve two basic goals, summed up in a slogan popularized during the early Meiji period: "Enrich the country, strengthen the military" *(fukoku kyōhei)*. This demanded a concerted program of Westernization, modernization, and industrialization to catch up with the West. Widespread domestic poverty and the threat of foreign encroachment upon Japanese sovereignty helped to rally support for these twin goals from all segments of society. The Ad Hoc Council finds evidence of both continuity and discontinuity between the prewar and postwar goals of Japanese education: continuity with the goal to "enrich the country," which resurfaced during the postwar "era of high economic growth" (*kōdo keizai seichō jidai*); discontinuity with regard to the goal to "strengthen the military," which was unequivocally renounced—together with militarism and ultra nationalism—by the nation following the Asia-Pacific War.

The second major reform of education, according to the Ad Hoc Council's account, commenced during the Allied Occupation, which had as its goal to remove all vestiges of the militaristic and ultra nationalistic education that had led the nation to war, and to replace it with education that would build a nation of peace and culture (*heiwa kokka ya bunka kokka*) dedicated to the realization of democracy, freedom, equality, and the perfection of human character (*jinkaku no kansei*).[28] During this period, education was opened up to the masses and expanded in response to the imperatives of the period of high economic growth and technological advance. Eventually, it helped Japan achieve its longstanding goals of catching up with the modernized West and enriching the nation. However, by the late 1960s, the costs of its success were also apparent: not only in the form of problems like industrial pollution, but also in a loss of respect for humanity and nature brought about by rampant materialism, and aggravated by an educational system that emphasized the dissemination of knowledge to the neglect of spiritual development, and uniformity to the neglect of individual character. It was these problems, coupled with the challenges posed by an increasingly interdependent international community in which Japan was expected to play a leading role, that the Central Council on Education sought to address in 1970 by attempting to institute Japan's third great educational reform. Although the Central Council's effort was unsuccessful, it has served as both an inspiration and a guide for the work of the Ad Hoc Council.

This interpretation of the historical context and contemporary significance of the 1980s reform movement has achieved orthodox status in the years since the Ad Hoc Council published its reports. With respect to internationalization, its principal argument is that while previously internationalization was motivated by the single-minded goal of catching up to the West, now that Japan has achieved that goal internationalization, like other components of the third reform movement, must serve a higher purpose, by preparing the Japanese to assume an active leadership role in, and contribute something to, the international community beyond the monetary donations that have made it a leading provider of international development aid. This conclusion certainly lends credibility to the ongoing reform measures instituted by the MOE, so it is no surprise that the MOE has faithfully adhered to this historical narrative in its own publications.[29]

To be sure, opponents of the Council's reform program, such as the teachers' union members in Hiroshima, have vociferously challenged the Ad Hoc Council's interpretation of its historical relationship to preceding reform movements, not to mention its implications for the future. Yet, their criticisms do not really challenge the three-stage paradigm of Japanese education reform set forth by the Council. The same has been true of the media's coverage of the reform campaign. Even some scholars have accepted this paradigm as the starting point for their analyses and commentaries.[30]

Their collective failure to acknowledge, much less examine, the interwar campaign to internationalize Japanese education as a predecessor to recent reform efforts has several adverse consequences. First, it obscures the persistence and complexity of Japan's struggle with problems of identity—individual, social, cultural, national—and power that has marked the country's modern intellectual, social, and political history. The interwar internationalization movement suggests not only that the alleged differences between his "healthy nationalism" and *kokkashugi* are not as clear-cut as Nakasone claims; it also suggests that the concept of "nationalism" used by his critics to attack Nakasone is too simplistic. *Kokkashugi*—literally, "statism,"—did not preclude some of the emperor's loyal subjects from publicly questioning many of its tenets during the interwar period, or from imagining a different ideology and a different set of political and social relationships in its place. By the same token, "healthy nationalism" does not guarantee that this longstanding problem of identity and power has been safely resolved, since it continues to grant the state—through agents like the MOE—final authority to define and disseminate a common "Japanese" identity and the set of social and political relationships that define "Japan." What, ask critics of Nakasone and the MOE, is healthy about whitewashing school textbook accounts of the Nanjing Massacre, biological warfare experiments on prisoners of war, the virtual enslavement of Asian "comfort women" to provide sexual gratification to Japanese troops, and other atrocities committed by the Japanese military during the Asia-Pacific War?

Second, it obscures the complexity of the education reform process itself by concentrating on the rhetoric and policymaking activities of Japan's political and bureaucratic elite, while paying scant attention to the opinions and activities of those working in the trenches, such as school administrators, teachers, textbook writers, and union representatives.

Ultimately, the superficial historical accounts of Japanese education that preface some of the scholarly studies and official reports devoted to the 1980s reform campaign obscure our understanding *both* of the history of Japanese educational reform (which, of course, is also part of the history of Japanese social and political reform) *and* of the contemporary reform movement itself.

Itō Akihiro and Kitamura Kazuyuki, in one of the few essays to take up the history of *kokusaika* discourse and its relationship to Japanese education, offer an alternative schema. They divide that history into five major periods, beginning with the era of "civilization and enlightenment" (*bunmei kaika*) during the early Meiji period, when education emphasized the dissemination of Western science and practical knowledge for the purpose of insuring Japanese national independence, power, and prestige in the face of Western overseas expansion. The second period was marked by a spirit of international cooperation during the second half of the Taishō era, epitomized by the international education movement following the Great War. According to the authors, the very term *kokusaika* likely originated with the proponents of this movement. The third period culminated in the Asia-Pacific War, when the concept of internationalization was co-opted by proponents of imperial Japan's Greater East Asia Co-Prosperity Sphere. They attempted to challenge Western domination of international norms and the international community by advancing a project of Japanese domination that was concealed in the rhetoric of Asian liberation. The fourth period was marked by Japan's so-called "second opening" to the West, centering on the Occupation era. It began with idealistic calls to reject militarism and nationalism, embrace the democratic, antimilitaristic policies championed by the American Occupation authorities, and reconstruct Japan as a trustworthy contributor to world peace and culture. However, the onset of the Cold War and the Occupation's reversal of its earlier policies prompted a resurgence of Japanese nationalism and a complicated political, economic and military alliance with the United States. During the fifth and final period, between the 1960s and the 1980s, the term *kokusaika* resurfaced, gained wide currency in economic, political, cultural, as well as educational circles, and in the process was manipulated to support multiple and conflicting meanings and nuances.[31]

The virtues of this schema are that it recognizes that: (1) there is a history behind the contemporary discourse on *kokusaika* that predates its rise to prominence in the 1980s; (2) the meanings attached to *kokusaika* and related terms in that discourse are historically determined and subject to change; (3) this discourse has not been monopolized by the state and its ruling elite; (4) even within the educational system, this discourse has been shaped by the voices of different interest groups. Its principal shortcomings are that it does not consider any pre-Meiji precedents to the *bunmei kaika* period, and it ignores important late-Meiji and early-Taishō era precedents to the authors' second stage (following the Great War).

SYNOPSIS

Accordingly, the narrative structure of this book is based loosely on Itō and Kitamura's five-stage schema, with provisions for the omissions noted above. It examines the ideological, political, and pedagogical dimensions of Japanese educational discourse using a variety of primary and secondary sources.

Chapter 1: Most scholarship on the history of Japanese education during the Meiji period has linked the introduction of compulsory schooling to the government's pursuit of a "rich country, strong military," and to one form of internationalization—imperialism and colonialism—that Japan emulated from those countries that had forced her to sign the "unequal treaties" in the

1850s. According to this account, by 1890 school teachers, principals and local officials faced increasing government pressure to produce a new breed of modern imperial subjects, exhibiting: a common national identity and patriotic spirit; absolute loyalty to an Emperor who embodied both divine right and divine purpose; and absolute obedience to those charged with governing in His name. In this way, Meiji educators and their successors contributed to the eventual triumph of ultra nationalism and militarism in the 1930s and early 1940s.

Chapter 1 challenges this orthodox historical account on two fronts. First, selected essays by late Tokugawa-era writers are examined to demonstrate that decades before Commodore Perry's storied "opening of Japan" to the West, some Japanese were mounting their own challenges to the Tokugawa policy of *sakoku*. These writers advocated Japanese engagement in overseas colonization *and* changes to Japanese education commensurate with such a policy. Second, the views of various Meiji-era figures are examined for evidence of opposition: not to the government's pursuit of imperialism and colonialism, per se; but to the specter of Japanese education becoming the handmaiden to ultra nationalism and militarism. The adoption of Western ideas and institutions, two major wars against China and Russia, and frictions with Western countries resulting from the expansion of Japanese trade, immigration, and territory prompted some Meiji-era reformers to caution that the state's educational policies designed to produce a nation of loyal, patriotic, obedient imperial subjects were out of sync with Japan's growing prominence on the world stage; circumstances which demanded a new generation of citizens capable of creative thought and independent action as trustworthy members of an international community. As explained in chapter 2, such criticisms helped set the stage for a new form of internationalization that I call "liberal internationalism," and for Japan's first organized movement to internationalize Japanese education.

Chapter 2: In Japan, as with other members of the Imperial Club that witnessed the Great War, the unprecedented scale of destruction fueled a lingering sense of peril, while the Treaty of Versailles and the League of Nations fueled a sense of hope that a new era in international relations based on the principles of multilateralism, humanitarianism, and peaceful coexistence had dawned. "Liberal" Japanese educators concluded that this new era demanded a coordinated international movement to harness education in countries throughout the world to the goals of the League. Working in concert with likeminded educators from other countries, they adopted a series of concrete proposals and then turned to the task of implementing them in Japan. These included: new guidelines for the teaching of history, geography and literature to impart "specific principles which directly promote international goodwill";

revising textbooks for these subjects by removing excessively nationalistic content and introducing lessons that illustrate our common humanity; and observation of International Good-Will Day, when schools throughout the world were to provide "instruction on the work of the Hague Conference and more recent efforts to bring the world together in a cooperative body, accompanied by national and international songs, plays, and pageants which carry out the spirit of the day."

It is no coincidence that the leaders of this interwar international education (_kokusai kyōiku_) movement in Japan were also at the forefront of a parallel movement for "liberal education" (_jiyū kyōiku_), which historians of Japanese education associate with "Taishō democracy." These parallel initiatives constituted a two-pronged attack on a school system that suffered from excessive centralization, standardization, regimentation, and bureaucratic interference. These men gravitated to the private sector, founding schools where they could experiment with new teaching methods that: embodied democratic, egalitarian principles; respected individual differences and encouraged individual creativity; and aimed to cultivate a new generation of imperial subjects who were also citizens of the world.

However, these ventures were hampered both by internal contradictions and external resistance. On one hand, the liberal internationalists who led the campaigns for international education and liberal education were at a loss to explain how their ideas related to schools serving Japan's colonial subjects (including Ainu and Okinawans), where the ostensible goal of education was political and cultural assimilation through the obliteration of indigenous cultures and local identities, and compulsory adoption of Japanese culture and identity. On the other hand, skeptics and critics speculated that international education, like the League of Nations itself, was simply another tool being manipulated by the Western powers to continue their prewar policies of colonial expansion at Japan's expense.

Chapter 3: Proponents of liberal internationalism who spearheaded Japan's first movement to internationalize education during the 1920s found themselves on the defensive by the end of the decade. Their ideological and political opponents, both inside and outside the government, pointed to a variety of evidence—passage of racist immigration exclusion laws in the U.S., Canada and Australia, America's failure to join the League, results of the Washington Conference's restrictions on Japanese naval development, Chinese boycotts against Japan, the growth of the international communist movement following the Russian Revolution—to warn of a future international conflict that would be waged on several fronts—military, economic and ideological. By the 1930s, following the Manchurian Incident and then the Japanese invasion of China, these liberal internationalists struggled to bridge their views with what would become an official doctrine that I call "Japanese imperial internationalism." This doctrine professed goals similar to its "liberal" predecessor—peaceful "coexistence and co-prosperity"—and advocated a similar formula to achieve them: a program of educational (intellectual and moral) and cultural enlightenment, designed by the most advanced countries and imposed upon the least advanced. Of course, there were major differences separating the two: Japanese imperial internationalism rejected the universal claims of western political philosophy and international law, in favor of Japan's own divinely sanctioned Imperial Way; and it authorized total war for the purpose of destroying the oppressive, exploitative world order constructed by the west, and "bringing the world under an eightfold [Japanese] roof" (*hakkō ichiu*).

Chapter 4: Following Japan's defeat in the Asia-Pacific War, educational policies backed by the Allied Occupation were supposed to repudiate the doctrine of Japanese imperial internationalism and help to reinstate a modified form of liberal internationalism that championed democracy at home and a foreign policy based on pacifism and humanitarianism. Political conservatives in the Diet and the Ministry of Education made temporary peace with these new policies, which sought to limit political influence and bureaucratic control over the curriculum, textbooks, and teachers. This feat was made easier by the onset of the Cold War and the so-called "reverse course." With the Occupation at an end, and conservatives staging a political comeback, the stage was set in the 1950s for a new type of ideological and political assault against organized teachers, textbook authors, and other supporters of the pacifist, humanist, democratic principles enshrined in the 1946 Constitution and the 1947 Fundamental Law of Education. This conflict is analyzed through a detailed examination of successive editions of the Ministry of Education's Course of Study guide (*gakushū shidō yōryō*) that were issued between 1958 and the end of the century; and through a parallel examination of successive editions of primary school textbooks published between 1958 and 2002, which were expected to conform to the Course of Study. The influence of the 1970 report on education produced by the Ministry's Central Council on Education, and of the reports prepared by Nakasone's Ad Hoc Council on Education in the 1980s, upon late-twentieth century discourse on the internationalization of Japanese education, is also discussed.

NOTES

1 In 2001, as part of a government-wide campaign to restructure a bureaucracy that has been widely criticized for its bloated size, redundancy, inter-agency competition over jurisdictions and resources, and resulting inefficiencies, the Ministry of

Education, (*Monbushō*) adopted both a new Japanese name (*Monbukagakushō*) and a new official English translation: Ministry of Education, Culture, Sports, Science and Technology. However, for the sake of consistency and simplicity, the name Ministry of Education and the acronym MOE will be applied throughout this book.

2. In 1989, internal political differences and concerns over declining membership resulted in the left wing of the JTU splitting off to form a new union named Zen Nippon Kyōshokuin Kumiai Keimeikai (or Zenkyō). See Marie H. Roesgaard, *Moving Mountains: Japanese Education Reform* (Aarhus, Denmark: Aarhus University Press, 1998), 113–18. For the sake of consistency and simplicity, unless otherwise noted, the name Japan Teachers Union and the acronym JTU will be used throughout this book to refer to the teachers union in postwar Japan.

3. Robert W. Aspinall, *Teachers' Unions and the Politics of Education in Japan* (Albany: State University of New York Press, 2001), 124–27. According to Aspinall, the national union leadership of the JTU gradually modified its position on this issue during the late 1990s, as part of a larger campaign to stem declining membership and regain its political clout by adopting a more centrist position in Japan's political spectrum. However, not all of the prefectural branches of the union followed suit, and some like Hiroshima continued to put up local resistance to the Ministry's demands.

4. See Hiroshima ken kyōshokuin kumiai kyōgikai, ed., *Dare no tame no "Hinomaru, Kimigayo"? Sono uso to oshitsuke* (Tokyo: Meiseki Tosho, 1999).

5. Aspinall, *Teachers' Unions*, 126.

6. Ibid., p. 124; Christopher P. Hood, *Japanese Education Reform: Nakasone's Legacy* (London and New York: Routledge, 2001), 72.

7. Hood, *Japanese Education Reform*, 52. As will be explained below, Hood himself is unaware of the irony stemming from the links he draws between Nakasone's "healthy" nationalism and the principal's very unhealthy suicide. This is not surprising, given that Hood voices support for Nakasone's initiative, as well as for the ensuing laws governing the legal status and educational use of the flag and the anthem.

8. Leonard James Schoppa, *Education Reform in Japan: A Case of Immobilist Politics* (London and New York: Routledge, 1991), 251–57. Schoppa identified five principal reasons for the failure of this education reform initiative: (1) "the absence of a conservative consensus" between the reformist camp, led by Nakasone and supported by likeminded business and academic leaders who formed his so-called "brain trust," and supporters of the status quo, notably officials in the MOE *and* politicians from Nakasone's own Liberal Democratic Party (LDP) (known collectively as the education *zoku*), who had worked closely with the MOE over the years to fashion the current system; (2) the LDP's longstanding "one-party dominance" in the Diet, which helped to sustain these relationships between ministry bureaucrats and *zoku* politicians while discouraging challenges to their authority; (3) "the narrow segmentation of the education sphere," which undercut Nakasone's attempt to involve outside supporters of his views in the policy-making process, including business leaders and officials from other ministries; (4) "the role of public opinion," or more precisely, conflicting interpretations of public opinion, which made the search for consensus even more elusive; (5) "the impact of history," stretching back to the eras of prewar militarism, wartime defeat, and the postwar Occupation, that "has shaped the lines of

cleavage which separate the progressive camp from the conservative camp" and their interactions in the policy-making arena.

9. Roesgaard, *Moving Mountains*, 15. While Roesgaard's analysis of the MOE's role in implementing reforms illuminates a crucial dimension of the policy-making process that governs Japanese education, it does not alter Schoppa's findings. Far from ignoring MOE influence, as she implies, Schoppa demonstrated that MOE officials, in collaboration with members of the LDP education *zoku*, were able to co-opt the reform agenda and dictate the outcome by consenting to those reforms which they had long advocated *prior to* the Nakasone initiative, while sidelining the rest by calling for "further study" or by offering non-committal support "in principle." See my review of Roesgaard's book in *The Journal of Asian Studies* 58:4 (November 1999), 1153–54.

10. Hood, *Japanese Education Reform*, 172. Like Roesgaard, Hood's criticisms do not do justice to Schoppa's study, while his decision to focus on Nakasone as the "key actor" in the reform campaign creates certain problems of its own. See my review of his book in *The Journal of Japanese Studies* 28:2 (Summer 2002), 508–12.

11. They include the following: Mark Lincicome, "Nationalism, Internationalization, and the Dilemma of Educational Reform in Japan," in *Comparative Education Review* 37:2 (May 1993), 123–51; Kaori Okano and Motonori Tsuchiya, *Education in Contemporary Japan: Inequality and Diversity* (Cambridge, UK: Cambridge University Press, 1999), especially chapter 6; Nobuo Shimahara, "Japanese Education Reforms in the 1980s: A Political Commitment," in James J. Shields, Jr., ed., *Japanese Schooling: Patterns of Socialization, Equality, and Political Control* (University Park: Pennsylvania State University, 1990, 1993), 270-281; and Brian J. McVeigh, *Japanese Higher Education as Myth* (Armonk, NY: M. E. Sharpe, 2002), especially chapter 10.

12. Teruhisa Horio, *Educational Thought and Ideology in Modern Japan: State Authority and Intellectual Freedom*, edited and translated by Steven Platzer (Tokyo: University of Tokyo Press, 1988), 365.

13. For example, see Yamashina Saburō, *21 seiki o ikiru Nihonjin to wa: shin gakushū shidō yōryō o yomu* (Tokyo: Gakushū no Tomo Sha, 1989), especially chapter 3.

14. See Monbukagakushō, ed., *Nijūisseiki no kyōiku kaikaku: Monbukagaku hakusho* (Tokyo: Zaimushō, 2001), 8–10.

15. Schoppa, *Education Reform in Japan*, 5–6. The other seven issues were: (1) "basic requirements for an education relevant to the twenty-first century"; (2) "organization and systematization of lifelong learning and correction of the adverse effects of undue emphasis on the educational background of individuals"; (3) "enhancement of higher education and individualization of higher education institutions"; (4) "enrichment and diversification of elementary and secondary education"; (5) "improving the quality of teachers"; (6) "coping with the information age"; (7) "review of educational administration and finance."

16. Michael W. Apple, *Education and Power* (Boston: Ark Paperbacks, 1982, 1985), 30; see also 12–29.

17. Hood, *Japanese Education Reform*, 52.

18. Novelist William Plomer turned a critical eye on these sacrificial acts for readers of English in his 1929 short story, "The Portrait of an Emperor," in which a school

principal commits suicide after the Emperor's portrait goes missing from the shrine that he had built on the school grounds to house it. See his *Paper Houses* (New York: Coward-McCann, Inc., 1929). For information on Plomer, see D. N. Lammers, "Taking Japan Seriously," in Robin Winks and James Rush, eds., *Asia in Western Fiction* (Honolulu: University of Hawaii Press, 1990), 201–04.

19. Yamashina, *21 seiki o ikiru Nihonjin to wa*, 10–12. See also Nakano Akira, *Kyōiku kenkyū chosaku senshū 3: Senkanki kyōiku e no shiteki sekkin* (Tokyo: EXP, 2000), 25–26; Ōtsuki Takeshi and Matsumura Kenichi, *Aikokushin kyōiku no shiteki kyūmei* (Tokyo: Aoki Shoten, 1970), 167–71.

20. Interview with Igasaki Akio, Director, Citizens' Institute for Educational Research, May 31, 1989.

21. Quoted in Hood, *Japanese Education Reform*, 52.

22. www.yasukuni.or.jp/english/ (6 August 2008). For information on the history of Yasukuni Shrine and the political controversies that have surrounded it in the decades since Nakasone's first official visit there, see the following: Harry Harootunian, "Memory, Mourning, and National Morality: Yasukuni Shrine and the Reunion of State and Religion in Postwar Japan," in Peter van der Veer and Hartmut Lehmann, eds., *Nation and Religion* (Princeton: Princeton University Press, 1999), 144–60; and Helen Hardacre, *Shintō and the State, 1868–1988* (Princeton, NJ: Princeton University Press, 1992).

23. Count Shigenobu Ōkuma, "Our National Mission," in Naoichi Masaoka, ed., *Japan's Message to America: A Symposium of Representative Japanese on Japan and American-Japanese Relations* (New York: G. P. Putnam's Sons, 1914), 1–2.

24. Ibid., 4.

25. In his classic treatise on nationalism, Ernest Gellner states:

> [N]ationalism is, essentially the general imposition of a high culture on society, where previously low cultures had taken up the lives of the majority, and in some cases the totality, of the population. It means the generalized diffusion of a school-mediated, academy-supervised idiom, codified for the requirements of reasonably precise bureaucratic and technological communication. It is the establishment of an anonymous, impersonal society, with mutually substitutable atomized individuals, held together above all by a shared culture of this kind, sustained by folk cultures reproduced locally and idiosyncratically by the micro-groups themselves.

Ernest Gellner, *Nations and Nationalism* (Oxford: Basil Blackwell, 1983), 57.

26. Stefan Tanaka, *Japan's Orient: Rendering Pasts into History* (Berkeley: University of California Press, 1993).

27. The following summary is taken from Lincicome, "Nationalism, Internationalization, and the Dilemma of Educational Reform in Japan," 148–49.

28. According to Kyoko Inoue, the strongly elitist, hierarchical connotations that prewar Japanese had attached to the phrase *jinkaku no kansei* ("moral character") managed to survive in Japanese educational discourse both during and after the American Occupation, when the same phrase was used to interpret "individual dig-

nity" in the Japanese translation of the postwar Constitution that was drafted by Occupation authorities. See her book, *Individual Dignity in Modern Japanese Thought: The Evolution of the Concept of Jinkaku in Moral and Educational Discourse* (Ann Arbor: Center for Japanese Studies, University of Michigan, 2001).

29. For example, see Monbukagakushō, ed., *Nijūisseiki no kyōiku kaikaku*, Op. Cit., 2–10.

30. See the following examples: Hood, *Japanese Education Reform*, 17–24; Schoppa, *Education Reform in Japan*, chapter 2; Edward R. Beauchamp, "The Development of Japanese Educational Policy, 1945–1985," in Edward R. Beauchamp, ed., *Windows on Japanese Education* (Westport, CT: Greenwood Press, 1991). Even scholars who do acknowledge the push for "liberal education" (*jiyū kyōiku*) in interwar Japan make little or no mention of the concurrent international education movement. For example, see Roesgaard, *Moving Mountains*, 39–41, and Byron K. Marshall, *Learning to be Modern: Japanese Political Discourse on Education* (Boulder, CO: Westview Press, 1994), chapter 4.

31. Itō Akihiro, Kitamura Kazuyuki and Ebuchi Kazuhiro, "Nihon ni okeru kokusaika shisō to sono keifu," in Sawada Akio and Kadowaki Kōji, eds., *Nihonjin no kokusaika: 'chikyū shimin' no jōken o saguru* (Tokyo: Nihon Keizai Shinbunsha, 1990) 9–48.

1

Reconsidering the Meiji Legacy

The literature on nationalism ascribes a pivotal role to schools in creating what Benedict Anderson calls an imagined community, through the formation and dissemination of a common national identity and a shared national consciousness where none existed before.[1] It is not unusual to find Japan cited as a prime example of this process of mythmaking, not only among theorists of nationalism, but among Japan specialists, as well.[2] In general, they portray the first two decades of the Meiji period, between 1868 and 1890, as the era when a modern national consciousness merged with a revivified nativist identity to form an "emperor-centered nationalism" that was institutionalized and propagated by the state, chiefly through a newly established compulsory, centralized school system. Frequently, this assertion is supported by citing the Imperial Rescript on Education (1890), which begins, "Our Imperial Ancestors have founded Our Empire on a basis broad and everlasting and have deeply and firmly implanted virtue; Our subjects, ever united in loyalty and filial piety, have from generation to generation illustrated the beauty thereof." This distinctive brand of Japanese nationalism is also regarded as a factor contributing to the subsequent development of Japanese imperialism and the country's pursuit of a colonial empire abroad, which began with its victory in the Sino-Japanese War (1894–1895), and concluded fifty years later with its defeat in the Asia-Pacific War.

The problem with this account is that it reifies nationalism, education, and the state and treats the relationships among them as static and unchanging. As a result, it tends to overlook, downplay or dismiss evidence of challenges to the status quo that was allegedly established by the early 1890s. To appreciate the dynamic, even contentious history of educational development in Japan *after* 1890, and its convoluted role in the dissemination of nationalism and the formation of Japan's imagined community before the Asia-Pacific War, requires that those challenges be examined more closely.

1

Accordingly, the first part of this book centers on an episode in the history of modern Japanese education that is not mentioned in the literature cited above. The episode in question, known as the "international education movement" (*kokusai kyōiku undō*), is intriguing for a couple of reasons. First, as the name implies, it involved a conscious, organized attempt to invert the relationship between education and nationalism, as traditionally conceived. For some of its proponents, at least, the goal of this movement was not merely to reduce the amount of time that teachers, as servants of the state, were obliged to spend inculcating loyalty and patriotism (*chūkun aikoku*) in the hearts and minds of their pupils, inside as well as outside the classroom. They sought, in addition, to use education to disseminate a different form of nationalism that was at odds with the one that privileged the bureaucratic state (*kokkashugi*). Their conception of nationalism centered, instead, on the individual and his dual citizenship as a member of the Japanese nation *and* of the universal brotherhood of man. This involved them in a contentious struggle to reconceptualize Japanese national identity, the proper relationship between Japanese and non-Japanese peoples, and Japan's role in the community of nations.

The international education movement is also intriguing because of who led it. Standard historical accounts imply that with the exception of faculty and students in the elite universities, the Japanese educational community was largely oblivious to the intellectual, political, and cultural ferment that swept over Japan (and elsewhere) at this time. Instead, it is alleged that the state viewed the schools as its first line of defense against the apostles of "radical" ideologies such as internationalism, democracy, socialism, and communism, and methodically controlled the schools to fend off these ideological challenges. The international education movement suggests, however, that other segments of the educational community participated in this ferment, especially since its most notable leaders were also active in the concurrent "new education" (*shin kyōiku*) and "liberal education" (*jiyū kyōiku*) movements that raised their own challenges to state-controlled education.[3]

They saw themselves as servants of the state and were committed to its preservation. They had spent all or part of their professional careers in the field of education: as teachers, administrators, officials, journalists, or some combination thereof. They were reformers, not revolutionaries, who nevertheless believed that the relationship between the state and the people, certain of the state's policies (both foreign and domestic), and the ideology of state-centered nationalism that were forged during the Meiji period were inappropriate in the twentieth century. Their discourse on international education was not only a critique of these shortcomings but an attempt to reconfigure state and society in light of the changing times.

RECONSIDERING NATIONALISM AND EDUCATION

Before examining their discourse on international education, it is worth asking why it has been neglected for so long. One reason may be that historians of Japan have been slow to appreciate the historical significance of Japan's flirtation with internationalism during the early twentieth century. Until recently, if it was mentioned at all, internationalism in prewar Japan tended to be recounted in one of two ways: (1) as a fringe movement sparked by a small group of Christians and socialists during and after the Russo-Japanese War (1904–1905), chiefly on pacifistic grounds; (2) as a calculated diplomatic initiative orchestrated by Foreign Minister Shidehara Kijūrō during the 1920s, which attracted, at best, modest support from a small band of allies in the foreign and finance ministries, and among a handful of business leaders and "bourgeois" intellectuals.[4] In neither case was internationalism judged to have represented a serious challenge to the prewar state's policies of imperialism, or to the public's support for those policies.

Over the past decade or so, a new generation of scholars has taken a fresh approach to the topic, producing a body of work marked by greater theoretical sophistication, a richer variety of primary and secondary sources, and more subtle interpretations of those sources. What made this possible was their rejection of the presumed binary opposition between internationalism and nationalism that characterized the work of earlier commentators. Instead, they begin with the assumption that "Nationalism and internationalism are not contradictory value systems. Each represents values and goals that often overlap with and interdetermine each other, and in fact they are so intertwined that it may be impossible to completely disentangle them."[5] As a result of this shift, the writings and speeches of early twentieth-century Japanese university professors and intellectuals now figure more prominently in the latest scholarship on the topic than before. Even so, the prewar international education movement and its leading advocates are still missing from this newer body of work, so we must look for another explanation for this omission.

I suggest that it may be the residual effect of a deeply entrenched historical narrative on nationalism and education in modern Japan that emphasized the monolithic character of the Japanese state and state-sponsored nationalism, as well as the hegemonic power of the state over the school system, and concluded that Japanese schools and educational personnel functioned as little more than conduits for the dissemination of that ideology. At least two generations of scholars traced this putative link between prewar Japanese education and state-sponsored, emperor-centered nationalism and imperialism back to the 1880s.[6] Having ushered in a hasty program of Westernization during the first decade of the Meiji period—including the establishment of Asia's first system of universal, compulsory schooling, in which Neo-Confucian metaphysics gave way to Western positivism and utilitarianism—the Meiji oligarchs, we are told, were persuaded by conservative elites that the pendulum had swung too far. This prompted a "conservative counterattack"[7] that culminated in such measures as: promulgation of the Imperial Rescript on Education; a stronger emphasis on moral education and the reintroduction of Confucian ethics into the curriculum; the introduction of military-style physical education (*heishiki taisō*) to instill discipline and respect for authority; and increased government control over curricula and textbooks. This assessment characterizes Japanese nationalism and its chief conduit, Japanese education, as increasingly conservative and particularistic; at the same time, it portrays the leadership as monolithic and authoritarian. While portions of this narrative have been convincingly challenged by various scholars since the mid-1980s,[8] its portrait of Japanese school teachers and administrators as compliant civil servants, bound to the dictates of state-centered nationalism, has not been erased from public consciousness.

One need not reject their unanimous conclusion that the Japanese state ultimately resorted to authoritarian control over education to quash dissent and garner ideological support for the Asia-Pacific War, in order to question scholars' neglect of organized attempts to resist that trend. The measure of their significance should not be limited solely to the failure of these efforts to stem the tide of ultra nationalism in the 1930s. On the contrary, given the long-held belief that the state methodically extended hegemonic control over education from the 1880s until Japan's defeat in 1945, is it not significant that attempts at resistance occurred at all? Katherine Verdery observes that scholarship on nation "should treat nation as a symbol and any given nationalism as having multiple meanings, offered as alternatives and competed over by different groups maneuvering to capture the symbol's definition and its legitimating effects."[9]

Writing in a similar vein, E. J. Hobsbawm observes, "What we need to discover is what precisely national slogans meant in politics, and whether they meant the same to different social constituencies, how they changed, and under what circumstances they combined or were incompatible with other slogans that might mobilize the citizenry, how they prevailed over them or failed to do so."[10]

Responding to this challenge, Satō Shigeki refers not to "Nationalism" but to multiple nationalisms that contend for legitimacy. Even "official nationalism" sponsored by the state does not exist in a vacuum, and hegemony is never so complete as to preclude challenges from disenfranchised or dissenting groups harboring different priorities and different conceptions of the nation.[11]

Kevin Doak applies Satō's observation to his historical survey of Japanese nationalism:

> Japanese nationalism can only be understood properly once we recognize that theoretical attempts to grasp Japanese nationalism as a singular thing often fail to grasp the true range of its historical forms. . . . Japanese nationalism was not constructed solely by the state, by capitalism, by the West, by the emperor, or even the "people." Japanese nationalism was the result of a specific series of historical and political events that created a plurality of agents in a contested arena, where each sought to expel, expunge or appropriate the others in the name of the true Japanese nation. As nationalism, however, this discourse has its defining limits around the question of the "people": who are they, where are they, and over whom/under whom do they have sovereignty, identity and meaning?[12]

This approach can also be applied to discourses on *inter*-nationalism, which, according to Tom Nairn, emerge in response to nationalism. Internationalism, says Nairn, "is not a mirror of internationality, but a complex range of reactions to nationalism: part defense, part disguise, and part staged adaptation. It is a constituent of the same nationalist universe."[13]

As noted in the Introduction, scholars are not the only ones guilty of shortchanging the interwar international education movement. Policymakers involved in more recent reform initiatives since the 1970s have also failed to cite it as a precedent to their own efforts to internationalize Japanese education. It is impossible to know whether this oversight—which also fails to acknowledge the better-known liberal education movement that took place concurrently—stems from simple ignorance or willful neglect. In either case, their omission robs us of an opportunity to gain a critical perspective on their own activities by comparing them with the experiences of their predecessors more than a half-century earlier.

The challenges to official nationalism that were made in the name of internationalism during the interwar period were not limited to marginalized groups like the socialists. As noted previously, one intriguing feature of the international education movement in early twentieth-century Japan is that its criticisms of official nationalism—and of the state itself—were made by leading educators and other members of the intelligentsia. While their goal was reform, not revolution, this fact does not diminish either the subversive character or the political potency of their movement. Inspired, in part, by the concurrent wave of "cultural internationalism" in other parts of the world,[14] Japanese educators questioned the state's unilateral authority to define national identity and safeguard national culture.[15]

Missing from the standard historical narrative summarized above is compelling evidence indicating that some prominent education officials and teachers actively contested the inwardly authoritarian, outwardly chauvinistic character of emperor-centered nationalism and sought to retain a place for the individual within the state apparatus, and a place for Japan within the international community. These self-described proponents of liberalism and internationalism in Japanese education did not always agree on policy particulars. However, most of them shared the conviction that state-centered nationalism (*kokkashugi*), which extolled loyalty and patriotism to the emperor above all else, would ultimately weaken rather than enhance Japan's position in the community of nations.

A better understanding of the relationship between nationalism and education, the relationship between the state and schooling, and the prospects for educational reform in twentieth- *and* twenty-first-century Japan requires that we scrutinize historical episodes such as the international education movement to ask: What concerns prompted career educators and other members of the intelligentsia to challenge "official nationalism" and the state's insistence that it be taught in the schools? What did they perceive as its shortcomings, and what remedies did they propose? What conceptual, practical, and political constraints confronted their calls for reform, and how did they respond?

To simply begin with this movement, however, would mean ignoring evidence of earlier debates and tensions between competing conceptions of the nation, the individual, the international community and their mutual relationships; and between competing conceptions of the proper role of education in their cultivation and dissemination. Accordingly, this chapter surveys some of these precedents before turning to an examination of the interwar international education movement in chapter 2.

KOKUSAIKA VERSUS INTERNATIONALIZATION

The most vigorous challenge to the state's manipulation of state-centered nationalism and its control over education in Japan occurred during the era that Andrew Gordon calls "Taishō imperial democracy"—here defined as the years between the Russo-Japanese War (1904–1905) and the Manchurian Incident (1931)—when opponents launched concurrent movements calling for liberal education and international education.[16] However, as the few Japanese scholars who have written about these twin movements have pointed out, there are important precedents that identified some of the ideas and issues that would become associated with these movements.[17]

As noted in the Introduction, Itō and Kitamura believe that the ideology of "civilization and enlightenment," which garnered support among government and non-government elites during the early years of the Meiji Renovation

(*Meiji ishin*),[18] marks the inauguration of internationalization discourse in modern Japan, some fifty years before the international education movement introduced the word *kokusaika* into the Japanese lexicon.[19] That depends upon how one defines "internationalization"; a term which, like "nationalism," "internationalism," and more recently "globalization," has become ubiquitous thanks, in part, to its vernacular imprecision. Adding to the problem, according to Ebuchi Kazuhiro, is that their meanings are not only historically determined but culturally distinct. He contends that the word *kokusaika* first appeared in a Japanese dictionary only in 1981, where it referred to a transformative process wherein the *subject becomes* someone or something international (*kokusaiteki na mono ni naru koto*). Ebuchi himself seems partial to this nuance, describing *kokusaika* as a two-stage process (practical and normative) of social and cultural change—or attempts at such—involving the integration of systems, values, and norms between nation-states that co-exist more closely than before. The word "internationalization," on the other hand, could be found in an English dictionary as early as 1864, which emphasized its transitive verb form, "internationalize," denoting an action that one or more parties *perform upon another*. In particular, writes Ebuchi, it was used by European colonizers to describe and justify their techniques for exerting control over other societies and exploiting them, for example, "The Suez Canal must be internationalized." And, since Europe's system of interstate alliances and its techniques for controlling other nations became the de facto global standard or framework, then as European colonialism advanced during the nineteenth century so did its doctrine and techniques of internationalization, which countries like Japan had little choice but to emulate.[20]

TOKUGAWA ANTECEDENTS

Ironically, if one accepts Ebuchi's contention that *kokusaika* and "internationalization" are historically as well as culturally distinct terms, then it can be argued that the appearance of Western-inspired internationalization discourse in Japan predates the Meiji period *and* "civilization and enlightenment," not to mention Japan's "native" *kokusaika* discourse. One is reminded, in particular, of late Tokugawa-era reformers like Honda Toshiaki, who accepted Western imperialism as a fact of life more than fifty years before Commodore Matthew Perry's ultimatum forced the Tokugawa bakufu to sign the Treaty of Kanagawa on March 31, 1854, which was soon followed by the "unequal treaties" granting America and its major European rivals extraterritoriality and the power to set tariffs on trade with Japan.[21] In his 1798 treatise, *A Secret Plan of Government* (*Keisei hisaku*), Honda braved the wrath of the bakufu to counsel its leaders on the specter of Western science and military might in the service of imperialism. But, unlike his Confucian opponents, who advocated moral reform of government and society in order to gird Japan against Western encroachment, Honda urged the bakufu to learn from the example of the West, asserting that "If the islands near Japan were colonized, they would be highly desirable places. By such colonization numerous possessions—some sixty or more—would be created, which not only would serve as military outposts for Japan, but would produce in abundance metals, grain, fruit, and various other products, thus greatly adding to Japan's strength."[22]

Honda also recognized that success in this endeavor required that the government accept a new form of knowledge, and encourage a new type of education to develop and disseminate that knowledge beyond the samurai ruling elite:

> Because astronomy, calendar making, and mathematics are considered the ruler's business, the European kings are well versed in celestial and terrestrial principles, and instruct the common people in them. Thus even among the lower classes one finds men who show great ability in their particular fields. The Europeans as a result have been able to establish industries with which the rest of the world is unfamiliar. It is for this reason that all the treasures of the world are said to be attracted to Europe. There is nowhere that the Europeans' ships do not go in order to obtain the different products of the world. . . . Their prosperity makes them strong, and it is because of their strength that they are never invaded or pillaged, whereas for their part they have invaded countless non-European countries. . . . Even countries that have not yielded to European might are devoting all their energies to producing things for Europe. The real objectives of the European nations are thus achieved anyway.[23]

Literate though some of his countrymen were, and imbued with the desire for self-improvement, in Honda's opinion that was not enough. Only when the *ruler* recognized the value of practical over classical learning and saw to its dissemination among the common people could Japan hope to emulate the power and sense of purpose that Honda perceived in Europe.

Practical learning, for Honda, was not limited to mathematics and the natural sciences. As he explained in a companion work, *Tales of the West* (*Seiiki monogatari*) colonization also required practical knowledge of other societies, cultures and languages:

> A person may acquire the reputation of being a great Confucian scholar and yet not be really familiar with the affairs of even one country. However, I understand that in the West a man who has a reputation for wide learning will know the languages of over thirty countries, and will be perfectly acquainted with their conditions and products as well. This must be because, having few letters [of the

alphabet] to learn [in comparison to thousands of Chinese characters], Western-ers can devote all their energies to the study of more important things.[24]

Honda's contemporary, Satō Nobuhiro, amplified some of Honda's themes two decades later, in a more strident discourse that has been labeled "totali-tarian nationalism" by some scholars and "national socialism" by another.[25] According to Komine Kazuo, whereas Honda viewed colonization as a means to fend off Russian encroachment from territories that originally belonged to Japan (Ezo, the Kurile Islands, the Kamchatka Peninsula), Satō drew inspira-tion from nativism (*kokugaku*) and Shinto to go even further, by champion-ing colonization for the purpose of extending Japanese influence throughout Asia. In so doing, writes Komine, Satō, in turn, provided inspiration and justification for Imperial Japan's declaration of a "Greater East Asian Co-Prosperity Sphere in 1940.[26] In his essay, *Confidential Plan of World Unifica-tion (Kondo hisaku)*, Satō borrowed the nativists' primordial vision of Japan as a divinely created civilization that is destined to lead the world:

> Our Imperial Land came into existence at the very beginning of the earth and it is the root and basis of all other countries of the world. Thus, if the root is attended to with proper care, the entire world will become its prefectures and counties, and the heads and rulers of the various countries will all become its ministers and servants. According to the scriptures of the Divine Age, the impe-rial progenitors, Izanagi and Izanami, instructed Susanoo [the Impetuous Male Diety] that 'our rule extends over the eight hundred folds of the blue immense.' And thus we learn that to make clear the divine teaching of production and pro-creation and thereby to set the peoples of the entire world at peace was, from the very beginning, the principal and urgent mission of our heavenly country. The salvation of the people of the world is an immense task which requires, first of all, a clear knowledge of geography and the state of affairs in the countries of the world.[27]

Satō outlined multiple courses of overseas expansion. One envisioned seizing the Philippines; opening the Ogasawara Islands; capturing Korea and Manchuria; occupying Beijing, Nanjing, and parts of the Chinese coast; and invading Formosa and the Ryūkyūs. Then, once "benevolent" government is carried out, Japanese and Chinese troops together can overwhelm Europe and America. A second, aimed at defending Japan against Russia, called for annexing Kamchatka and controlling the Sea of Okhotsk. A third, aimed at countering British imperialism, called for placing military garrisons in places like the Philippines, Java and Borneo.[28]

Satō's "totalitarian" vision was not limited to Japan's international rela-tions, but applied equally to domestic relations between the government and people at home. The state was to exercise absolute authority over the education, socialization and occupational training of the Japanese people through a bureaucratic apparatus composed of three departments (education, religion and justice) and six bureaus (agriculture, natural resources, construction and manufacture, commerce and treasury, defense, and maritime affairs). Satō went beyond Honda's general advocacy of practical education to outline a comprehensive system of schooling that provided for: a ministry of education that would design the curriculum and select teachers; a state university consisting of ten divisions (philosophy, religion, social institutions, music, law, military defense, medicine, astronomy, geography, and foreign languages), responsible for training government officials; and provincial schools open to all children beginning at age eight, each of which would also administer an institute of general relief, free dispensaries, asylums for indigent children, playgrounds and kindergartens.[29]

COMPETING MEIJI NATIONALISMS

Elements of Honda's and Satō's proposals for educational reform, considered radical in their own day, were elevated to orthodoxy seventy years later by the founders of the Meiji regime, whose first statement of the new government's aims, the Charter Oath of Five Articles (*gokajō no goseimon*), was promulgated by the emperor in April 1868. Eager to reach across the class divisions and sectional loyalties that were mainstays of the Tokugawa political economy, drafters of the Charter Oath resorted to broadly worded assurances that: (1) all classes would unite in promoting the nation's economy and welfare; (2) an assembly would be established and matters of state would be decided by public discussion; (3) all classes would be allowed to fulfill their just aspirations, so as to avoid discontent; (4) base customs of the past would be abandoned, and all actions would conform to universally recognized principles of justice; (5) knowledge would be sought throughout the world to strengthen the foundations of imperial rule. Implicit in this statement was not simply Honda's and Satō's charge to embrace Western scientific and practical knowledge, but also their expectation that the government would disseminate that knowledge to the people, which the people, in turn, would use to serve the nation. Thus, from its inception in 1872, Japan's system of universal, compulsory education was expected to advance "civilization and enlightenment" in order to build a "rich country and strong military."

Yet, the Charter Oath also departed from Satō's "totalitarian" plan of government in several important respects. First, it appears to distinguish between the public interest (the nation's economy and welfare) and private interests (just aspirations). Second, it grants to all classes of people a responsibility to pursue the former, and a concurrent right to pursue the latter. Third, it links these two domestic spheres of interest—public and private—with the international sphere: by calling for universal principles of justice to replace outmoded traditions; and by making the pursuit of knowledge "throughout the world" part of the people's public duty to strengthen the "foundations of imperial rule." These features of the Charter Oath, inspired by Western political philosophy, are significant because their incorporation into the discourse on "civilization and enlightenment" rendered the discourse itself open to popular participation and multiple interpretations. As a result, the harmonious relationships that the framers of the Charter Oath had envisioned in their blueprint for national renovation—between high and low social classes, public and private interest, and between native customs and international principles—soon proved elusive in nearly every policy arena: from domestic politics to war and diplomacy; from intellectual thought and journalism to literature and art; and from religion to education. Indeed, each of these would become contested territory, frequently pitting the various branches of government (the Meiji oligarchs, bureaucracy, and after 1890, the Diet) against private interest groups *and* against one another.[30]

As I have discussed elsewhere,[31] education is a good example of how such conflicts were exacerbated by contradictions and inconsistencies in the government's own policies to civilize and enlighten. During the 1870s, for example, through its fledgling network of normal schools, the government encouraged primary school teachers to abandon the practice of teacher-centered lectures and rote memorization associated with Tokugawa-era Confucian learning, in favor of the "developmental education" (*kaihatsushugi*) doctrine that was gaining adherents in America and Britain. Inspired by the pedagogical experiments and writings of Johann Pestalozzi and his followers, developmental education advocated a pupil-centered, discovery-based approach to learning that not only accorded greater respect to the child as a unique individual, blessed with natural abilities that should be nurtured from within rather than instilled from without. It also accorded greater respect to the individual teacher as a trained professional, capable of structuring the classroom experience to best suit the needs of the pupils in his or her care. By the 1880s, however, conservatives in the government began to view this individualized, decentralized approach to education as a threat to the government's authority and power, as well as to national unity. Those fears were fanned by the concurrent "movement for freedom and popular rights" (*jiyū minken undō*) whose supporters included a number of teachers.

With respect to internationalization, it was the government, as well, that championed a curriculum devoted to "practical learning" (*jitsugaku*) in Western-oriented subjects such as the physical sciences and history. In some cases, these were taught using abridged translations of Western text-books. By the 1880s, this policy, too, came in for criticism by conservative ideologues and government officials for neglecting to instill pupils with sufficient knowledge of, and respect for, Japanese history, customs, and ethical values to insure they would become loyal subjects of the emperor and servants of the state.

In short, the same compulsory education laws that were essential to cultivate human capital needed for commerce and industry also exposed a literate public to other intellectual currents from abroad which critics considered not merely impractical, but potentially dangerous to the divinely ordained, imperially sanctioned "national polity" (*kokutai*). At the top of their list of dangerous thoughts was not Christianity, as in Honda's and Satō's day, but a variety of secular "doctrines" (*shugi*) that went by such names as *kojinshugi* (doctrine of the individual, or individualism), *jiyūshugi* (liberalism) and *hakuaishugi* (humanitarianism). What made them dangerous were not their putative Western origins, although that label was routinely affixed to them in an effort to discredit them as inappropriate for Japan. Rather, they were dangerous because they appeared to undermine government authority and threaten the pre-eminence of the nation-state in the lives of the people.

DILEMMAS OF EMPIRE

At stake were not simply the specific problems of determining the constitutional rights of the citizenry or the professional authority of teachers, important though these were. For the outcomes of these struggles would, in turn, impact the fundamental issue of identity. Who, and what, would define "Japan" in the era of civilization and enlightenment and the modern nation-state? What did it mean to be "Japanese": as a private citizen, as an imperial subject, and as a citizen of the world?

According to Frederick Dickinson, it is this issue of identity that explains why the Meiji leaders, after successfully renegotiating the unequal treaties in 1894, lost no time implementing a series of foreign and domestic policies that would have made Honda and Satō proud. The three pillars supporting these policies were "empire, arms, and oligarchic rule."

> Like her fundamental political choice, Japan's drive for empire originated in the 1880s as an essential component of the project of national self-definition. Like constitutional government, empire had become in the "age of imperialism" a critical gauge of a civilized state. Great nations vied for power based upon the size of their armies, the range of their fleets, and the sweep of their territories. Granted by the great powers the relative freedom to construct their own empire

at will, modern Japan's founders looked to imperial expansion as a principal element of their quest for international power and respect.[32]

In other words, the Meiji oligarchs did not render their own definition of Japanese identity solely in terms of domestic culture and politics, through a doctrine of state-centered nationalism. They also incorporated the classic European doctrine of internationalization in the service of empire, just as Honda had urged their Tokugawa predecessors to do.[33]

Dickinson downplays concerns over external threats to the nation as motives for the Meiji oligarchs and the military to adopt an expansionist foreign policy. Those reasons, which continue to be cited by most historians of Japan, include Japan's alleged concerns about military security (with the Unites States gradually replacing Russia as the most potent threat), economic security (due to Japan's lack of natural resources), and overpopulation (compounded by a series of racist anti-immigration regulations that the United States pressed upon Japan, beginning with the Gentlemen's Agreement in 1907–1908). More important than these, argues Dickinson, was the oligarchs' pressing need to shore up their political power and legitimacy among a skeptical public; and, in the process, to rescue the nation from internal disorder and weakness by inciting public support for "empire, arms, and oligarchic rule" at home, while soliciting diplomatic acquiescence abroad. [34] For good measure, they also took another page from the Western manual on internationalization, and soon began espousing a uniquely Japanese mission within the international community, although the description of that mission shifted over time. It was initially defined as civilizing the rest of Asia, whose persistent backwardness was decried as a threat both to the entire region and to Japan. Her mission was soon expanded to include serving as a bridge to understanding between East and West; the very claim made by Ōkuma Shigenobu in the essay quoted in the Introduction. Ultimately, as the possibility of war against the United States loomed larger in the twentieth century, Japan's mission was redefined again: this time as the liberation of Asia from Western imperialism *and* (echoing Satō Nobuhiro in the 1820s) world renovation under Japanese tutelage.[35]

Dickinson's assertion that the Meiji government's pursuit of imperialism had more to do with political problems it faced at home than with threats from abroad is supported by Doak's trenchant analysis of competing nationalisms that grew out of the government's attempt to create a modern nation-state during the 1870s and 1880s. If the Charter Oath represented the government's original commitment to liberal, civic nationalism (*kokuminshugi*), then its authoritarian responses to the public's demands that it deliver on its promises soon undermined public support for the government and, in some quarters of society, support for civic nationalism itself. The government attempted to counter the threat of public disaffection and outright opposition by turning to state-centered nationalism (*kokkashugi*). The public, in turn, began to split along class lines: while some early advocates of "civilization and enlightenment," such as Fukuzawa Yukichi, defended civic nationalism, others began to articulate a "populist kind of nationalism that turned to indigenous forms of civic and cultural identity (*minzoku*)."[36] The resulting "triangular competition within Japanese nationalism between the state, civic (liberal) nationalism and ethnic nationalism," writes Doak, "provides the foundation for subsequent debates over nationalism, liberalism and internationalism during the 20th century."[37]

If, as Dickinson argues, domestic political considerations favored international conflict and the pursuit of empire over international cooperation and the pursuit of peace, then the public's response to Japan's wars against China and Russia between 1894 and 1905 would seem to prove that the government's strategy was successful, at least in the short run. Historians generally agree that as Japanese soldiers marched off to a succession of overseas conflicts in the space of a decade, people representing every socioeconomic class, occupation, and age group could be heard proclaiming the righteousness of Japan's cause, disparaging that of their Chinese and Russian foes, and calling upon fellow Japanese to unite behind their emperor and sacrifice themselves to defend the sacred land.[38] Many school teachers, principals, local and national education officials, textbook writers and educational journalists did even more by helping to disseminate these ideas to students and parents. And among those who may have harbored doubts about either the morality or the wisdom of their government's foreign adventures, few during that decade were willing to risk imprisonment, or ostracism, or loss of their jobs by condemning the enterprise outright.[39]

However, the benefits that the government derived from these wars proved to be ephemeral. To begin with, the treaty settlement that ended each conflict did nothing to sustain public support for the government or confidence in its rule: the Triple Intervention by Germany, France and Russia forced Japan to relinquish its claim to the Liaodong Peninsula following its war against China, while the paltry concessions extracted from Russia in the Portsmouth Treaty of 1905 sparked angry riots in Tokyo and elsewhere. The public mood also soured on the sheer costs of war, both in taxes paid and lives lost, which party politicians in the Diet—whose numbers now included a few of the regime's founders, like Ōkuma Shigenobu and Itō Hirobumi—seized upon to challenge government plans for further military expansion.[40]

IMPERIALISM OR INTERNATIONALISM?

Dickinson himself is quick to state that party politicians' resistance to the oligarchs' policies following these two conflicts was limited to the pursuit of "arms" and "oligarchic rule," and did not challenge the pursuit of "empire."[41] However, the three are not so easily separated, nor so easily generalized. Some appreciation of the range of opinions that marked Japanese debates about nationalism versus internationalism, the individual versus the state, and the role of education during this time may be gleaned by examining the views of leading thinkers and government policymakers. In so doing, one soon discovers the difficulty of classifying these individuals as "nationalist," "imperialist," "internationalist," "pacifist," "liberal," or "conservative": both because the meanings of these labels were open to continual debate and reinterpretation; and because such individuals often exhibited an extraordinary range of opinions during their careers.

Nowhere is this more apparent than in the case of noted journalist and educator Tokutomi Sohō, whose views as a young writer in the 1880s have been described by Kenneth Pyle as "the culmination of *bunmei kaika* themes."[42] At a time when the government was forging its plan for "arms, empire, and oligarchic rule," Tokutomi, under the influence of Herbert Spencer, was assuring his countrymen that the militant phase of civilization was destined to be superseded by industrialism, and that warfare would give way to internationalism, marked by free-trade policies and economic interdependence that would overcome national divisions. To prepare itself for an age in which economic rather than military strength would determine national survival, Japan should redouble its efforts to adopt modern technology, civilized institutions, and liberal values common to advanced industrial societies.[43]

What set Tokutomi apart from most of his contemporaries, according to his biographer John Pierson, was his willingness to apply these liberal values to the private, individual sphere, rather than limit them to the public sphere in the service of purely national goals. This conviction guided Tokutomi's own enlightenment activities during the early part of his career. He became involved in the Sōaisha (Mutual Benevolence Society), which was founded in 1878 to push for "freedom and popular rights" in his native Kumamoto. While the Society offered some support to candidates in local elections, most of its work concentrated on educating the local people about current political issues and about the foundations of popular government.[44]

By the time the Society disbanded in 1883, Tokutomi was already engaged in another project in Kumamoto: opening his own private academy for young men, the Ōe Gijuku. He referred to his educational program as Japanese Studies (*Nihongaku*) because it was geared to preparing his students to take an active role in the political and social modernization of the nation. However, the curriculum was notably "international" in scope: combining Japanese books like Rai Sanyō's *Nihon Gaishi*, the *Tale of Genji*, and the *Kokinshū* with Confucian texts in Chinese, as well as English-language works by Spencer, Mill, Bentham, and deTocqueville. The academy closed when Tokutomi moved to Tokyo in 1886, where he would launch a new magazine, *The Nation's Friend* (*Kokumin no tomo*).[45]

His magazine gave Tokutomi a forum and a larger audience for advocating a citizen-centered society built upon the common man (*heiminshugi*). Rejecting the excessively Westernized, intellectualized, utilitarian character of the Meiji government's early education ordinances, as well as reactionary moves by traditionalists to revive Confucianism, Tokutomi argued that education must be rooted in the nature of humanity itself (*ningen kyōiku*) and strive to cultivate the whole person. Above all, it should emphasize learning by doing (*rōsaku kyōiku*), in order to nurture the spirit of independence and self-reliance. This spirit is essential for the practice of constitutional government, which is the surest guarantee of individual happiness and national strength in the modern world.[46]

Yet, by the early 1890s, Tokutomi began to shift his position: from champion of individual freedom and laissez-faire to collectivism and interventionism; and from pacifism to war and expansionism. According to Pierson, this had less to do with the government's strategic pursuit of "arms, empire, and oligarchic rule," or even with the rising tide of nationalism as Japan positioned itself for war against China, than with Tokutomi's determination that Western societies were already moving in that direction in response to the new social and political conditions produced by modernity. It was at this time that he began to turn to East Asia for the building of a "Greater Japan."[47]

Scholars disagree over the degree and significance of this shift in Meiji thought, politics, and education between the late 1880s and early 1890s: from civic nationalism to ethnic nationalism; individualism to collectivism; "liberalism" to "conservatism"; pacifism to militarism and expansionism; laissez-faire to interventionism. Pyle concludes, "The successive public controversies over the unequal treaties with the powers diminished the appeal of the *bunmei kaika*'s benign view of international relations and helped make the conservatives' case for preserving cultural autonomy a basis for maintaining the strength of the Japanese state."[48] Frustrated by the Western powers' continued refusal to admit Japan into the ranks of civilized nations, Tokutomi told the readers of *The Nation's Friend* in August 1894 what the war with China was really all about:

Why do some Japanese say we fight in order to reform Korea, or to vanquish Peking, or to establish a huge indemnity? They should realize that we are fighting to determine once and for all Japan's position in the world. . . . If our country achieves a brilliant victory, all previous misconceptions will be dispelled. The true nature of our country and of our national character will suddenly emerge like the sun breaking through a dense fog.[49]

Others point to the inauguration of parliamentary government as a major incentive for conservatives in government to reemphasize national unity and loyalty to emperor and state. According to Alistair Swale, Tokutomi himself came to share this concern, which provided another incentive for him to modify his position:

The acrimonious and combative muddle of the first Diet assembly, followed by the outright failure of the second to survive its full term, did not provide encouraging signs of political maturity and further highlighted the difficulty which the Japanese people would have in escaping from a traditional political culture that was prone to exclusive oligarchy and deeply polarized clan affiliations. By 1894 *Kokumin no Tomo* was in decline, as the traditional Freedom and People's Rights message, which after all relied to a large degree on the notion of emulating the "successful" democracies of the West, was quickly losing traction in the consciousness of the reading public.[50]

Thus, observes Swale, "Tokutomi was therefore increasingly forced to accommodate the rhetoric of national integrity and patriotism" in his writings, even going so far as to forge links with rival pundits like Miyake Setsurei, whose own publications "had succeeded in creating an intellectual climate that made addressing Japanese national identity a sine qua non of contemporary political commentary."[51]

However, Swale, like historian Motoyama Yukihiko before him, believes that historians have exaggerated this alleged shift by misinterpreting the writings of Tokutomi and Miyake, who like Tokutomi, turned to journalism to help shape public opinion. According to Motoyama, although Miyake was widely regarded as a proponent of cultural nationalism (*kokusuishugi*) as the publisher of the magazine *The Japanese* (*Nihonjin*), he brought a global perspective to bear upon his theory of the preservation of the national essence (*kokusui hozon ron*). Miyake viewed the world, the nation, and the individual as cells in the great organism that was the universe. Each of these cells has its own particular role and capacity: the free development of the capacities of these national and individual cells promotes the evolution of world culture and leads toward the future realization of truth, goodness, and beauty.[52] "To exert oneself on behalf of one's country is to work on behalf of the world," he wrote. "Promoting the special nature of a people contributes to the evolution of mankind. Defense of the homeland and love of mankind are not at all contradictory."[53]

In practical terms, Miyake believed that due to racial, geographical, and historical factors, Japan was uniquely equipped to contribute to the pursuit of truth by promoting the study of East Asian history, society, and culture—including, of course, her own—which Western scholars had failed to treat adequately. Japan could advance the cause of goodness in the international arena by using its military power to protect its weaker neighbors from Western imperialism. And Japan could contribute to the world's appreciation of beauty by preserving and developing its own unique conception of beauty.[54]

Motoyama believes that Miyake's global outlook was shared by prominent officials in the MOE, and even found expression in some of the very policies that historians have blamed for promoting conservatism and nationalism during the early 1890s. For example, if one examines the provisions of the Revised Primary School Ordinance (Kaisei Shōgakkōrei, 1890) and the written commentary of Egi Kazuyuki who helped to draft it, one finds that its provision for moral education, emphasizing loyalty to the emperor, was coupled with other provisions emphasizing the acquisition of knowledge and skills, and respect for the self. Furthermore, its call to respect the Japanese nation was not meant to single out Japan as superior to other nations. Rather, according to Egi, the intent was to teach that every nation has its own distinctive character, and that each nation deserves the respect of its people. Far from promoting nationalistic education, Egi and his colleagues sought to prevent primary education from being co-opted by overzealous nationalists.[55] Similarly, examining the commentary provided by Ōki Takato regarding the Course of Study Outline (Kyōsoku Taikō) that was promulgated during his tenure as minister of education (June 1891 to August 1892), Motoyama concludes that Ōki worked to integrate Japan's unique, nation-centered morality with a universalistic morality grounded in a faith in human goodness; he did not mean to champion the former at the expense of the latter.[56]

A less charitable interpretation of these early accommodations by Meiji government officials like Egi and Ōki to the views of cultural nationalists like Miyake contends that they were attempts to co-opt the appeal of cultural nationalism and neutralize the threat that it represented to state-centered nationalism. It was a strategy that the state would continue to employ in the twentieth century in defense of both its domestic policies of social and political control and its imperialist policies abroad.[57]

One prominent official who left no doubt about his views on these issues was Saionji Kinmochi: scion of a Kyoto noble family who twice served as minister of education (1894–1896 and 1898) before becoming prime minister in 1906 and an influential elder statesman (*genrō*). During his tenure at the ministry, which began during the Sino-Japanese War, Saionji warned against a narrow, one-sided emphasis on inculcating the "national essence" through moral education that preached the virtues of loyalty and filial piety. By doing so, Japan risked falling behind the progress of world civilization, and, ultimately, losing out in the economic competition with other nations. For the sake of the nation, as well as of the individual, more attention must be given to science education, foreign language instruction, and the education of women. Saionji even advocated making English a compulsory subject and eliminating national literature (*kokubungaku*) from the curriculum. Through these reforms he sought to prepare postwar Japanese youth for citizenship in what he grandly termed *sekai no Nihon* ("Japan of the world"). He eventually resigned his ministerial post over a proposal he made to replace the 1890 Imperial Rescript on Education with a new one that would recognize egalitarian principles and promote a morality that accorded greater respect for all peoples.[58]

By substituting *sekai no Nihon* for *dai Nippon teikoku* ("great empire of Japan"), emphasizing the sciences and foreign languages over moral education, and proposing a new rescript on education, Saionji championed not only liberal nationalism but a form of liberal internationalism as well, albeit one that accepted imperialism as a reality. He raised a rhetorical, conceptual, political, and practical challenge to those who defined nationalism and imperialism in oppositional terms, in which the former pitted the interests of the state against those of the individual, while the latter pitted the interests of one state against another. Instead, he spoke of complementarity, saying that Japan's interests were bound up with those of the international community (or at least, with the interests of the Western powers). Japan's emergence as a colonial power in 1895 meant that it must act more responsibly and accept a greater role in world affairs, in accordance with internationally recognized norms. At the same time, Japan's interests and those of the international community could only be advanced when they were linked with those of the individual. Hence, Japanese education in the age of imperialism must respect individual differences, nurture individual talents, and socialize individual personalities so that citizens will come to identify their own interests with those of Japan and the world at large.

Saionji's "liberal" views on the relationship between the individual, the state, and the international community; the nature and purpose of nationalism and internationalism; and the role of education in their formation, may have been unusual among Japanese ministers of education. But they were not unique among his contemporaries, some of whom shared their opinions with the readers of *The Japan of the World* (*Sekai no Nihon*), the magazine

that Saionji co-founded with Takekoshi Yosaburō in 1896.[59] This magazine
initially resembled a high-brow international relations journal: the masthead,
written in English, billed the publication as "A Monthly Political, Financial,
Social, and Literary Review." However, according to Nozawa Masako, it soon
developed a more popular following as a forum for discussing topics ranging from Tokutomi's *heiminshugi* to French republicanism, popular rights,
and even socialism. It reflected Saionji's own brand of internationalism by
debating the prevailing ideologies of Japanism (*Nihonshugi*), state-centered
nationalism (*kokkashugi*) and imperialism; by examining the pros and cons of
international cooperation and pacifism; and by championing peaceful diplomacy over intimidation and the use of force.[60] As Takekoshi explains in the
editorial that opened the first issue, the magazine was born out of a conviction
that identity is shaped by one's consciousness of the world:

> Once they understood that it is was impossible for Japan to close its borders,
> seclude itself and survive on its own, [Japanese] then sought to protect them-
> selves by closing the borders of the Orient (*tōyō*), having come to recognize the
> fundamental law of co-existence and joint governance (*kyōzon kyōsei no taihō*)
> among nations of the world. But once it is understood that this fundamental
> law operates among the citizens of countries everywhere, then how can anyone
> claim that it operates only in the Orient, and not in the rest of the world? Going
> a step further, once the world beyond Japan is recognized, then why stop at the
> Orient and exclude the rest of the world? When citizens' ideas are confined to
> the area of the Orient, they come to think in terms of racial and ethnic similari-
> ties and differences, of the strong dominating the weak, and of Western coun-
> tries as implacable enemies.[61]

Later issues carried various articles that applied this editorial viewpoint
to criticize the Meiji government's educational policies. In the third issue,
for example, Kiono Tsutomu contributes an essay criticizing the harmful effects of *kokkashugi*, whose abstract appeals to the "national essence" and the
"national spirit" tend to promote the government's authority at the expense
of the people, thus depriving society of the vitality that comes from the
grassroots. Writing in a similar vein on the topic of education and religion
for Issue Seven, Kutsumi Yasunori attacks the Imperial Rescript on Education as the officially sanctioned foundation of moral education in Japan.
Kutsumi objects to both the content of the Rescript and to the authoritarian
manner in which it was forced upon the people. The result makes a mockery of morality because students only pay lip service to the Rescript when
required to do so, without internalizing its maxims. Genuine morality must
blossom from within each individual, just as the doctrine of developmental
education (*kaihatsushugi*) advocated a decade earlier, rather than be forcibly
"poured into" (*chūnyū*) pupils in a heavy-handed, arbitrary manner. And in

Issue 21, Kutsumi follows up with an attack on the concept of public morality (*kōtoku*), which together with *kokkashugi* violates the "universal law" of individual liberty and authority underlying private morality (*shitoku*). The strength of the nation does not exist independently of its people, who must be allowed to maximize their individual abilities through an education system that takes this as its primary goal.[62]

It was no accident that Saionji, Miyake, and their contemporaries who voiced these comparatively liberal and internationalist proposals did so in the 1890s. Their revisionist interpretation of nationalism and accompanying calls for educational reform were prompted by an acute awareness of changes both at home and abroad, especially following the Sino-Japanese War. The growth of capitalism at home, which received an important boost from the war, created new demands from industry for skilled workers, and new demands from workers for the education and training needed to compete for those positions. Japan's abrupt emergence onto the world stage also created demands for a new generation of talented cosmopolitans, whose knowledge of foreign languages and cultures could be employed to advance Japan's diplomatic and economic interests in the international arena in an era marked by increasing global economic competition.

Osaka banker Koyama Kenzō, writing in the January 1, 1904, edition of the magazine, *Pacific Ocean Business World* (*Jitsugyō sekai Taiheiyō*) notes that while business education in Japan has experienced impressive quantitative growth over the past ten years, the mediocre quality of that education puts Japan at a disadvantage in the "twentieth century's peaceful international war" (*nijusseki ni okeru taigai heiwateki sensō*) that will be waged on the commercial front. If Japan is to keep up with the likes of France, Germany, England and the United States, where business education is more comprehensive, then Japanese educators must implement the following reforms. First, they must not be content to instruct students solely in business-related skills, which does nothing to combat the narrow-minded ideas exhibited by many recent graduates of various types of schools. Those who intend to pursue careers in international business need to possess sophisticated ideas and sound moral character (*jinkaku*) if they hope to earn the trust and respect of foreigners. Second, educators must place more emphasis on foreign language education. In addition to improving the quality of foreign language instruction in middle schools, it should be made a required subject at higher primary schools located in Japan's major cities. [63]

Another important characteristic of the Taishō-era "new education" and "international education" movements that was already discernable by the turn of the century was their multinational, or transnational scope. That is, these efforts to reform Japanese education had their counterparts in other countries, especially Europe and North America, from which they drew both inspiration and direction. (It is ironic that less than a decade after the "conservative counterattack" against the excesses of Westernization had culminated in the Imperial Rescript on Education, Japan's emergence as a global imperial and capitalist power prompted some Japanese reformers to examine, once again, how Western societies were trying to cope in the face of similar imperatives.) This fact is significant, not simply because it reopened the door to Western influence upon Japanese education, but because it presented Japanese reformers with an opportunity to ally themselves with like-minded reformers abroad, and to seek legitimacy for their campaign at home by linking it to a worldwide movement calling for international peace, equality, and justice.

CONCLUSION

As noted in the Introduction, when it comes to the development of educational policy and practice in modern Japan, many scholars still characterize the Meiji legacy as the product of state-centered nationalism (*kokkashugi*) at home and imperialism (*teikokushugi*) abroad; two complementary ideologies rooted in the principle of absolute loyalty to the emperor as the fountainhead of Japan's sovereignty, national unity and identity, and even her "mission" abroad. While not denying the hegemonic *potential* of these state-sponsored ideologies, this chapter has painted a more complex picture of the Meiji community of intellectuals and educators; a community which retained the capacity to challenge that hegemony because it was less homogenous and more contentious than commonly believed. Throughout this period, the members of that community—journalists, MOE officials, school administrators and teachers—debated such fundamental questions as: Who are the Japanese and what defines them as a nation? What should be the relationship between the individual and the state? What should be Japan's relationship to the international community of nations? And what kind of education is required to make this vision a reality? In the process, they not only disagreed with each other but occasionally shifted their positions in response to changing political, social, economic, or strategic considerations.

Thus, while conservatives applauded the promulgation of the Imperial Rescript on Education in 1890 and pressed for its formal recognition as the cornerstone of Japanese education, critics like Kutsumi challenged the very authority of the government to legislate private and public morality. And while many, if not most, school principals, teachers, and textbook writers cooperated during the Sino-Japanese and Russo-Japanese Wars to drum up support for "arms and empire" among the younger generation inside the nation's classrooms, others sympathized with the fledgling antiwar and peace movements that were precipitated by these conflicts.

This mixed legacy of Meiji is illustrated by historian Nakano Akira, who recounts the extraordinary steps taken by the MOE to glorify the moral character and loyal service of General Nogi Maresuke, who is best known for joining his wife in a double suicide on September 13, 1912, just as the late Emperor Meiji's funeral procession was leaving the imperial palace. In 1906, the MOE had commissioned poet Sasaki Shinko to write verses for a song extolling Nogi's heroism during the Russo-Japanese War as the epitome of the old *bushidō* ideals of loyalty and sacrifice. Four years later, in 1910, the MOE included Sasaki's verses in its fifth-grade Japanese language textbook and it also approved the song for singing exercises. According to Nakano, this initiative should not be taken as a sign of state hegemony over education. Rather, it was a defensive measure prompted by concerns that the state's ideology of emperor-centered nationalism was losing support among a population that had paid a heavy price during that bloody and costly war, and that had rioted in the streets when the terms of the treaty ending the conflict were announced. [64] The irony, of course, is that it was the Meiji government's early and consistent advocacy of universal, compulsory education, framed by the goals it set forth in the Charter Oath of 1868, which supplied educators and the general public with the intellectual tools to challenge its attempts at hegemony.

NOTES

1. Benedict Anderson, *Imagined Communities: Reflections on the Origin and Spread of Nationalism.* (London: Verso, 1983, 1991). See also: E. J., Hobsbawm, *Nations and Nationalism Since 1780: Programme, Myth, Reality* (Cambridge: Cambridge University Press, 1990); and Anthony Smith, *National Identity* (Reno: University of Nevada Press, 1991).

2. See the following examples: Edward Beauchamp, "Education," in Takeshi Ishida and Ellis S. Krauss, eds., *Democracy in Japan* (Pittsburgh, PA: University of Pittsburgh Press, 1988), 226–29; William Cummings, *Education and Equality in Japan* (Princeton, NJ: Princeton University Press, 1980), 17–25; Takashi Fujitani, *Splendid Monarchy: Power and Pageantry in Modern Japan* (Berkeley: University of California Press, 1998); Janet Hunter, *The Emergence of Modern Japan: An Introductory History Since 1853* (London: Longman, 1989), 192–97; Saburō Ienaga, *The Pacific War, 1931–1945* (New York: Random House, 1978), 19–32; Kenneth Pyle, *The Making of Modern Japan*, 2nd ed. (Lexington, MA: D. C. Heath and Company, 1996), 125–30; Schoppa, *Education Reform in Japan*, 29–31; J. E. Thomas, *Modern Japan: A Social History Since 1868* (London: Longman, 1996), 254–62; Stephen Vlastos, ed., *Mirror of Modernity: Invented Traditions of Modern Japan* (Berkeley: University of California Press, 1998).

3. The terms *shin kyōiku* (new education) and *jiyū kyōiku* (liberal education) have been appropriated by numerous social and educational reformers both before and since the Asia Pacific War, although they were most commonly used between the turn of the century and the 1930s. Consequently, it is impossible to assign concise definitions to either one. The former has been associated with Western educational reformers as diverse as J. E. Demolins (*L'education nouvelle*, 1898), Maria Montessori, Ellen Key, and John Dewey. The latter has been attributed to Japanese followers of neo-Kantianism. For present purposes, it is sufficient to bear in mind that among the generation of reformers discussed in this book, both terms generally referred to education that respects and nurtures individual interests, talents, and abilities (instead of subjecting all pupils to a single, standardized curriculum); that encourages pupils to be active participants in the learning process (rather than passive participants whose thoughts and actions are prescribed by teachers and administrators); and that strives to cultivate well-rounded, fully developed human beings (instead of placing undue emphasis on knowledge acquisition, moral training, etc.). See Ōta T. and Nakauchi Toshio, eds., *Minkan kyōiku shi kenkyū jiten* (Tokyo: Hyōronsha, 1975), 67–69, 72–75; and Ōi Yoshio, *Nihon no "shin kyōiku" shisō: Noguchi Entarō o chūshin ni* (Tokyo: Keisō Shobō, 1984), 161–71.

4. Nobuya Bamba and John F. Howes, eds., *Pacifism in Japan: The Christian and Socialist Tradition* (Kyoto: Mineruba Shobō, 1978); Ian Nish, *Japan's Struggle with Internationalism: Japan, China and the League of Nations, 1931–33* (London: Kegan Paul International) 8–14; Sadako Ogata, "The Role of Liberal Nongovernmental Organizations in Japan," in Daniel Borg and Shumpei Okamoto, eds., *Pearl Harbor as History: Japanese-American Relations, 1931–1941* (New York: Columbia University Press, 1973), 459–86.

5. Kevin M. Doak, "Liberal Nationalism in Imperial Japan: The Dilemma of Nationalism and Internationalism," in Dick Stegewerns, ed., *Nationalism and Internationalism in Imperial Japan: Autonomy, Asian Brotherhood, or World Citizenship?* (London and New York: Routledge Curzon, 2003), 19.

6. For a critique of this scholarship, see Mark Lincicome, "Local Citizens or Loyal Subjects? Enlightenment Discourse and Educational Reform," in Helen Hardacre, ed., *New Directions in the Study of Meiji Japan* (Leiden: Brill, 1997), 451–55.

7. Herbert Passin, *Society and Education in Japan* (New York: Teachers College, Columbia University, 1965).

8. Some notable exceptions to this literature are: Carol Gluck, *Japan's Modern Myths: Ideology in the Late Meiji Period* (Princeton, NJ: Princeton University Press, 1985); Marshall, *Learning to be Modern*; and Motoyama Yukihiko, *Proliferating Talent: Essays on Politics, Thought, and Education in the Meiji Era*, edited by J. S. A. Elisonas and Richard Rubinger (Honolulu: University of Hawai'i Press, 1997). However, Gluck does not mention either the liberal or international education movements, while Marshall merely refers to them in passing (pp. 105–06). See also the conclusion to Mark E. Lincicome, *Principle, Praxis, and the Politics of Educational Reform in Meiji Japan* (Honolulu: University of Hawai'i Press, 1995).

9. "This means that we should not treat nationalism itself as a social actor and ask whether it is good or bad, liberal or radical, or conducive to democratic poli-

tics. Rather we should ask: What is the global, societal, and institutional context in which different groups compete to control this symbol and its meanings? What are the programs of the different groups? Radical? Liberal? Reactionary? What are the social conditions that predispose towards success for one group and one program over another? This approach takes the 'ism' out of nationalism and lodges agency back in human beings, constrained by social structures. It also leads us to wonder if the term nationalism is adequate to the inflation of its meanings and uses." Katherine Verdery, "Whither 'Nation' and 'Nationalism'?" in *Daedalus* 22, no. 3 (Summer 1993), 39.

10. Hobsbawm, *Nations and Nationalism Since 1780*, 110.

11. Satō Shigeki, "Nēshon, nashonarizumu, esunishitei." in *Shisō* 854 (1995), 115–17. See also the following essays by Kevin M. Doak: "Colonialism and Ethnic Nationalism in the Political Thought of Yanaihara Tadao (1893–1961)," in *East Asian History* 10 (1995), 79–98; and "Culture, Ethnicity, and the State in Early 20th Century Japan," in Sharon A. Minichiello, ed., *Japan's Competing Modernities: Issues in Culture and Democracy, 1900–1930* (Honolulu: University of Hawai'i Press, 1998), 181–205.

12. Kevin M. Doak, *A History of Nationalism in Modern Japan* (Leiden: Brill, 2007), 45.

13. Tom Nairn, "Internationalism and the Second Coming," in *Daedalus* 22, no. 3 (1993), 155–70.

14. See Akira Iriye, *Cultural Internationalism and World Order* (Baltimore, MD: Johns Hopkins University Press, 1997), especially chapter 2.

15. The state could not afford to ignore this challenge because, as Zygmunt Bauman observes:

> As the sovereignty of the modern state is the power to define and to make definitions stick, everything that self-defines or eludes state-legislated definition is subversive. . . . Resistance to definition sets the limit to sovereignty, to power, to the power of the sovereign state, to order. That resistance is the stubborn and grim reminder of the flux which order wished to contain but in vain; of the limits to order; of the necessity of ordering. State ordering creates chaos. But the state needs chaos to go on creating order.

Zygmunt Bauman, "Modernity and Ambivalence," in Mike Featherstone, ed., *Global Culture: Nationalism, Globalization and Modernity* (London: Sage Publications, 1990), 166.

16. Andrew Gordon substitutes his term for the more common "Taishō Democracy," which he criticizes as "chronologically inaccurate and analytically empty." See his book, *Labor and Imperial Democracy in Prewar Japan* (Berkeley: University of California Press, 1991), 5–10.

17. Ishizuki Minoru, "Kokuminshugi to jiyūshugi," in Motoyama Yukihiko, ed., *Meiji kyōiku yoron no kenkyū*, Vol. 1 (Tokyo: Fukumura Shuppan Kabushikigaisha, 1972); Nozawa Masako, "Sekaishugi," in Motoyama, ed. *Meiji kyōiku yoron no kenkyū*, 175-217; Motoyama Yukihiko, *Kindai Nihon no seiji to kyōiku* (Kyoto: Mineruba Shobō, 1972).

18. Following the lead of Frederick Dickinson, I have elected to substitute the word "Renovation" for the more common "Restoration" when referring to the

Meiji Ishin. While "Restoration" highlights the "return" of political power from the Tokugawa shogun to the Meiji Emperor that took place in 1868, "Renovation" is now acknowledged to be a more literal translation of the Japanese. Equally important, it better captures the spirit that inspired at least some of the participants to dismantle the Tokugawa system and its accompanying traditions in the years that followed, and to undertake the ambitious series of reforms that marked the first half of the Meiji period.

19. Itō, Kitamura and Ebuchi, "Nihon ni okeru kokusaika shisō to sono keifu," 11.

20. Ibid., 49–66.

21. The text of the 1854 Treaty of Kanagawa is reprinted in Peter Booth Wiley, *Yankees in the Land of the Gods: Commodore Perry and the Opening of Japan* (New York: Penguin Books, 1990), 501–03. The first of the "unequal treaties," the Treaty of Amity and Commerce (known informally as the Harris Treaty), which was concluded between Japan and the United States on July 28, 1858, is reprinted in David Lu, ed., *Japan: A Documentary History* (Armonk, New York: M. E. Sharpe, 1997), 289–92.

22. Quoted in Donald Keene, *The Japanese Discovery of Europe, 1720–1830* (Stanford: Stanford University Press, 1952, 1969), 180.

23. Ibid., 192.

24. Ibid., 207.

25. The phrase "totalitarian nationalism" appears in Ryūsaku Tsunoda, Wm. Theodore deBary, and Donald Keene, eds., *Sources of Japanese Tradition*, Vol. 2 (New York: Columbia University Press, 1958), 56. Grant K. Goodman likens Satō's vision to "a sort of modified national socialism" in his *Japan: The Dutch Experience* (London and Dover, NH: The Athlone Press, 1986), 220.

26. Komine Kazuo, "Kaikokuki ni okeru kaigai shokuminron," in Asada Kyōji, ed., *"Teikoku Nihon" to Ajia* (Yoshikawa Hirofumi Kan, 1994), 43–44.

27. Quoted in Tsunoda et. al. *Sources of Japanese Tradition*, 70–71.

28. Goodman, *Japan: The Dutch Experience*, 220–21.

29. Ibid.; Tsunoda et. al. *Sources of Japanese Tradition*, 58. Another late Tokugawa era proponent of Western learning that also advocated greater attention to education (especially science and technology) and promoted territorial expansion through foreign trade and colonization was the painter Watanabe Kazan. See W. G. Beasley, *Japan Encounters the Barbarian: Japanese Travellers in America and Europe* (New Haven, CT: Yale University Press, 1995), 33–34.

30. The Charter Oath went through several drafts, which are translated in Lu, ed., *Japan: A Documentary History*, 308–09. For additional analysis of the political challenges that promulgation of the Charter Oath posed to the Meiji regime as it moved to act upon its five articles during the remainder of the period, see Mark Lincicome, "Meiji Period," in David Levinson and Karen Christensen, eds., *Encyclopedia of Modern Asia*, vol. 4 (New York: Charles Scribner's Sons, 2002), 129–35.

31. See Lincicome, *Principle, Praxis, and the Politics of Educational Reform in Meiji Japan*.

32. Frederick R. Dickinson, *War and National Reinvention: Japan and the Great War, 1914–1919* (Cambridge, MA: Harvard University Asia Center, 1999), 15.

33. Robert Eskildsen argues that this "drive for empire" had begun to influence Meiji foreign policy even earlier, with the government's decision to mount a punitive expedition against a group of aborigines on Taiwan in 1874, ostensibly in retaliation for the murder of fifty-four people from the Ryūkyū Kingdom who were shipwrecked there in 1871. See his essay, "'Leading the Natives to Civilization': The Colonial Dimension of the Taiwan Expedition." Harvard University, Edwin O. Reischauer Institute of Japanese Studies, *Occasional Papers in Japanese Studies*, Number 2003-01 (March 2003).

34. Dickinson, *War and National Reinvention*, 12–17.

35. In addition to Satō Nobuhiro, another late-Tokugawa ideologue whose writings anticipated Japan's early twentieth-century mission of world renovation was Ōkuni Takamasa. Ōkuni rejected Western insistence that all nations must conform to the Western discipline of international law "simply because there exists no single ruler over all the nations of the world":

> There are good and bad people; everybody respects the good and everyone despises the bad. There are good and bad, noble and base countries, too. This explains, of course, why Westerners have adopted the practice of granting "titles" to nations; "imperial" nations, "royal" nations, "noble" nations and so forth. The nations of the world should, therefore, select the best among those of "imperial" rank, style it a "greater imperial nation," and refer to its ruler as the greater ruler of all the world. Amongst the nations bearing the title "imperial," it is Japan alone whose Emperor's rule extends from the Age of the Gods. What could be more natural, then, than to elevate the Japanese Emperor to a position of "greater emperor," and have all nations revere him? It remains, however, that knowledge of the Japanese imperial line has yet to reach other nations, and they are bound to reject all this as "national" theorizing. We have no choice but to wait for the day when all nations acknowledge this truth.

Quoted in Ōkuni Takamasa, "Bankoku Kōhō" [New True International Law], translated by John Breen, in *Readings in Tokugawa Thought*, 2nd ed., Select Papers, Vol. 9 (Chicago: The Center for East Asian Studies, The University of Chicago, 1994), 234–35.

36. Doak, "Liberal Nationalism in Imperial Japan," 25.

37. Ibid., 27.

38. Gordon, *Labor and Imperial Democracy in Japan*, 50–52; S. C. M. Paine, *The Sino-Japanese War of 1894–1895: Perceptions, Power and Primacy* (Cambridge: Cambridge University Press, 2003), 135–36.

39. The reluctance of educators to criticize or oppose government policies in support of "empire, arms, and oligarchic rule" was surely heightened by the widely publicized case of Uchimura Kanzō, who felt compelled to resign his teaching position at the First Higher Middle School in 1891 following his failure to bow with sufficient reverence before a copy of the Imperial Rescript on Education containing the Emperor's signature, as stipulated by the school principal. See Robert Lee, "Service to Christ and Country: Uchimura's Search for Meaning," in Ray A. Moore, ed., *Culture and Religion in Japanese-American Relations: Essays on Uchimura Kanzō, 1861–1930* (Ann Arbor: Center for Japanese Studies, University of Michigan, 1981), 86–87. For a slightly different interpretation of this event, see Marshall, *Learning to be Modern*, 59–60.

40. Dickinson, *War and National Reinvention*, 27–28. See also Gordon, *Labor and Imperial Democracy in Japan*, 52.

41. Ibid., 32.

42. Kenneth B. Pyle, "Meiji Conservatism," in *Cambridge History of Japan*, Vol. 5 (Cambridge: Cambridge University Press, 1989), 688.

43. Ibid.

44. John D. Pierson, *Tokutomi Sohō, 1863–1957: A Journalist for Modern Japan* (Princeton: Princeton University Press, 1980), 83–90, 115–18.

45. Ibid., 90–105.

46. Motoyama Yukihiko, *Proliferating Talent*, 357.

47. Pierson, *Tokutomi Sohō*, 244–46.

48. Pyle, "Meiji Conservatism," 695.

49. Quoted in Kenneth B. Pyle, *The New Generation in Meiji Japan: Problems of Cultural Identity, 1885–1895* (Stanford, CA: Stanford University Press, 1969), 173.

50. Alistair Swale, "Tokutomi Sohō and the Problem of the Nation-State in an Imperialist World," in Dick Stegewerns, ed., *Nationalism and Internationalism in Imperial Japan* (London and New York: Routledge Curzon, 2003), 74.

51. Ibid., 75.

52. Motoyama, *Proliferating Talent*, 358.

53. Quoted in Pyle, "Meiji Conservatism," 692–93.

54. Pyle, *The New Generation*, 150–55.

55. Motoyama Yukihiko, "Meiji kokka no kyōiku shisō: Taishō kyōiku to no kanren o chūshin ni," in Ikeda Susumu and Motoyama Yukihiko, eds., *Taishō no Kyōiku* (Tokyo: Dai Ippō Ki Shuppan Kabushikigaisha, 1978), 59–66.

56. Ibid., 70–72. In the same vein, Motoyama also believes that historians have unfairly characterized as statist and nationalistic the better known education ordinances attributed to Mori Arinori during his tenure as minister of education (December 1885 to February 1889).

57. See Kevin M. Doak, "Nationalism as Dialectics: Ethnicity, Moralism, and the State in Early Twentieth-Century Japan," in James W. Heisig and John C. Maraldo, eds., *Rude Awakenings: Zen, the Kyoto School & the Question of Nationalism* (Honolulu: University of Hawai'i Press, 1994–1995), 174–96.

58. Nozawa Masako, "Sekaishugi," 177–82; Motoyama, *Kindai Nihon no seiji to kyōiku*, 276–87; Motoyama, "Meiji kokka no kyōiku shisō, 88–92; Oka Yoshitake, *Five Political Leaders of Modern Japan*, trans. by Andrew Fraser and Patricia Murray (Tokyo: University of Tokyo Press, 1986), 185–86.

Takekoshi Yosaburō, Saionji's accomplice in this and other endeavors, offers a slightly different version of events. According to Takekoshi, Saionji approached the emperor with a proposal to instruct the people in a new morality better suited to the requirements of modern society; one that rejected the vertical relationships which anchored the old class system, and promoted horizontal relationships and emphasized common bonds between all members of society. The emperor replied by instructing Saioji to draft a new imperial rescript. Takekoshi says that he prepared the draft in consultation with Saionji, which the emperor accepted. However, before it could be issued, appendicitis forced Saionji to resign from his ministerial position. See Yosaburō Takekoshi, *Prince Saionji*, translated by Kozaki Nariaki (Kyoto: Ritsumeikan University, 1932), 154.

59. Takekoshi credits Saionji with coining the phrase *sekai no Nihon* to serve as the title of the magazine, which they conceived in consultation with Mutsu Munemitsu, Tomii Masaaki, Ume Kenjirō, Motono Ichirō, and Sakai Yūzaburō. See Takekoshi, *Prince Saionji*, 137. See also Yoshitake Oka, *Five Political Leaders of Modern Japan*, 185. The English translation, "The Japan of the World," appeared briefly on the cover of the magazine, along with a description of the publication as "A Monthly Political, Financial, Social, and Literary Review"; see, for example, Issue Number 15 (May 1, 1897).

60. Nozawa, "Sekaishugi," 177–82.

61. "Shasetsu: Sekai no Nihon," *Sekai no Nihon* 1:1 (July 25, 1896), 1–2.

62. Ibid., 182–84.

63. Koyama Kenzō, "Jitsugyō kyōiku zōkan," *Jitsugyō sekai Taiheiyō* 2:1 (January 1, 1904), 8–9.

64. Nakano Akira, *Taishō demokurashī to kyōiku: 1920 nendai no kyōiku* (Tokyo: Shin Hyōron, 1977, 1990), 9–15. Nakano notes the irony of the MOE's choice of Nogi for "deification" as a war hero and a paragon of the *bushidō* tradition, inasmuch as his management of the siege of Port Arthur, which claimed the lives of more than 50,000 soldiers — among them, his younger son — was criticized within military circles at the time, while the meaning and appropriateness of his suicide became a subject of heated debate among intellectuals and in the media.

2

The Great War, International Education, and the Politics of Peace

"TAISHŌ DEMOCRACY" AND EDUCATIONAL REFORM: CHALLENGING STATE AUTHORITY

Among students of Japanese history, the term "Taishō Democracy" has long been synonymous with the political reforms advocated by Yoshino Sakuzō under the banner of "the people as the base" (*minponshugi*), or the constitutional reinterpretation proposed by Minobe Tatsukichi through his "emperor organ theory" (*tennō kikansetsu*). Among historians of Japanese education, however, "Taishō Democracy" is just as likely to elicit references to a group of early twentieth-century Japanese educators who sought to reform the Meiji school system through the introduction of "liberal education," "new education," and "international education." In both cases, "Taishō Democracy" is shorthand for a wave of public resistance to the concentration of power amassed by the Meiji state through its management of Japan's military, economic, political, and social modernization after 1868. However, the term also masks a broad range of contending ideological and policy positions that threatened to divide, as much as to unite, critics of the status quo. Some participants accused the government of betraying the founding principles which the emperor had enshrined in the Charter Oath of Five Articles: a government based on public discussion, social mobility, the freedom of all persons to pursue their respective callings so that there may be no discontent, the adoption of international standards of behavior in place of base customs of the past, and the pursuit of knowledge throughout the world. Others objected that specific government policies, enacted in the ensuing decades, had placed the interests of the state ahead of the interests of the people, perhaps in contravention of the Imperial Will.

Resistance against state power and objectionable government policies likewise took different forms and involved different segments of the population. At one extreme were dramatic grassroots protests like the Hibiya Riots of 1905, which were triggered by the announcement of the modest terms of the peace treaty ending the Russo-Japanese War, and the Rice Riots of 1918 that protested the effects of wartime inflation and government manipulation of rice prices. At the other extreme were peaceful campaigns organized by members of Japan's new middle class that promoted specific reforms, including the "new education" and "international education" initiatives that will be examined in this chapter.

The term "new education," like the term "Taishō Democracy," encompasses a variety of reform initiatives launched between the turn of the century and the mid-1920s. The best known of these aimed to introduce "progressive" or experimental teaching methods, curricula, and techniques of school governance pioneered by European and American educators. At the risk of overgeneralization, what these experimental doctrines had in common was a child-centered philosophy that defined learning as a process of self-discovery, self-expression, and the cultivation of each child's interests and inborn talents. The appeal of these doctrines among Japanese educators stemmed from their frustration with the Meiji education system. As noted in chapter 1, during its formative period between the early 1870s and the mid-1880s, the major components of that system—from teacher training and teaching methods to curriculum and textbooks—were based on an earlier developmental, child-centered doctrine (*kaihatsushugi*) which recognized the child as an individual possessing a unique set of inborn traits and talents, and which recognized the professional teacher as the person responsible for guiding each child to a realization of his or her potential. By the turn of the century, however, some members of that profession were warning that developmental philosophy, and the respect it accorded both to the individual child and to the individual teacher, were being sacrificed for the sake of bureaucratization, standardization and militaristic regimentation.

This was not the first time that Meiji-era political reformers and educational reformers found themselves standing on common philosophical ground, deriving support from one another in their respective campaigns. During the early 1880s, when the doctrine of *kaihatsushugi* was at the height of its popularity in Japanese normal schools and primary schools, many teachers also openly supported the Freedom and People's Rights Movement (*jiyū minken undō*), which pressed for the adoption of a "modern" national constitution and representative form of government. However, the stakes were much higher, and the situation vastly most complicated, for would-be reformers in the era of Taishō Democracy than was the case in the 1880s, because the Japan that they hoped to reform had already changed during the interim. On the domestic front, Japan no longer bore the stigma of a backward nation, but boasted many of the trappings of modernity. And on the international front, the late-Tokugawa vision of overseas empire was fast becoming a reality, with the acquisition of Taiwan and the Pescadore Islands in 1895, southern Sakhalin Island and the Liaodong Peninsula in 1905, and Korea in 1910. That fact would create a major dilemma for this new generation of reformers: Were political democracy and liberal education to be extended to *all* subjects of the burgeoning Japanese Empire, including ethnic Chinese, Taiwanese Aborigines, and ethnic Koreans, or were they to be reserved for "homeland Japanese" (*naichijin*)? At a more fundamental level, they were confronted with the question: Are political democracy and liberal education compatible with imperialism and colonialism?

This chapter examines the writings and activities of some of these educational reformers between the turn of the century and the mid-1920s, four of whom receive special attention: Noguchi Entarō, Sawayanagi Masatarō, Shimonaka Yasaburō, and Harada Minoru. It finds that they exhibited a range of responses and shifting positions as they wrestled, both individually and collectively, with this ideological, moral and political dilemma.

NOGUCHI ENTARŌ
AND THE CRISIS IN PUBLIC SCHOOLING

These reformers were not revolutionaries. Their goal was to renovate the school system that had provided them with their own education and professional training, not to destroy it. Initially, therefore, most of them attempted to reform that system from within. Moreover, some officials managing the educational bureaucracy were initially willing to let them try, so worrisome had the symptoms of malaise become.

A case in point is Noguchi Entarō, who earned his teaching license and began teaching primary school at age seventeen in his native Fukuoka Prefecture, after graduating from public primary and middle schools there. He soon left to seek additional training: first at the prefectural normal school, and then at the Tokyo Higher Normal School, from which he graduated in 1894. Noguchi's reputation as a "new education" reformer was born shortly after he was named the first principal of the new Himeji Normal School in 1901. By this time, Japan's normal schools—the very institutions responsible for training teachers—were facing what seemed like an epidemic of disorderly student behavior. Noguchi concluded that the phenomenon was spawned by the rigid, impersonal, militaristic atmosphere that pervaded the normal schools, particularly during the decade between the Sino-Japanese War and the Russo-Japanese War. With the blessing of the MOE, he introduced reforms at Himeji that were inspired by sources as disparate as the elite British public school system, the Ōyōmei branch of Confucianism, and the Tokugawa-era agricultural reformer and moralist, Ninomiya Sontoku. They included abolishing the examination system, permitting self-government in student dormitories, short-term student stays in the homes of their teachers, and nonsectarian religious study in support of moral education. Noguchi's goal was to nurture a family-like (*kazokushugi*) community based on mutual respect, friendship and cooperation between teachers and students, and between older and younger students; experiential learning; and a love of nature and humanity among students and teachers.[1]

Initially, Noguchi's reforms were considered a success: the MOE held them up as a model for the nation and awarded him a special commendation in 1908. Noguchi, for his part, returned from a study tour of Europe and America in 1914 eager to do even more, having found new inspiration in the work of educators like Maria Montessori and Ellen Key, and in new American approaches like the Dalton Laboratory Plan. The resulting "Himeji Plan" was designed to further loosen the structure of the daily school regimen; to give teachers more flexibility to tailor the curriculum to their students' abilities; and to treat math and science not simply as intellectual education, but also as moral education.

But in the years between the Russo-Japanese War and the Great War, as the Taishō Democracy phenomenon spread among disaffected members of the middle and lower classes, the government took an increasingly dim view of liberal educational doctrines (*jiyū kyōiku*) that seemed to encourage a self-indulgent individualism (*kojinshugi*) at the expense of state-centered nationalism. Noguchi's frustration grew in 1917, when he discovered that other normal schools were either unwilling or unable to jettison their military-style regimen and incorporate his Himeji Plan. Eventually, like some other "new education" proponents, Noguchi concluded that the best way to put his liberal, humanistic ideas into practice was to leave the public sector in favor of private education.[2] His opportunity to do so came in 1919 at the invitation of Sawayanagi Masatarō—another defector from the public sector—who persuaded Noguchi to resign his position at Himeji and move to Tokyo to undertake a very different assignment.

SAWAYANAGI MASATARŌ
AND THE MEANING OF THE GREAT WAR

Sawayanagi was the most prominent educator of his generation to make this move from the public to the private educational sphere; although, in truth, the division between the two has never been absolute, and relations between public authority and private educational organizations and institutions have, at different times, ranged from contentious to conciliatory.[3] A native of Matsumoto city in Nagano Prefecture—a region famous for its avid support of schooling and educational modernization throughout the late-Tokugawa and Meiji periods—Sawayanagi began his formal education at the Kaichi Shōgakkō; one of the first public elementary schools to open in the new era of "civilization and enlightenment." When his family moved to Tokyo in 1875, ten-year-old Masatarō entered the laboratory primary school affiliated with the Tokyo Normal School, where he was exposed to the child-centered teaching practices inspired by the developmental education doctrine. Three years later, he proceeded to a public middle school in Tokyo, and then to the Tokyo Daigaku Yobimon, a preparatory boarding school, before entering Tokyo Imperial University in 1884.[4]

After graduating from the Department of Philosophy in 1888, Sawayanagi went on to wear many hats during a long and distinguished career that straddled the public and private spheres. After a brief stint at the MOE, he resigned in 1892 and spent the next six years as a principal at both public and private middle schools. In 1898 he was appointed principal of the government's elite First Higher School. In 1908, he returned to the MOE to assume the powerful post of vice minister, but not before making two trips abroad: an eight-month sojourn in 1902 to observe educational conditions in Europe and the United States; and a visit to London in 1906, where he lectured on the history of Japanese education. In 1911 he was appointed president of Tohoku Imperial University, and two years later he was named president of Kyoto Imperial University. However, his forced resignation in 1914 over the so-called Sawayanagi Incident (*Sawayanagi jiken*) brought his formal career as a public servant to an abrupt end.[5]

His reentry into the private sector did not have to wait long. In 1916, Sawayanagi became the principal of the newly established Seijō Middle School, and the very next year he oversaw the establishment of an affiliated elementary school, where he could develop his liberal education philosophy and experimental teaching methods without having to cater to the demands of the government and business community for purely practical training geared to the creation of an obedient workforce.[6]

Perhaps even more important to the history of international education in Japan was Sawayanagi's appointment in 1916 to take over the reins of the Imperial Education Association (Teikoku Kyōikukai). The Association was ostensibly a private membership organization serving the interests of educators throughout the country. However, much of its funding came from the government, and under the direction of Baron Tsuji Shinji the Association had come to be regarded as a conservative, moribund government mouthpiece by increasingly vocal critics of Japanese education. Tsuji's death in December 1915 created the opportunity to bring in Sawayanagi—who had built a reputation as a straight-talking reformer who favored limiting government's role in education—to assert the Association's independence from the MOE. And it was Noguchi, in turn, whom Sawayanagi invited from Himeji in 1919 to serve as executive director, in order to help Sawayanagi reorient this stagnating Association toward the new education movement.[7]

One tool at their disposal was the Association's magazine, *Imperial Education* (*Teikoku Kyōiku*), whose nationwide distribution provided a forum to influence the opinions of teachers, school administrators, government officials and journalists regarding leading educational issues of the day. Under their direction, the magazine began to publish a wider range of articles, reaching beyond purely pedagogical matters to encompass educational thought and politics, domestic and foreign events impacting education, and so forth that, on occasion, struck a surprisingly critical tone. One notable example, which appeared in the December 1921 issue under the title, "Shortcomings of Imperial Japan that should be Considered," amounts to an editorial, inasmuch as it was written by Miura Tōsaku, whom Sawayanagi had hired the previous year to edit the magazine.[8] Miura opens with a scathing post mortem on the political legacy of Prime Minister Hara Kei following his assassination on November 4. Miura criticizes those who idolize Hara as the man who ushered genuine party politics into Japan: while Hara was indeed a master of the machinery of politics, he was motivated not by higher ideals, but solely by a desire to empower his own political party, the Seiyukai, and its friends. His policies contributed nothing to the people's welfare or to advancing the nation's cultural enlightenment, writes Miura; witness Hara's reduction of the budget for education, and his selection of political cronies to serve in the top positions of the MOE.

Miura revisits this theme at the end of his essay, which decries the unprecedented decline in public respect for the MOE, surpassing even the period during 1903 and 1904, when the government debated abolishing the MOE altogether. Hara stacked the MOE's top positions with political appointees; they, in turn, chose subordinates based on academic pedigree rather than ability. Yet, simply injecting new blood into the MOE and investing these officials with more authority is not enough, Miura writes. The true mark of an enlightened nation is a government that supports education in order to advance science and industry, and to build a cultural country (*bunkateki kokka no kensetsu*).[9]

Noguchi and Sawayanagi also contributed articles to *Imperial Education* on a regular basis, such as a two-part essay on democracy and its relationship to education by Noguchi that appeared in 1920. In the face of conservative skeptics who insist that democracy is incompatible with Japan's emperor-centered *kokutai* and would undermine the nation, Noguchi argues that the nation-state risks disappearing altogether if it fails to adopt democracy, while also adapting democracy to suit Japan's monarchical tradition. Historically, he explains, education has played an indispensable dual role in the advance of democracy throughout the world. On one hand, the demand for democracy grows as access to education spreads from the few to the many, empowering them with a new consciousness of themselves and knowledge of their world. On the other hand, the spread of education is essential for a democratic system of government to function properly. Japan's own transition to a democratic, parliamentary system of government can be facilitated by the fact that education has already spread widely among its people, and by Japan's long history of assimilating foreign ideas and doctrines, such as Buddhism, which also faced similar resistance when it first arrived on Japanese shores.[10]

Sawayanagi's contributions to *Imperial Education*, and to other periodicals such as the research journal published by his faculty at Seijō, document his circuitous path from champion of national education to advocate of international education between 1914 and 1923. They leave no doubt that for Sawayanagi and his contemporaries the principal catalyst for this shift was the Great War, which prompted him to move gradually from particularism toward universalism, in a three-stage process that took him from Japanism, to Asianism, and finally to internationalism.

In 1914, as hostilities commenced in Europe, Sawayanagi, sounding very much like an MOE official, issues a warning to his Japanese readers in an essay entitled, "A Discussion of Citizens' Future Resolve and its Application to Education." After nostalgically recounting Japan's impressive transformation into a powerful, advanced nation during the Meiji period, Sawayanagi cautions that her very success has made Japan the target of suspicion and enmity among other nations, which now see Japan as their rival: witness the mounting hostility in the United States, Canada and elsewhere toward Japanese immigrants. In the wake of Japan's success, its people no longer have a common sense of purpose capable of uniting them and encouraging them to contribute to the good of the nation. Instead, they have become absorbed in individualism and flirt with an influx of new ideas from the West.

Contrast Japan with Germany, he writes, where the people are convinced of German superiority and are prepared to devote themselves to achieving what they see as Germany's destiny to become the world's mightiest nation. Japanese must take their cue from the Germans, recognize that the rest of the world has turned against them, and commit themselves to the survival and prosperity of their nation in the face of this adversity.[11]

As the war in Europe dragged on, however, Sawayanagi grew more pensive about its impact on civilization, whereupon he began to publish a number of articles devoted to the question: What kind of education will be needed after the war is over? One of the earliest of these essays, published in 1916, opens with Sawayanagi speculating on whether militarism or pacifism will be the legacy of the war. What could convince the nations of the world, now locked in battle, to forsake war in the future, he asks rhetorically. His answer: the utter senselessness of this war, which will produce no real winners, only victims on both sides of the conflict; the war's unprecedented scale of devastation; and its enormous cost in lives and money wasted. Hence, those educators who seek to make militarism and morality the basis of postwar education are shortsighted and fail to consider Japan's long-term needs. Rather, they should press for practical reforms that will demonstrate the people's loyalty to the emperor by preparing them to live and work abroad, and contribute thereby to maintaining Japan's position as an economic, cultural, and scientific leader in Asia and throughout the world.[12] If, as seems likely, the war serves to revitalize Western civilization and renew the spirit of its people, then Japan must prepare to respond to a new wave of Western economic and political influence in Asia, as well as to a new wave of Western social and political ideas.[13]

He elaborates on this theme the following year, in several essays devoted to presenting what he terms a "new doctrine" (*shin shugi*) to guide educational policy following the war. Specifically, he advocates going beyond merely continuing the prewar mix of doctrines, e.g., militarism, "family-ism" (*kazokushugi*), science education, and the like to consider what new educational policies will be called for in light of the Great War and its impact on global conditions. He urges the Japanese to study carefully the prospects for negotiating a permanent peace, which, if it comes about, will have a tremendous impact upon national systems, social organization, and human thought, not to mention international relations.

In the meantime, however, he urges the adoption of "Asianism" (*tōashugi, tōyōshugi, ajiashugi*) as the new doctrinal foundation of Japan's postwar education. The aims of this new doctrine are many. Inspired by ethnic creeds (*minzokushugi*) already rampant in the West, such as Anglo-Saxonism and Germanism, which share a common antipathy toward the Yellow Race, its first goal must be to liberate Asia from the White Peril and promote peace and happiness in the region. This aim, in turn, serves three other functions. First, since Japan is the only Asian nation capable of bringing about Asia's liberation and advancement, Asianism provides the Japanese people with the sort of shared mission that is necessary to foster a healthy nationalism at home. Second, Asianism will inspire the Japanese people to overcome their infatuation with the West and their disdain for their fellow Asians, especially Chinese and Koreans, leading to better relations with China and more effective colonial administration in Korea. Third, Asianism will encourage the Japanese people to acquire greater knowledge of Asian civilization, which is a prerequisite for Japan to contribute to "world culture" (*sekai no bunka*) by acting as a bridge between the Orient and the Occident.[14]

The logic, and much of the rhetoric, of Sawayanagi's Asianism evokes thoughts of Japan's scheme to establish a New Order in East Asia that was announced in November 1938, and its call for a Greater East Asia Co-prosperity Sphere two years later, both of which were intended to justify Japanese aggression during the Asia-Pacific War.[15] There is a good reason for this, according to Barak Kushner, whose study of Japanese wartime propaganda between 1931 and 1945 concludes that it was "actually a subset of the imperial propaganda project that dates back to the 1890s. . . . In the first decades of the twentieth century, not only did many of the nonmilitary educated Japanese elite support Japan's imperial aims, but Japan's message of 'Asia for the Asiatics' also held broad popular appeal."[16] As a result, Japanese historians accuse Sawayanagi of distorting the principles of humanism and internationalism in order to rationalize and defend Japanese ethnic nationalism and imperialism. Ozawa Yūsaku, for example, contends that Sawayanagi conceived of the world in three units: an inner unit, dominated by the modern Japanese nation-state, which encompassed the colonies of Korea and Taiwan and joined their peoples to native Japanese as subjects of the Japanese empire; an intermediate unit populated by Chinese and other Asian "related peoples," as described in his doctrine of Asianism; and an outer unit dominated by the West. This tripartite conception of the world skewed Sawayanagi's understanding of ethnic groups and riddled his policies to educate and assimilate them with contradictions.

Thus, continues Ozawa, while Sawayanagi recognized and respected the distinctive cultures developed by native Japanese and Westerners, he dismissed those of Korean, Taiwanese and other Asian ethnic groups as inferior and insignificant. On one hand, convinced that Japan had achieved parity with the West as a modern, advanced nation, Sawayanagi was open to viewing Japan from a Western perspective and to advocating Western "liberal" educational reforms that would imbue his Japanese students with the "modern" ideals of individuality, democracy, and love for humanity. On the other hand, convinced that Japan was superior to other Asian nations by virtue of her unique culture and her unique ability to emulate the modern West without falling victim to Western colonialism, Sawayanagi was incapable of viewing Koreans, Taiwanese, Chinese or other Asians except from a Japanese perspective. So even as he worked to formulate a new, "liberal" educational plan at Seijō Gakuen that would respect the individuality of his native Japanese students and cultivate in them a modern Japanese consciousness, Sawayanagi supported educational policies aimed at Japan's non-Japanese imperial subjects—Ainu, Okinawans, Koreans, Taiwanese—which, under the guise of providing humanitarian assistance to help civilize these backward peoples, denied both their individuality and any inherent value in their distinctive ethnic identities.[17]

Prompted more by a pragmatic mission to secure the blessings of the empire for the Japanese people than by a humanistic mission to secure those blessings for Japan's colonial subjects, Sawayanagi advocated education that would not only improve the lives of the latter, but would also assimilate (*dōka*) them into Japanese society. In theory, this meant that Japan's colonial subjects could expect to enjoy the same respect, legal rights and civic responsibilities as native Japanese, provided that they shed their own cultural heritage and embraced Japanese culture and a Japanese identity. To that end, Sawayanagi helped to develop the Meiji government's program of colonial education emphasizing moral education and Japanese language acquisition. In a 1909 Japanese translation of a series of lectures which he first delivered in English to London audiences three years earlier, Sawayanagi explains that Japanese language instruction is a humanitarian measure that is beneficial to the people of Taiwan because it is a vital means of communication, it contributes to their cultural development (*bunka hattatsu*), and because it is the most effective aid to their assimilation.[18]

In practice, however, colonial education served to reinforce the alien status and inferiority of the colonized, just as Sawayanagi's descriptions of it served to reinforce Japanese claims of educational and cultural superiority. This can be seen in two essays that he published in the autumn of 1910, shortly after the ink had dried on the Japan-Korea Annexation Treaty that was signed on August 22. In the first essay Sawayanagi welcomes the treaty and expresses confidence that Koreans and his fellow Japanese will, too. The treaty, he writes, presents Koreans with their first real opportunity to realize a better future. It allows Japanese to heal the domestic divisions that sparked the Korea Controversy, the Saga Rebellion, and the Seinan War during the first decade of Meiji, and to neutralize the threat to Japan's security that led to wars with China and Russia. It establishes a foundation for peace in the Orient (*tōyō no heiwa no kiso*) that will enable both Koreans and Japanese residents in Korea to experience the benefits of civilization under the Japanese emperor. He also expresses optimism about the prospects for a smooth process of cultural assimilation. Among the world's many different ethnic groups, he writes, there are none more closely related than Japanese and Koreans, as evidenced by linguistic analysis of their respective languages and by physiological analysis of their physical characteristics. These scientific facts, coupled with a history of cultural, economic and diplomatic relations reaching back some two thousand years, mean that it is only natural for that shared history to culminate in their union under a common national sovereignty and a single state (*kokka*).[19]

However, in the second essay (published in the magazine *Imperial Education* six years before he became president of its parent organization) Sawayanagi strikes a more cautionary note on the prospects for the speedy assimilation of Koreans through education. While the ultimate goals of colonial education should be the same as those for education of native Japanese, a provisional policy must first be developed, based on an investigation of the reasons for Koreans' docility. Koreans are not inherently stupid or completely backward. The reason why Korean culture is not as advanced as Japanese culture is due, instead, to Korea's geographic location sandwiched between China and Japan—making it the target of periodic invasions and plunder—and to its small size and population. Chances are that Japanese would have suffered the same fate, if positions had been reversed.[20]

Elaborating on his earlier prescription for educating the people of Taiwan, Sawayanagi reiterates the importance of immersing Koreans in the study of Japanese language, since it is through the Japanese language that Japanese ideas will be conveyed. To this end, more primary schools must be built in Korea and Japanese language textbooks must be supplied to them. Official correspondence should be written in Japanese, and popular Korean novels about family life (*katei shōsetsu*) should be presented to them in Japanese translation. Provisions for supplementary education (*hoshū kyōiku*) and evening classes should also be made. Through these steps Koreans can be assimilated and groomed to contribute to the advancement of civilization alongside Japanese.[21]

Sawayanagi, it is safe to say, would not have admitted to any contradictions in his educational thought. As a proponent of internationalism he professed to respect ethnic and cultural differences as assets for the enrichment of humanity. And as for Japanese expansion in Asia, this was not the same as Western imperialism, according to Sawayanagi, since the purpose was to help the rest of Asia, not to exploit it. True, he admits, weaker ethnic groups like the Ainu and the Ryūkyū people have found it difficult to adjust to modern ways, but the Japanese government has always been committed to their assimilation. The same holds true for Koreans, who are ethnically and culturally related to the Japanese. The Chinese, while not related ethnically, nevertheless share a common cultural heritage that provides a unique foundation upon which to base a close, cooperative relationship as China strives to become a modern nation.[22]

The ambiguities and contradictions embedded in Sawayanagi's characterization of Japan's colonial subjects and in his prescription for their education were common among his contemporaries, including other prominent "internationalists" like Nitobe Inazō, whose career included service as a colonial administrator in Taiwan, headmaster of the elite First Higher School in Tokyo, professor of colonial policy at Tokyo Imperial University, and under-secretary-general of the League of Nations.[23] They were also embedded in the very policies that colonial administrators tried, with little success, to implement on the ground. For example, even though Sawayanagi, Nitobe, and other members of their generation pointed to the introduction of compulsory education as a major factor in Japan's swift and successful nation-building effort during the Meiji period, the state moved much more slowly to extend the advantages of schooling to the people of Taiwan and Korea, where school attendance did not become compulsory until the early 1940s, by which time schools throughout the crumbling Japanese empire had ceased to function as places of learning. Even assimilation (*dōka*) did not become official policy until the early 1920s. Instead, early colonial policy took a gradualist approach that Leo T.S. Ching labels "accommodation and association," which left attendance voluntary and allowed local schools taught in the native language to coexist with a small number of Japanese-language schools, most of which were concentrated in the cities and served children of the local elite. Nitobe, writing in 1912, offered a "scientific" rationale for this gradualist policy:

> I think that assimilation will be found easier in Korea, for the reason that the Korean race is very much allied to our own. In Formosa, assimilation will be out of the question for long years to come, and we shall not try to force it. We put no pressure upon the people to effect assimilation or Japanization. Our idea is to provide a Japanese milieu, so to speak, and if the Formosans adapt themselves to our ways of their own accord, well and good. Social usages must not be laid upon an unwilling people. . . . If the Formosans or the Koreans approach us in customs and manners, we will not repulse them. We will receive them with open arms, and we will hold them as our brothers; but if they do not desire to adopt our way of living, we will not pursue them. We leave their customs and manners just as they are disposed to have them, as long as they are law-abiding. Our principle is firmness in government and freedom in society.[24]

However, E. Patricia Tsurumi cites lest lofty and more pragmatic reasons for this policy of "accommodation and association." For native Japanese living and working in the colonies, the education of the native populace represented a threat to their privileged existence. Moving to a full-fledged policy of assimilation would siphon off government funding that went into maintaining higher quality, segregated schools that served "homeland Japanese" (*na-ichijin*) exclusively. It would prompt demands from the native population for access to those exclusive schools. It would reduce the pool of undereducated, low-wage native laborers employed by Japanese industry in the colonies, while increasing the pool of educated natives who would demand to compete with the Japanese for the better-paying, higher status positions. Worst of all, assimilation, if successful, would ultimately obliterate the very claims of cultural difference and superiority that the Japanese used to justify colonization in the first place.[25]

Seen in this light, it was not surprising that assimilation only became official policy in Taiwan and Korea in the 1920s, in a belated effort to neutralize more immediate threats to Japanese control stemming from the Korean independence movement and demands in both colonies for representative government. Furthermore, as Ching explains, "Japanese colonialism, on the ideological level at least, could not abandon the rhetoric of *dōka* because . . . Japanese colonial discourse had legitimized itself on the basis of its difference from Western colonialism. If Japanese colonialism abandoned the discourse of *dōka*, it would also, by definition eliminate legitimacy of Japanese colonial rule itself."[26]

Even so, the policy of *dōka* failed to achieve its goals because it failed to appeal either to the colonial administrators responsible for implementing it or to the colonized, who showed a continued preference for private schools taught in their native tongue. Thus, it was also no surprise that *dōka* was, in turn, replaced in 1937 by *kōminka* (imperialization); a shift which, as Ozaki Hotsuki observes, allowed the colonized "not to live as Japanese, but to die as Japanese"[27] as the empire became embroiled in the Asia-Pacific War. Under *kōminka*, mandatory school attendance and study of the Japanese language, ethics, history, and military drill were accompanied by new laws that declared the use of one's native tongue a punishable offense, expected ritual submission to the emperor, and even pressured Koreans and Taiwanese to adopt Japanese surnames.[28]

Sawayanagi was not the first person to justify Japanese imperialism by appealing to Asianism, and he would not be the last. But while it is true that Sawayanagi's intellectual passage from particularism to universalism was halting, and prone to contradictions and reversals, such criticism must be tempered by two observations. First, at this time internationalism itself was still Eurocentric, which limited the options available to him. According to Akira Iriye, "Asian writers . . . had somehow to hope that the blatantly racist arguments they saw in the West did not represent the prevailing view and that ultimately internationalism would be broadened enough to accommodate the whole of humanity—otherwise, they would either have to counter this formulation by developing their own definition of internationalism or abandon the effort and retreat to an exclusionary stance comparable to some Western writers."[29]

Japanese critics of Western discourse on internationalism that echoed through the Palace of Versailles during the Paris Peace Conference had good reason to be skeptical of the sincerity of the Allies' proclamation of a new world order based on the principles of peaceful coexistence, equality, and self-determination. None other than President Woodrow Wilson, the chief architect of this new world order, had advised his Cabinet in February 1917 that the United States should stay out of the Great War "to keep the white race or part of it strong to meet the yellow race—Japan, for instance, in alliance with Russia, dominating China." Wilson carried his anxieties about the "yellow race" through the final years of the war and into the peace conference in 1919.[30] One example of this was Wilson's capitulation to Australian Prime Minister Billy Hughes, who adamantly opposed Japan's proposal to insert the phrase "the principle of the equality of Nations and the just treatment of their nationals" into the League of Nations Covenant because Hughes feared it would undermine Australia's whites-only immigration and naturalization policy.[31]

Western racism toward Asians was nothing new, of course, as the Japanese who watched the proceedings at Versailles knew only too well. Long before Australia had announced its White Australia Policy in 1901 and before Kaiser Wilhelm II had proclaimed Japan's victory over China the harbinger of a "Yellow Peril" in 1895, the United States had enacted a series of laws targeting Orientals. As Roger Daniels observes, the abolition of slavery in 1865 prompted Congress five years later to amend a naturalization statute that the first Congress had passed in 1790, which stated that "free white persons" who had lived in the US for at least two years could be naturalized in any American court. But rather than make the Naturalization Act of 1870 color-blind and simply refer to "persons,"

> Congress chose instead to broaden the law to allow the naturalization of "white persons and persons of African descent." Asians were pointedly excluded, and in the brief debates it was clear that a desire to exclude Chinese from citizenship was, for the majority, the main point. . . . This meant that the thousands of Chinese already in the United States and the hundreds of thousands of other Asians who would come in the following eight decades were in a new category: "aliens ineligible to citizenship" by federal law.[32]

Twelve years later, in 1882, Congress followed up with the Chinese Exclusion Act, which sought to appease white workingmen living on the West Coast who railed against cheap Chinese labor, without jeopardizing American trade with China. Under this Act, immigration of Chinese laborers was "suspended," but Chinese merchants could still be admitted. Ironically, these restrictions on the supply of cheap Chinese labor opened the door to a new wave of cheap Japanese labor to take its place. By 1900, Japanese immigrants to the continental US and their descendants numbered 24,326, three-quarters of whom resided on the Pacific coast. Predictably, this growing Japanese presence triggered another wave of nativist legislation aimed at stemming the tide of Oriental economic and cultural influence in the US, with California again taking the lead. In 1906, the San Francisco School Board tried to force Japanese students in that city to attend the already established segregated school for Chinese. The Board rescinded the order only after President Theodore Roosevelt intervened. Daniels believes that only concern about provoking a militarily powerful Japan deterred the federal government at that time from passing a Japanese version of the 1882 Chinese Exclusion Act. To forestall that possibility, Roosevelt negotiated the Gentlemen's Agreement of 1907–1908, which effectively ended the immigration of Japanese laborers to the US by having the Japanese government refrain from issuing passports to them. The Gentlemen's Agreement delayed, but did not prevent, more stringent exclusionary legislation directed against Japanese immigrants. In 1913, the California legislature passed the Webb-Heney Alien Land Act, which barred Japanese from owning land in that state. And in 1924, at the very moment when the international education movement in Japan was at its height, Congress passed the Immigration Act, which abrogated the Gentlemen's Agreement and barred all Japanese as "aliens ineligible to citizenship."[33]

Of course, Western racism toward Asians did not have to wait for their arrival on Western shores. It was a longstanding component of imperialist ideology and a prominent feature of the colonial discourse articulated by generations of Western politicians, colonial administrators, missionaries, and popular writers to justify their occupation and exploitation of Asia. Thus, it is no coincidence that the rhetoric of Asian racial inferiority which marked American debates over Asian immigration during and after the late nineteenth century was soon accompanied by American claims of a divine mission—Manifest Destiny, and the White Man's Burden—to civilize Asia as the United States staked its own territorial claims in the Asia-Pacific, beginning with the acquisition of the Philippines, Hawaii, Guam and Wake Island following the Spanish-American War.[34] If Meiji-era imperialists like Sawayanagi, or Showa-era proponents of a Greater East Asia Co-Prosperity Sphere, required any rhetorical inspiration to help advance the cause of Japanese empire, they need not have looked any farther than U.S. Senator Albert J. Beveridge of Indiana, who invoked the very same arguments—racial and moral superiority, divine mission, national security, "commercial supremacy of the world"—to push for annexation of the Philippines and the pursuit of American empire in the Pacific. Speaking before the Senate on January 9, 1900, Beveridge explained why America must not waiver in its bloody war against the Philippine independence movement, which would eventually claim the lives of over 200,000 Filipinos:

The Philippines are ours forever, "territory belonging to the United States," as the Constitution calls them. And just beyond the Philippines are China's illimitable markets. We will not retreat from either. We will not repudiate our duty in the archipelago. We will not abandon our opportunity in the Orient. We will not renounce our part in the mission of our race, trustee, under God, of the civilization of the world. And we will move forward to our work, not howling regrets like slaves whipped to their burdens but with gratitude for a task worthy of our strength and thanksgiving to Almighty God that He has marked us as His chosen people, henceforth to lead in the regeneration of the world.[35]

Many hoped that Wilsonian internationalism and the League of Nations would check the lust for empire and temper the ideology of Manifest Destiny by proclaiming that "the well-being and development" of subject peoples "form a sacred trust of civilization." However, the League merely repackaged the nineteenth-century rhetoric of paternalism and moral mission,[36] such that echoes of Senator Beveridge's speech were still audible in 1927, when Stanford University President Ray Lyman Wilbur addressed the delegates at the second conference of the Institute of Pacific Relations on America's foreign policy in the Pacific:

> The enthusiastic confidence with which the American government entered upon the program of education for the people of the Philippines has been tempered by the realization that it takes time for modern representative popular government to become reasonably efficient. America at present has a parental attitude toward the people of these Islands and is in the mood of the father of an ambitious adolescent boy who is not yet thought to be capable of making his own way in the world, but who needs more training and education.[37]

These facts shed some light on the dilemma that Sawayanagi and many other members of his generation faced in Japan during the era of Taishō imperial democracy. Although Japan joined the colonial club at virtually the same time as the U.S., the racist ideology of Asian inferiority that was easily adopted by American imperialists served to exacerbate the problem of Japanese identity and the relationship between Japanese and other members of the Yellow Race.

The second observation with respect to Sawayanagi's reputation as an imperialist is that Asianism was not the last stop on Sawayanagi's intellectual journey, even though he never renounced his support for Japanese colonialism or for the policy of assimilation. In one of his last statements on the subject—a public lecture that was published in September 1919—Sawayanagi speaks pragmatically of Asianism, Europeanism, Americanism and other ethnic creeds (*minzokushugi*) as a transitional stage between the preceding era of "jingoistic" and "chauvinistic" nationalism and a future age of globalism and human equality (*sekaishugi jinrui no byōdō*). As such, Asianism itself must uphold the principle of human equality: by making room for democracy, intellectual engagement, and creativity among the Japanese people, and by instilling Japanese with genuine respect for Chinese, Koreans, and other Asians whom they continue to disdain. Sawayanagi appears to sense the contradiction between his declaration of human equality and Japanese subjugation of their Asian relatives (*shinrui*) who they are supposed to be rescuing from European exploitation and from their own backwardness. He confides that he has heard from a knowledgeable friend that in spite of their nominal integration into the Japanese body politic, the Ryūkyū people continue to be uneasy in their relations with "us homeland Japanese" (*ware ware naichijin*) and have not fully assimilated themselves. Turning to the tense situation in Korea, he states that he does not think that the current movements for independence from Japanese rule are in the best interest of either Korea or Japan. Yet, he asks his audience to put itself in the shoes of those Korean secessionists who defiantly declare, "Japan has a mere three thousand-year history, while our Korea has a history of five thousand years!" How, he asks, should we regard this very real problem in Korea? How should we regard China? How should we deal with Siamese, Indians and Vietnamese, who have also begun to arrive on our shores?[38]

With the war nearing its end, Sawayanagi appeared ready to commit his nation to the construction of a new political and social order, both at home and abroad. In a September 1919 essay, "On the Upheaval in Thought," he writes that it is time for Japanese to break out of their traditional ways of thinking about the individual's relationship to society and Japan's relationship to the world. Democracy, justice, and humanity are the watchwords everywhere, and the time has come for Japanese to embrace them, as well. The Great War demonstrated the folly of militarism and despotism, and vindicated the universal principles of humanity (*jindō*) and justice (*seigi*). Patriotism (*aikokushin*) will persist as long as people think in terms of countries. But is it appropriate to take the position "My country, right or wrong!" and to undertake any action, even if it is unjust, merely for the sake of one's country? In a striking reversal of his praise for Germany five years earlier, Sawayanagi holds German patriotic chauvinism up for ridicule and warns that Japan, too, has its share of people who not only claim Japan is superior, but who interpret that belief as a license to engage in unjust activities in order to "unify the world." By turning a blind eye to Japan's shortcomings, such people actually inhibit the nation's ability to advance further.

In particular, Japanese must accept the fact that in contrast to Koreans, Chinese, and Westerners, they have never contributed anything to world culture in return for all they have acquired from abroad. Only when they admit this shortcoming will they be able to make it their national mission to contribute to the advancement of world culture in the future. This, in turn, is the surest way to meet the economic and diplomatic competition that has followed in the wake of the war.[39] However, insuring Japan's survival and earning the world's respect hinges upon Japan staying abreast of the West in the race to reform and expand education.[40]

In spite of his gradual transformation from defender of historical, cultural, and geographic particularism to proponent of universalism, it was not until February 1923 that developments at home and abroad convinced Sawayanagi that the time had come for Japan to commit itself to a policy of international education. In his view, however, this demanded nothing less than the elimination of statist education (*kokka kyōiku*). In an article titled "Proceeding from Statist Education to International Education," he cites the establishment of the League of Nations as a milestone on the road to human happiness and progress. Acknowledging that more time and collective effort are needed before its future is guaranteed, the League marks the first time that nations have tried to establish a new world order based on collaboration rather than sheer self-interest. Therefore, he calls on Japan and other nations to help insure its success by nurturing the spirit of collaboration among their own citizens through the promotion of international education, in place of statist education. International education, he explains, does not deny the importance of patriotism, but it places patriotism in proper perspective by emphasizing the common bonds of humanity and the importance of working together for the common good.[41]

Sawayanagi's views on postwar educational reform were further informed by an extended trip he took to Europe and America between August 1921 and June 1922 to meet some of his Western counterparts and to observe the latest educational practices there. He is credited with introducing some of their innovations into Japan. In one such initiative, he secured funding from the president of the Kawasaki Shipbuilding Company and other donors to bring Harold Palmer from Britain to improve English language education. He is even better known among historians of the new education movement for championing the Dalton Laboratory Plan, which advocated a philosophy of individualized, experiential learning in place of the traditional teacher-led, subject-centered model of instruction. Sawayanagi brought the Plan's founder, American Helen Parkhurst, to Japan to lecture on her laboratory plan, and he formally adopted her Plan at Seijō Primary School.[42]

SHIMONAKA YASABURŌ AND RADICAL ACTIVISM

Yet another educational reformer who turned to the private sector was Shimonaka Yasaburō, although his training and early career in public education followed a very different path from those of Noguchi and Sawayanagi. Shimonaka is reminiscent of the proverbial "self-made man of Meiji,"[43] with the difference that he never forsook his working class consciousness that he acquired in his youth. Forced by circumstances to leave primary school after the third grade in order to help put food on the family table, Shimonaka studied privately in his spare time until in 1899, at age twenty-one, he embarked on what would become an eventful dual career in education and publishing: earning a primary school teacher's license in his native Hyōgo Prefecture while using his own money to write and publish a manual for teaching Japanese language at primary school. Moving to the Kantō area in 1902, he spent the next fifteen years teaching: first at the Japan Women's Art School; and then at the Saitama Prefecture Normal School. At the same time, he wrote for, and edited, publications like the *Children's Newspaper* (*Jidō Shinbun*) and the *Women's Newspaper* (*Fujo Shinbun*). In 1914 he founded Heibonsha, which would become one of Japan's largest publishing houses.[44] Shimonaka's departure from the Saitama Prefecture Normal School in 1918 marked the end of his career as a public school teacher and the start of a new career as educational reformer in the private sector, which got off to a bold start in 1919 when he and some of his former Saitama students founded the nation's first teachers union.[45]

The Japan Teachers Union Enlightenment Association (Keimeikai), as it came to be known, defended individual aspirations against the demands of the state, democratic rather than oligarchic rule, and equality of opportunity in education.[46] As such, it posed a competitive challenge to the Imperial Education Association, where Noguchi had just assumed his new post alongside Sawayanagi. The union manifesto reflected the humanism and idealism that characterized the new education movement as a whole. Article One declared, "Our ideal is to bring about a way of living in society that is based on man's true way of living. Therefore, we affirm all just and fair human demands, and all just and fair social existence." Article Three announced, "We are educators. We aim to become conscious of our mission as educators and claim our freedom, to help and to guide as friends of the people, and to awaken a passionate love for humanity."[47]

Yet, even as Shimonaka's union took aim against the Japanese government through its campaign for a more democratic, just and equitable society, it was also careful to proclaim its loyalty to Japan's national polity. Article Two of the manifesto proclaimed, "We are Japanese. We will demonstrate our pure-heartedness as [members of the] Japanese ethnic nation (*minzoku*) and strive on behalf of the fair, just, grand national essence (*kokuhon*). We will forcefully eliminate every irrational, unnatural structure, custom, or idea that would obstruct it."[48]

PURSUING A "CENTURY OF EDUCATION"

While some philosophical differences remained between the Imperial Education Association and the fledgling teachers union, Shimonaka, Noguchi and
Sawayanagi managed to set them aside to cooperate in two noteworthy reform
initiatives in the early 1920s, when the Taishō Democracy phenomenon was
at its height. The one best known to historians of Japanese education is the
establishment of the Century of Education Society (Kyōiku no Seikisha) in
1923. As indicated by its name—adapted from the title of a book by European
educationist Ellen Key, which Noguchi translated into Japanese—these men
regarded their Society as a bridge between the "new education movement" in
the West and its counterpart in Japan. According to one source, Noguchi was
inspired to establish the Century of Education Society by progressive educator
Beatrice Ensor, who together with likeminded members of the British Theosophical Society and the Theosophical Educational Trust, founded the New
Education Fellowship in 1921 and published an influential journal, *Education
for a New Era*. Ensor first wrote to Noguchi in May 1922, in his capacity as
executive director of the Imperial Education Association, to inquire about
Japanese interest in "new education." After exchanging correspondence, Ensor invited Noguchi to establish a branch of the New Education Fellowship in
Japan, which culminated in the Century of Education Society. [49]

Under the Society's auspices, Noguchi and Shimonaka collaborated in
opening an experimental private school, the Children's Hamlet Primary
School (Jidō no Mura Shōgakkō) in Noguchi's Tokyo home the following
year, and in launching a journal of pedagogical theory and practice, the
Century of Education (*Kyōiku no seiki*). The first issue announced the organization's five-point manifesto, "Ethos of the Century of Education Society,"
which was inspired by that of the New Education Fellowship:

1. We believe in education that brings about the unfettered development
   of each person's individual, inborn talents, and that contributes to the
   advancement of human culture through the activation of those talents;
2. We believe in education that fully respects the child's individuality,
   which is possible only through a form of cultivation that fully guaran-
   tees [the child's] liberty (*jiyū*);
3. We believe in education that respects the child's self-generated activity, which is only possible when fresh guidance is given to [the child's]
   internal interests;
4. We believe in school life in which students and teachers, by governing
   themselves, obviate the need for outside interference or internal group
   interference;

5. In the education we believe in, we expect [the child] to recognize his or her own dignity while learning to respect others, and [we] encourage [the child] to fulfill his or her duties to humankind.[50]

The Society's manifesto is an unambiguous expression of the desire for greater personal liberty and self-government that fueled the Taishō Democracy phenomenon in its various manifestations: in this case, the "new education" movement. Even so, postwar critics have charged that the proponents of "new education" and their Taishō Democracy brethren suffered one crippling shortcoming: by tacitly accepting Japan's imperialist ambitions abroad, they promoted political, social, and economic liberty for the Japanese "ethnic nation" while ignoring the cries for liberty voiced by other exploited peoples around the world, including neighboring China, not to mention Japan's own colonial subjects in Korea and Taiwan.[51]

GOING INTERNATIONAL

Such a blanket condemnation gives insufficient attention to a second reform initiative that brought Noguchi, Shimonaka and Sawayanagi together: the promotion of "international education" (*kokusai kyōiku*). To be sure, this 1920s campaign to reform school curricula in order to instill Japanese students with an "international consciousness" (*kokusai ishiki*), with the knowledge and foreign language skills needed to integrate Japan into the global community (*sekai no naka no Nihon*), and with a respect for cultural differences necessary for peaceful coexistence, is partly attributable to Japan's emergence as a colonial power following her military victories over China and Russia some two decades earlier. As noted in chapter 1, by the late Meiji period prominent educators and statesmen like Saionji Kinmochi and Ōkuma Shigenobu were asserting that Japan's new status meant that it must act more responsibly and accept a greater role in world affairs, in accordance with internationally recognized norms. At the same time, Japan's interests and those of the international community could only be advanced when they were linked with those of the individual: hence, the need to push for "new education" and "international education" simultaneously. Japanese education in the age of imperialism must respect individual differences, nurture individual talents, and socialize individual personalities so that citizens will come to identify their own interests with those of Japan and the world at large.[52]

Another impetus for the "international education" movement was the understandable desire to advance world peace in the aftermath of the Great War. Here, too, there are important precedents dating from the dawn of

Japan's colonial era. According to Yamazaki Yuji, during and after the Russo-Japanese War the issue of international education received an important boost from the incipient peace movement; itself the product of diverse interest groups. At one extreme stood the Commoners Society (Heiminsha), a political group whose advocacy of socialism, liberty, equality, humanitarianism, and pacifism found support among some educators, even as it incurred the government's wrath. At the other extreme was the Greater Japan Peace Association (Dai Nihon Heiwa Kyōkai), which enjoyed the support of Japan's political and business elite, and which stressed the peaceful resolution of diplomatic and security issues, notably the movement in the western United States to exclude Japanese immigrants, "in order to secure world peace and advance human happiness."[53]

Yamazaki concludes that the influence of these organizations persisted after the Great War. In 1920, members of the Greater Japan Peace Association joined with others involved in American-Japanese relations to form the nucleus of a new League of Nations Association, which worked within the framework of the League to promote peace and educate public opinion on international affairs. Although the Commoners Society had disbanded years before the war, its platform found renewed expression in Shimonaka's teachers union, the Keimeikai. In Yamazaki's view, the Taishō-era movement to internationalize Japanese education was born when the Keimeikai, at Shimonaka's urging, petitioned the League of Nations in 1920 and 1921 to establish an international education council. Through this council the petitioners sought to promote international cooperation and friendship that would not only support the League's own stated goal of furthering international economic cooperation, but would encourage all nations to substitute peace education for education that glorified militarism and imperialism. The 1921 petition stated in part:

> No peace can last without cultural bases; without the rational coordination of the cultural heritage and outlook of each people with the rest—the coordination that will do away with ignorance and prejudice. But as we look critically into the prevailing education of each nation we see all sorts of old prejudice still wittingly or unwittingly inculcated into innocent souls. The education of people, we dare say, is still predominantly influenced by national egoism. So long as egoism is allowed to persist, all other efforts toward peace and understanding, we are afraid, will be of no permanent value. We cannot, therefore, too strongly insist that without an international organization of educational influences, which shall effectively counteract all the hidden forces tending toward imperialism and militarism, no league of nations can possibly attain its object.[54]

Eight people signed this petition, including Shimonaka, Noguchi, Sawayanagi, and another reformer, Harada Minoru.[55] Harada was born and raised in Chiba prefecture, where his father worked in the prefectural government. After completing primary school and middle school there, he enrolled at Waseda University, graduating from the Department of English Literature in 1913. Harada worked briefly as a reporter and editor for the *Educational Review* (*Kyōiku jiron*), and also taught at the Children's Hamlet Primary School before returning to Waseda, where he spent the rest of his career teaching in the Higher Normal School Division and at the university level in the Faculty of Education.[56]

Although the League of Nations rejected both of these petitions, this fact helped to rally support from members of Shimonaka's teachers union, the League of Nations Association and other groups to establish the International Education Society of Japan (Kokusai Kyōiku Kyōkai) in 1922, with Sawayanagi as its president and Harada, Noguchi and Shimonaka serving on its board of directors. Sawayanagi was an obvious choice to head the Society, having met with various American educators to promote the idea of an international education conference during his eleven-month long (August 1921–June 1922) study tour in the United States. Its stated goals were to promote humanitarianism (*jinrui ai*), mutual understanding, and friendship among peoples of all nations, and thus contribute to genuine world peace. To that end, the Society pledged to convene an international education conference and to conduct comparative research on education abroad.[57] To attract the support of members of the Imperial Education Association to the Society, Noguchi recounted the circumstances of its creation and summarized its goals in the February 1922 issue of *Imperial Education*; the first of many articles on international education and peace education that would appear in the magazine during the 1920s.[58]

The ideas and aims that inspired Shimonaka to take the lead in founding the Japan Teachers Union Enlightenment Association, the Century of Education Society, the Children's Hamlet Primary School, and the International Education Society of Japan between 1919 and 1923 were first expressed to union members in a series of essays published in its journal, *Keimei*, and then republished in book form by the union for a larger audience in 1920 under the title, *The Reconstruction of Education* (*Kyōiku saizō*). Although not an avowed Marxist, in this work and in other essays dating from this period Shimonaka offers what sounds like a Marxian critique of bourgeois capitalist exploitation of the working classes at home, and imperialist exploitation of colonized and semi-colonized peoples abroad. In particular, he highlights the role that education has played in perpetuating political, economic, social, and cultural inequalities, and he explains how education, along with other key institutions in society, must be "reconstructed" in order to rectify those inequalities. It is not simply a matter of tinkering with new methods to make the educational enterprise more efficient. Rather, it requires reconstructing the fundamental spirit and overall structure of education, by equalizing educational opportunity, increasing local control over schools, introducing democratic principles into the curriculum and school governance, as well as internationalizing education.[59]

DEBATING THE AIMS OF INTERNATIONAL EDUCATION

Shimonaka's litany of complaints against Japanese education begins with the qualitative differences between education available to the children of the well-to-do versus education for the masses. The state perpetuates these class differences by devoting a disproportionate share of funding to secondary education, which is dominated by the former group, while limiting its support for elementary schooling serving the masses. The state also exerts power over the Japanese people through its control over school teachers and the curriculum. Teachers are not only prohibited from participating in politics, but are expected to devote class time to instructing children in their duties to the state (e.g., paying taxes, military conscription), rather than discussing their constitutional rights (e.g., political participation).

Furthermore, he warns that a dangerous strain of state-centered nationalism (*kokkashugi*) has permeated Japanese education over the past decade, as the so-called "citizens' morality" doctrine (*kokumin dōtoku*) has become rooted in teachers' minds. This is not to say that popular nationalism, per se, is bad: there is nothing wrong with popular nationalistic activities (*kokuminshugiteki katsudō*) which aim to contribute to world culture (*sekai no bunka*), since the true meaning of popular nationalism (*kokuminshugi*) respects the principle of human coexistence. What prevails in Japanese education, however, is an aggressive, chauvinistic form of state-centered nationalism that proclaims the superiority of one's own country and people. Even this strain of state-centered nationalism might be acceptable, if it somehow advanced the welfare of all citizens. However, the reality is that under the banner of national progress it violates the true meaning of civic nationalism by benefiting the ruling class at the expense of the citizenry.[60]

The principal source of these class inequities and divisions is bourgeois capitalism and its claim to have produced a superior form of culture that is only accessible to those who acquire a civilized education (*bunmeiteki kyōiku*). This situation is harmful to the upper classes and lower classes alike, and can only be remedied by discarding bourgeois capitalist culture altogether and nurturing a grassroots culture of the masses (*minshū bunka*) in its place. It is the lower classes who have held fast to the essential spirit of morality—the principles of equality, justice, sincerity, love, humility, simplicity—and who are now beginning to rise up around the world and clamor for democracy: equality, justice, liberty, selfhood (*jiko*), and liberation of individual dignity (*jinkaku kaihō*). The only way to bring about world peace and universal human happiness is to elevate and equalize the level of civilization (*kyōka*) of people everywhere. Only then can a world state (*seikaiteki kokka*) and a people's alliance (*kokumin dōmei*) become a reality. Responsibility for doing so rests with the advanced countries of the world (Britain, America, France, Italy, Japan) and with the ruling classes within each country. Further attempts to suppress these popular demands will only exacerbate deteriorating relations between the advanced "capitalist countries" and the culturally undeveloped "labor countries" (e.g., India, Korea, and China, whose recent clashes with Japanese authorities and boycotts of Japanese goods are symptomatic of this tension), as well as relations between capitalists and labor. In place of the growing nationalism that lies behind their progressive-sounding rhetoric, the advanced capitalist countries must practice humanitarianism (*zenjinrui ai*), liberate the underdeveloped labor countries and help them achieve the equality necessary to ensure their survival.[61]

This program of social reconstruction must begin at home: Japan should grant industrial workers more days off; open Sunday schools and universities where workers can use that free time to expand their practical knowledge and skills; address the adversarial thinking that exists between workers and capitalists, and that also infects Japan's colonies of Korea and Taiwan; and rid education of the old Asian principle, "Make the people submit to authority and keep them ignorant."[62]

Shimonaka displays little confidence in the new League of Nations to contribute to this reconstruction. Instead, he finds hope in humanity's growing calls for a true people's league (*kokumin renmei*) that will supersede the League of Nations once it becomes fully internationalized. When that time comes, national education (*kokumin kyōiku*), which has hitherto impeded international interactions among the people of the world, will become an anachronism. The problem is illustrated by Japan's own national education policy, which has become captive to a narrow nationalism that poses a danger to the world because it promotes developing the people's energies and national power to prepare for a future war. The chief conduit for propagating this narrow nationalism is the teaching of history, which has been based on a strong-country doctrine (*kyōkokushugi*) that fans the flames of animosity. To end this practice, history education itself needs to be reconstructed upon the doctrine of international coexistence and mutual aid. In addition, an international education conference should be convened to help disseminate antiwar teaching methods on a global scale.[63]

The announcement that a major international conference on education would, at long last, convene in San Francisco in the summer of 1923 under the auspices of the National Education Association in the United States, sparked various preparations in Japan. The International Education Society of Japan, together with eight other groups, chose Armistice Day (November 11) 1922 to announce the formation of a new Japan League for Peace (Heiwa Undō Nihon Renmei). With the top officials of the League hailing from the International Education Society—Sawayanagi was elected president by a vote of the League's board of directors, which included Harada, Noguchi, Shimonaka and Sawayanagi—it is not surprising that the top item on its agenda was to draft proposals to present at the meeting in San Francisco.[64]

The International Education Society of Japan also published, on the eve of the San Francisco conference, a collection of essays entitled, *Theory and Practice of International Education* (*Kokusai kyōiku no riron oyobi jissai*): the first book on the subject of international education to appear in Japanese. Agreement on the Society's goals did not preclude its members from voicing different opinions about the specific problems that international education was supposed to address or the kind of reforms that were needed. Their common invocation of terms like *jiyū kyōiku* (liberal education), *kokusai kyōiku* (international education), *kokusai rikai kyōiku* (education for international understanding), and even *heiwa kyōiku* (peace education) were also points of discussion and debate. Their disagreements might be construed as a sign of weakness in the interwar education reform movement. However, it is also possible to see them as a sign of vitality; a sign of resistance to the state's sporadic attempts to preempt debate and pedagogical experimentation altogether by increasing its bureaucratic control over schooling, and by mandating a uniform ideology based on emperor-centered nationalism.

Writing in the Foreword to this volume, Noguchi observes that in spite of the welcome trend toward the internationalization of education (*kyōiku kokusaika no keikō*) that emerged after the Great War as a result of humanity's desire for peace, the pursuit of this goal should not be left to political and economic forces. Thus, the International Education Society of Japan was founded in order to promote the common welfare of humanity (*jinrui kyōdō no fukushi*). Unfortunately, among Japanese of all social classes the concept of international education has failed to take root and spread. This book, he says, is being published to contribute to their understanding of the "true mission of the international education movement" (*kokusai kyōiku undō no shinjitsu naru shimei*), and to help make it a reality.[65]

The irony of this last statement is that the "true mission" of the movement depended on which contributing author one chose to believe. To their credit, at least, a number of essays in this volume, including Noguchi's own contribution, acknowledge the lack of consensus over the "true" meaning, goals, and methods of international education. Thus, the real function of this book was not to present a definitive mission statement to "the people," but to involve them in a spirited debate over this question, and in a collective search for its resolution. In the process, these writers also questioned a number of related concepts formerly defined by the state: national identity; nationalism; the relationship between the individual and the state; and the relationship between education, foreign policy, domestic politics, economics, and culture.

Izumi Tetsu opened this debate in his essay, "People Under a Constitution and International Education." A devout Christian who spent sixteen years studying in the United States, Izumi's advocacy of international education was inspired by the same democratic impulse that informed his positions on colonial policy and international law: subjects which he taught at Meiji University (1914–1927), and, later, at the imperial university in Seoul (1927–1935). According to Asada Kyōji, Izumi was critical of his government's policies for assimilating its colonial subjects in Taiwan and Korea. On the one hand, they discriminate against the colonized by imposing the same duties upon them as upon the home population, while extending none of the rights enjoyed by the latter. On the other hand, they throw those societies into confusion by trying to replace their distinctive languages, cultures, and customs with those of Japan. However, Izumi recognized that these repressive policies were closely related to his government's repressive practices at home. Self-government and independence would only come to the colonies after the authoritarian structure of the Japanese government had been liberalized.[66] Both of these ends could be served by international education.

The distinguishing feature of modern constitutional government, Izumi writes in his essay, is that the people of the nation, the *kokumin*, participate in the politics of the state (*kokka no seiji*). Based on this principle, foreign policy, too, should be based on public opinion and discussion (*kokumin no yoron*). In the modern era, especially in the wake of the Great War, it is no longer permissible to leave the resolution of important diplomatic problems impacting the security of the *kokumin* solely in the hands of the authorities. This, in turn, requires that changes be made to national education (*kokumin kyōiku*), so that they will be prepared to participate in resolving important diplomatic issues. In particular, national education must be purged of its existing chauvinistic state-centered nationalism (*henkyō naru kokkashugi*), in favor of a global perspective and the broad dissemination of international knowledge (*kokusai chishiki*).

Izumi blames Machiavelli for spreading the doctrine of nationalism, and for the consequent destruction of learning, religion, culture, and moral values in Europe. Since then, Europeans have gradually come to recognize the dangers inherent in chauvinistic nationalism. In Japan, on the other hand, the people still labor under the deleterious effects of statist education (*kokka kyōiku*), which cultivates a myopic brand of patriotism, false character, and irrational fears of the West. This education forsakes the goal of educating the whole person in order to create narrow-minded, submissive patriots. No matter how diligently Japanese youth are taught that their culture and greatness have no equals in the world, once they learn the truth—that there really are other truly great, civilized nations—they will react either with slavish respect toward, or outright fear of them. This is why Japan's diplomacy is so conservative and passive, and why its people suffer feelings of inferiority when they interact with foreigners over matters like trade.

Izumi goes on to castigate statist education for causing men to forget their responsibility to their families. They forsake their parents, wives, and children in the name of sacrificing themselves for the sake of the nation. This, he says, violates the sanctity of human life. Moreover, it goes without saying that if all citizens followed this path the nation itself would ultimately collapse.

Izumi's third indictment against chauvinistic nationalism of the sort promoted through Japan's state-controlled education is that it ignores the sovereignty of other nations and injures the people of other countries. The recent war against Germany demonstrates both the evil of this aggression and the newfound determination of other countries to resist it.

Most wars, says Izumi, are manipulated by leaders to unite their nations, or to preserve their positions; in either case, the result is that the ruling class sacrifices the happiness and security of the people. Since the Great War, however, the democratic trend in diplomacy has meant that the people's opinions should influence diplomacy. The advent of the League of Nations has contributed to this trend by discouraging secret diplomatic deals. This, in turn, creates a demand for a new form of national education: one that goes beyond instilling a narrow, chauvinistic nationalism in the people to one that provides them with the requisite knowledge and ability to resolve diplomatic issues in a timely manner.[67]

Izumi's sentiments were echoed by Noguchi in his own essay, titled "The International Education Conference and Its Goals." However, whereas Izumi emphasized the role of international education in bringing about political change both at home and abroad, Noguchi was more concerned with its role in advancing domestic pedagogical and social reform: areas in which he had been active throughout his career. Like Izumi, Noguchi asserts in his 1923 essay that international education and national education (*kokumin kyōiku*) are complementary. Indeed, the former presumes the existence of the latter, since the term *international* refers to nations. Problems arise when either is carried to extremes: national education that preaches narrow, chauvinistic patriotism;

or international education that preaches a utopian globalism predicated upon the replacement of nation states by a single world state (*sekai kokkashugi*). International education shares perfectly the goals of general education (*ippan kyōiku*), since both aspire to contribute to the happiness and prosperity of humanity, cultivate moral character, teach self-respect and respect for others.

Noguchi specifies the kind of pedagogical reforms that are necessary to successfully implement international education. Beyond the obvious need to purge the narrowly patriotic content of history, geography, ethics, language, and music textbooks to make room for information about other countries, teaching methods themselves must be changed. Uniform, graded methods of instruction that make students passive participants in the learning process bear too much of a military cast: while they may be effective in instilling patriotism, they fail to cultivate the critical thinking skills required for international education. Accordingly, they must be replaced with liberal educational methods that respond to the changing needs of individual pupils at different stages of development, in order to produce creative, individual personalities who can think for themselves.

Systemic reforms are also needed to raise the general level of national education and equalize educational opportunity, because most people now receive only rudimentary instruction, which is inadequate to make world peace a reality. Like Izumi, Noguchi pins the blame for wars on the vain desires of the privileged few to avenge their pride or to seek personal gain. By disseminating knowledge of other countries more broadly and sharpening the people's judgment, the prospect of war can be reduced.[68]

Harada's contribution to the Society's volume, entitled "Principles of the Globalization of Education," sets forth the central themes that he would emphasize in subsequent books and essays through the rest of the decade. His essay opens with the bold statement that

> The discovery of the individual (*kojin*) has no equal in human history; it can be said that the modern era (*kindai*) truly begins with this discovery. But mankind (*jinrui*) has since made another great discovery; the discovery of society (*shakai*). With the discovery of society, the individual, for the first time, has been able to secure a path leading to self-fulfillment. This is becoming clear through the study of the relationship between the individual and society.

Neither entity can survive without the other, and each influences the other. When their mutual influence is maximized, the livelihood of the individual is also maximized.

But through the development of communications, the borders (*han'i*) of society have expanded. Whereas society formerly consisted of a single hamlet, and later of a single state, today it encompasses the whole world. The

livelihoods of individual states have, in some cases, become more closely
entwined than those between neighboring households. On an emotional as
well as a material level, matters affecting the interests of the individual are no
longer necessarily determined by nationality. An advocate of a particular idea
living in Country A may have more in common with likeminded individuals
in Countries B and C than with those of his own countrymen who oppose his
ideas. So, too, may workers in Countries A, B, and C have more in common
with one another than with capitalists in their home country. So, for individuals living in this mammoth global society, regardless of their nationality,
they must not only pursue their own livelihoods with a positive attitude, but
remember to link those pursuits in a positive way to a relationship of mutual
assistance extending to others throughout the world. This requires that every
individual be imbued with the spirit of brotherhood.

While this spirit exists in every country through religion and moral doctrines, in practice it has been overshadowed by an emphasis on nationalism
and national needs that has pervaded education in countries everywhere.
This kind of narrow, self-serving education, which helped to bring about
the World War, must be jettisoned and replaced by the spirit of universal
brotherhood.[69]

The most critical assessment of the fledgling international education movement contained in the International Education Society's publication was contributed by Shimonaka. After bemoaning the failure of earlier international
conferences to contribute to world peace, his essay critiques the statement of
purpose published by the organizers of the upcoming international education
conference in San Francisco.[70] According to Shimonaka, that statement lists
among its goals a desire to apply proven educational principles to improve
education worldwide, without, however, abridging the existing rights and
privileges of individual nations. A second goal of the conference is to gain
international recognition of each nation's rights and privileges, regardless
of race or creed. A third goal is to foster respect for the value of the unique
national traits or characteristics (*kokuminsei no kachi*) of all peoples, as well
as their unique talents and abilities.

Far from applauding these goals, Shimonaka interprets this statement of
purpose as a thinly disguised attempt by the advanced capitalist, imperialist
nations of the world to maintain their economic and cultural hegemony over
developing countries, at a time when the latter are finally beginning to break
their silence and give voice to their own desires. Having endured the repeated
failures of the capitalist-controlled League of Nations to adopt proposals to
convene an international education conference, Shimonaka originally welcomed news of the San Francisco conference, until he saw its statement of
purpose. The spirit of international education, he insists, must be based on

the spirit of love for humanity (*zenjinrui ai no seishin*), which affirms human equality and the equality of ethnic nations (*minzoku*). It means substituting a global perspective for a national perspective (literally, "viewing one's fellow countrymen through the eyes of humanity, instead of viewing humanity through the eyes of one's own countrymen").

Echoing the themes he raised three years earlier in *The Reconstruction of Education*, Shimonaka warns that if true world peace is to be achieved, then political and economic agreements alone are not enough. They must be accompanied by cultural cooperation. Cultural cooperation, which takes place through education, demands that the level of international culture (*kokusai kyōka*) achieved by advanced countries and the cultural level reached by smaller and weaker underdeveloped countries be the same. To equalize educational opportunity in this way, the most critical issue on the agenda of the San Francisco conference ought to be how to bring education to the underdeveloped countries as soon as possible. Lame excuses like, "It is impossible to educate backward peoples" are unacceptable. The purpose of education must be to liberate human beings *as* human beings. Education here does not necessarily mean modern schooling; other types of education are possible. Once an oppressed class or oppressed citizenry is freed from that oppression, it can and will develop brilliantly. Ultimately, however, this requires that advanced countries sacrifice their positions of superiority over the so-called backward countries, because their superiority is based upon naked exploitation, not upon their possession of superior qualities or talents that supposedly distinguish one people from another.[71]

While Izumi, Noguchi, and Shimonaka all took the state to task for emphasizing nationalism and neglecting internationalism in its educational policy, conservative philosopher Inoue Tetsujirō felt compelled to defend *his* conception of national education from radical or utopian reformers in the international education movement. In keeping with his credentials as interpreter and defender of the Imperial Rescript on Education, Inoue's essay purports to examine the relationship between international morality (*kokusai dōtoku*) and national morality (*kokumin dōtoku*). It is a mistake, he says, to conclude that the subjects of national morality, national history, and national language and literature are concerned only with instilling warlike sentiments to prepare the people for war. In every country there are plenty of teaching materials available for each of these subjects to support pacifism, humanism, and internationalism. Promoting international education will help to ensure that proper choices are made when planning the curriculum of national education.

But the need for international education does not eliminate the need for national education, because people in each country are different. They belong to different nation states (*kokka*), each with its own interests, which do not always agree with the interests of other nations. For example, Japan's colonial subjects are beneficial to Japan, yet the United States objects to them. America's insistence on the sovereignty of China and Manchuria is likewise unacceptable to Japan.

Inoue finds further grounds to defend national education as he surveys contemporary world conditions, which belie all the talk of peace and internationalism. Looking at the strained relations between Germany and France, France and England, and the situation in Yugoslavia, it is clear that the worst offenders are the civilized nations of the West, which talk of peace yet aggressively pursue their own interests. Perhaps their talk of peace is a ploy to make Japanese drop their guard. Japanese must never lose their power to resist, or allow their country to be occupied. The fact that they have so far avoided that fate is due to their encouragement of national education.

Turning to the subject of international versus national morality, Inoue equates the former with pacifism, humanism, liberty, and equality: values perceived to be universally applicable to all people. While these values originated long ago, through the work of Confucius, Buddha, and Jesus, it is only in the modern era, as a result of improved communications and, in particular, in the wake of the Great War, that people in different countries have come to recognize that they share a common destiny. The growing attractiveness of international morality in the modern era is evident in numerous social reform movements that go under names like socialism and communism.

Yet, while claiming that international morality and national morality are complementary, Inoue again insists that the former will never completely displace the latter. His argument for the continued importance of national morality hinges on his defense of national, cultural, and historical differences. This is especially true in Japan, with its unique *kokutai* (national polity): a moral *kokutai* rooted in the character of its unbroken line of Japanese emperors. At the same time, Japan's *kokutai* already embodies the universal values he earlier identified with international morality: humanism, pacifism, and benevolence.[72]

FROM NATIONAL DEBATE TO INTERNATIONAL DISCOURSE

The foregoing selection of essays demonstrates that international education was a highly politicized concept in interwar Japan. Those by Izumi, Noguchi and Harada take exception to state-centered nationalism, which promotes authoritarianism and particularism in domestic as well as foreign relations, in violation of internationally recognized principles of justice and equality. Nations must, therefore, be encouraged to conduct international education, which seeks to disseminate those principles to individuals throughout society. Justice and equality will then govern domestic affairs in each nation where international education is practiced and, by extension, affairs between those nations. These writers stop short of addressing the issue of imperialism, but their remarks suggest that they favor a new form of nationalism that does not promote or condone imperialist aggression.

Shimonaka exhibits no such reservations in his essay, which, like his earlier book, *The Reconstruction of Education*, offers an extended critique of imperialism in the postwar era of the League of Nations. For him, international education is an obligation that every nation, particularly the advanced countries, must accept and carry out in close cooperation, so as to rectify political, economic, and cultural inequalities that imperialism established between the advanced nations and those underdeveloped nations that they continue to exploit and dominate.

Finally, at the other end of the political spectrum, is the essay by Inoue, who neither bemoans the state's power and its ideology of emperor-centered nationalism, nor apologizes for Japanese expansionism. "International morality" and "national morality" can coexist, he writes, although his description of each makes it difficult to see how.

The World Conference on Education was held in San Francisco from June 28 through July 5, 1923. The participants, representing "more than thirty distinct racial groups and over fifty national divisions," included a twelve-person delegation from Japan and a separate delegation representing Japan's principal overseas colony, Korea.[73] For Sawayanagi, who was the most prominent Japanese delegate at the conference, the experience marked a new phase in his career, and contributed to his posthumous reputation as an internationalist.

Prior to the conference, in his own contribution to the volume of essays examined above, entitled "Global Trends and International Education," Sawayanagi seeks to assure his countrymen that international education is not a new concept; it is merely attracting renewed attention in the wake of the Great War. Its fundamental goal, "person-oriented education" (*hito to shite no kyōiku*), can be traced back to the distant past, in the Orient as well as the Occident: it was present in Confucianism, and also in ancient Greece and Rome. Having thus reassured his readers that international education is neither foreign to Japan nor a radical departure from its own philosophical tradition, Sawayanagi states that if human society should one day reach its final, ideal stage of development, then the current distinction between nationalism and internationalism will disappear.[74]

He develops this theme further in a lengthy speech at the third and final general meeting of the conference delegates in San Francisco on July 5, entitled "New Ideals of the Nation." Again he credits the Great War with forcing nations to question their penchant for war, and with demonstrating that the only assurance of national progress is to heed the longstanding calls of educators and religious leaders to choose peaceful means over war. To that end, educators must continue to strive for peace; every individual must become both a model national citizen and a model world citizen, and nationalism must harmonize with internationalism; patriotism that fails to recognize other countries must be rejected.[75]

Delegates to the San Francisco conference formally adopted a number of recommendations. To promote international cooperation they supported: appointment of an educational attaché for each embassy or legation; graduate scholarships for students in international civics, economics and comparative education; and "greater unification in science," primarily through the universal adoption of the metric system. To aid the dissemination of education information they recommended the exchange of educational periodicals and articles, the creation of a universal library service, the exchange of teachers and professors, and research on the feasibility of establishing a world university. To improve "conduct between nations" the delegates recommended: an exchange of textbooks "with a view to correcting misrepresentations about any country and to furnishing material that will foster international friendship"; preparation of "a series of international readers . . . based upon the biographies and the best literature of all nations"; "that especially history, civics, and geography textbooks (including international law) emphasize the interdependence of all members of the human family, and the necessity of peace as an essential condition of the highest human development"; the development in each country of a course in world civics and ethics that would permeate all subjects in the school curriculum, at all age levels; and correspondence among school children in different countries.[76]

The delegates also approved specific recommendations to cultivate "international ideals." These included: an outline plan for character education "to be worked out in detail by each cooperating nation, the object being to develop in children and the youth of the world 'a sense of justice and an attitude of good will toward all mankind together with habits of action in accord with justice and love of humanity'"; guidelines for the teaching of history, geography and literature designed to impart "specific principles which directly promote international good-will" (e.g., impartial judgment, justice, national and personal modesty, cooperation, honor, interdependence, courage, enterprise, neighborliness, mutual understanding, courtesy, unselfishness, service, truthfulness, and human sympathy); and the observation of International Good-Will Day on May 18, the anniversary of the First Hague Conference, when schools throughout the world are to provide "instruction on the work of the Hague Conference and more recent efforts to bring the world together in a cooperative body, accompanied by national and international songs, plays and pageants which carry out the spirit of the day."[77]

Sawayanagi emerged from the San Francisco conference as the chief spokesperson for international education in Japan and the principal Japanese advocate for the conference's slate of recommendations on the international stage. This was due, in part, to his appointment as vice president of a new World Federation of Educational Associations (WFEA) that was also announced at the San Francisco conference. Having devoted his entire career to the reform and advancement of Japanese education, including his advocacy of education for international understanding and peace education, Sawayanagi was now given the added task of promoting these same innovations abroad, having pledged himself to support the founding goals of the WFEA: "to secure international cooperation in educational enterprises, to foster the dissemination of information concerning education in all its forms among nations and peoples, to cultivate international good will, and to promote the interests of peace throughout the world."[78]

It was a responsibility that Sawayanagi took seriously, judging from his subsequent record of professional activities. He would, for example, travel to Beijing in 1925, where he lectured to an audience of Chinese educators about the crucial role that teachers play in maintaining world peace by cultivating humanitarianism (*jinrui ai*) and an international spirit (*kokusai seishin*) among the next generation of citizens.[79] Two years later, in August 1927, he would travel to Toronto to represent Japan at the second international conference of the WFEA.[80] He was also an active member of the Japanese Council of the Institute of Pacific Relations (JCIPR), and headed the Japanese delegations that attended the IPR's first two international conferences, which took place in Honolulu in 1925 and 1927, respectively.[81]

Even so, historians question the motives behind Sawayanagi's peripatetic, globetrotting activities as the face of Cosmopolitan Japan abroad, and the extent of his commitment to the humanitarian, egalitarian ideals that he professed in his speeches and writings. According to Tomoko Akami, for example, his membership in the JCIPR, and his speeches at the IPR's international conferences, were largely public relations exercises. "JCIPR members," she remarks, "played a significant role as non-official, voluntary international publicists for the Japanese nation/state/empire." Sawayanagi and the other JCIPR members "tried to promote cooperative relations with the powers, particularly the United States, by stressing an image of a liberal and peace-loving Japan. They argued that militarism was dying, and that liberalism and democratic movements were the trend,"[82] in order to convince skeptical Western observers that Japan was an enlightened imperial power, deserving equal status with the Western powers and a prominent role in a new US-led regional order that was enveloping the Pacific in the wake of the Great War.[83]

The controversy over Sawayanagi's reputation as an internationalist and a champion of international education is destined to continue, if only because the historical record lacks any evidence of Sawayanagi's views as the era of Taishō Democracy gave way to Shōwa-era militarism. His sudden death from illness in December 1927, at age sixty-two—little more than a month after returning from what would be his final overseas conference appearances—spared him from having to reconcile his liberal internationalism with another that arose in Japan to take its place. As the next chapter will document, his contemporaries, including Shimonaka, Noguchi, and Harada, were not so fortunate.

As fate would have it, then, Sawayanagi's last words as a "publicist" for Japan, for internationalism, and for international education, were delivered in the summer of 1927: first at the Second Conference of the IPR in Honolulu in July; and then at the second international meeting of the WFEA in Toronto the following month. One theme common to both speeches was the West's practice of racial discrimination toward the "yellow or brown race" in general, and toward Japan in particular. In Honolulu, Sawayanagi cites it as an irrational, unjust reaction to Japan's attempt to alleviate its problems of population growth and inadequate food supply by encouraging Japanese emigration to the "vast territories still undeveloped and sparsely settled" in Australia and North and South America. While promising his fellow IPR conferees that "Japan . . . will never entertain the thought of going to war over the question of population," he asserts that nations bordering the Pacific must recognize "the natural right of all humankind to share the resources of the world on some equitable basis and to enjoy freedom of movement and residence."[84]

In Toronto, Sawayanagi addressed the prospect of educating a generation of "world citizens" bound together by "the idea of human brotherhood" that will shield them from the racial prejudice that perverts the minds of adults. "Children are by nature international," he proclaims. Hence, "The idea of world citizenship is not unnatural or new. Simply cease giving children national bias and racial prejudice, and they will naturally become world citizens."[85]

Rejecting the idea of racial superiority propounded by the white race, he substitutes the idea of "cultural superiority," which is more just because "it depends upon education and not upon fate." This does not guarantee that all races will achieve their common human potential, since effort is required:

[F]rom the standpoint of science, or from a fundamental point of view, no one race can justly be regarded either as superior or inferior. There may be a sense in which we can speak of the Ainu of Japan or the Aborigines of America as inferior because they are recognized to be dying races; but apart from these we cannot speak of any virile or progressive race as inferior. For example, none of you would say that the Japanese people are inferior to the Aryan peoples, and we educators should see to it that no harmful spirit of race prejudice or national bias be cultivated in the minds of our children.[86]

In line with Akami's critique, there is no denying the strident tone that Sawayanagi adopts when he turns briefly to defend Japan's commitment to education for world citizenship; like many of his cosmopolitan Japanese contemporaries, he saved his criticisms of Japanese education for audiences of Japanese educators back home. For example, on the matter of reforming the teaching of history and geography in order to "avoid giving a national or racial bias by placing too much emphasis upon the achievements and glories of our own country," he asserts that

the Japanese people have a right to be proud of what they have achieved. They have earnestly studied and assimilated foreign civilization. They have learned to appreciate all that is good and helpful in western lands, consequently they respect western people much more than western people respect them. Western people do not know Japan as well as Japan knows the West, and therefore racial antipathy is not being so strongly developed in Japan as it is in the West.[87]

In a similar vein, Sawayanagi touts Japan's concerted efforts to teach about "the meaning of the League of Nations and what it stands for" as "one concrete method of developing a spirit of world citizenship in our children":

Since the close of the Great War this has been done to a greater or less extent in most countries. Children should get as thorough a knowledge and understanding of the constitution of the League of Nations as of the government and constitution of their own country. In this matter Japan is second to none. She has inserted information about the League of Nations in her regular text-books and has organized League of Nations Associations not only among adults, but student organizations are promoted throughout the country.[88]

Two observations may be offered here in response to Akami's accusation that Sawayanagi was just a PR man for Imperial Japan in his appearances abroad. First, the pedagogical claims he made in Toronto were true. A League of Nations Association of Japan was, indeed, founded in April 1920 through the initiative of scholars and diplomats who were in Paris during the Peace Conference at Versailles. Its membership grew to become the largest of any League-related body in the world: from 683 in 1920 to 11,771 by 1932, including 5,652 students. Student members were organized into 48 campus-based groups.[89] And it is also true that Japanese textbooks published in the 1920s not only conveyed information about the League of Nations, but also lessons about Japan's responsibilities as a member of the international community.

The second observation is that Sawayanagi actively pursued the goal of transforming Japanese youth into "world citizens" through his multifarious educational activities back home, even in the face of public skepticism and political wrangling over the fairness and efficacy of the League of Nations, and the wisdom of Japan's membership therein.[90] To those activities which have already been discussed—president of the Imperial Education Association, principal of Seijō Elementary School, co-founder of the International Education Association of Japan, essayist, lecturer—it is appropriate here to add the title, textbook author. Appropriate because like the collection of magazine essays and books that he wrote for fellow educators before and after the Great War, Sawayanagi's school textbooks also document his struggle to moderate the influence of nationalism and imperialism upon Japanese educational thought and practice, in order to accommodate the postwar crescendo of calls—both at home and abroad—for liberty, equality, peaceful coexistence and collective prosperity.

CREATING A COSMOPOLITAN CURRICULUM

Consider, for example, *Middle School Ethics* (*Chūgaku shūshinsho*): a series of textbooks authored by Sawayanagi that went through four major revisions and nine printings between its debut in 1909 and 1923. Some of his revisions are subtle, as in a chapter from the first edition entitled "The Japanese," which echoes the familiar Meiji-era refrain that Japanese identity emanates from the people's unity under an unbroken line of emperors, and from their unique history as the only nation never to suffer foreign invasion. Key to Japan's rise to prominence as the leading civilized nation in Asia, and as one of the most advanced nations in the world, is the ability of her people to acquire knowledge from various sources and then apply it systematically, coupled with adherence to a national morality (*kokumin dōtoku*) founded on loyalty and filial piety (*chūkō*) and on choosing goodness over evil.[91] Aside from altering the chapter title to "The Dignity of the Japanese," the only change that Sawayanagi makes to this chapter in the 1923 edition is to instruct his audience of middle school students to be loyal, filial, and just (*seigi*) in their behavior in order to advance world culture and contribute to human happiness (*sekai no bunka o hattatsu seshime jinrui no kōfuku o zōshin suru koto ni tsutomu beki de aru*).[92]

Sawayanagi takes a similar approach, to a similar theme, in a chapter whose original title, "Middle Class Citizens of the Enlightened Meiji Period," aptly reflects the highly stratified, elite orientation of middle school education at that time. His message here to Japan's nascent middle class is that it bears a twofold responsibility: (1) to ensure that the modern system of representative government and attendant right of free speech, which the emperor has entrusted to his subjects, are exercised responsibly; (2) to expand the state's sovereignty and elevate its stature in an era of intense global competition that is shifting more and more to Asia.[93] In the 1923 edition, Sawayanagi drops his reference to the middle class by re-titling this chapter, "The Mission of Educated Citizens," and by expunging his nationalistic exhortation to expand Japanese sovereignty and elevate the state's stature in the competition among states. Instead, he exhorts all Japanese to apply their education to the mission of providing support and leadership to the developing nations of Asia, contributing to world culture, and promoting the welfare of humanity.[94]

More conspicuous is the addition of various chapters to the 1923 edition that were not part of the original. One, entitled "Our National Flag," states that while every country employs a flag to symbolize and honor the nation, foreigners typically respect their national flags more than Japanese do theirs. Citizens should be aware of the characteristics of their national flag and respect it, while also showing respect for the flags of foreign countries. National symbols, such as flags, reflect the particular histories and characteristics of the nations they represent. Japan's flag is a reflection of its ancestral ties to Amaterasu, the Sun Goddess, and to the unbroken line of emperors who, like the sun, radiate virtue. This is the source of the ideals of the Japanese people, who reject the practice of racial discrimination that divides east and west, and who demonstrate fairness at home and abroad, just as the sun illuminates the four seas. We Japanese, rich in humanitarian spirit, help those who are weak, enlighten those shrouded in darkness, guide people in developing countries and shower them with the blessings of culture, just as the sun radiates light and heat to nurture all creation.[95]

In another new chapter, "Coexistence and Co-Prosperity," Sawayanagi states that while their differing beliefs create opposition and occasional conflict, people everywhere still aspire to live together in peace. The current clamor for more individual liberty is a natural reaction to the restrictions placed on the individual's political and economic activity in the past. However, liberty without limits poses a risk to members of a society seeking to coexist peacefully and prosperously. Coexistence and co-prosperity should be the governing principle in the home, village, city, and nation, and also between nations. Germany's fate is a reminder of what happens when one country pursues its own gain at the expense of another; an action that has been rendered illegitimate following the establishment of the League of Nations. Our country currently faces anti-Japanese sentiment in China, he writes, but rather than worry about that, our response should be to uphold the ideal of coexistence and co-prosperity in our relations with China. We should not retaliate against those who spurn us by spurning them.[96]

Another chapter in the 1923 edition, "Our Country's Standing in the World," offers a sobering analysis of Japan's reputation abroad. Although Japan is recognized as a first-rank military power, it remains a second- or third-rate economic power. Its people have failed to achieve independence over the material and spiritual components of their lives, and their intellectual powers lag behind foreigners'. Meanwhile, anti-Japanese sentiment is widespread—in the United States, Canada, Australia, even China—creating the impression that Japan is becoming isolated and is under siege. Rather than fault Japanese policies abroad for contributing to these sentiments, however, Sawayanagi describes them as manifestations of a Yellow Peril doctrine fueled by fear and resentment of Japan's unexpected challenge to Western superiority. Japanese must reflect upon these developments and redouble their determination to maintain their country's international standing in the face of economic competition that has increased in intensity and shifted to Asia in the wake of the Great War.[97]

As if to offer Japanese middle school students hope and encouragement in the face of this rather weighty task, Sawayanagi also adds a new chapter on "The League of Nations and the International Spirit" to the 1923 edition of his ethics textbook. Throughout the world and throughout recorded history, he writes, humans have preached the ideals of equality, cooperation and peace, even as their natural penchant for war has repeatedly violated those ideals. At first glance, one is likely to conclude that the Great War that took place in Europe recently is simply another instance of man's power to destroy. However, that perspective does not do justice to the historic establishment of the League of Nations, which marks the first time that humanity's longstanding ideals have taken concrete form as an organized system. The League, like every new organization, has experienced growing pains, but that is no reason to denigrate it. Given that it is still in its infancy, he asks rhetorically, is it fair to expect the League to resolve all international disputes to everyone's satisfaction? Rather, it is remarkable that in the few years since it was established the League has quickly tackled a number of international disputes. Although the United States, Germany and Russia have yet to join, there is no doubt that the League will gradually reach maturity. Being an international political organization, the League can only do so much to advance the cause of world peace, however. That goal ultimately depends upon employing education to cultivate an international spirit (*kokusai seishin*) in the citizens of every nation. This international spirit encompasses the concept of coexistence and co-prosperity, and eschews pursuit of the national interest at others' expense. Japan's contribution to the cause of international peace and human happiness lies in promoting this international spirit, both at home and abroad.[98]

CONCLUSION

What is most notable about these excerpts from Sawayanagi's ethics textbook is how closely the lessons he sought to convey to Japanese middle school students in 1923 echo the points he sought to convey to his foreign counterparts through his overseas conference speeches between 1923 and 1927. Whatever public relations value his appearances abroad may have had for Imperial Japan was secondary to Sawayanagi, who along with contemporaries like Noguchi, Shimonaka, and Harada, had more pressing reasons to campaign for international education, both at home and abroad. Like other "enlightened" members of the Meiji generation, they were acutely aware of the precarious nature of modernization and increasingly troubled by its inherent contradictions, even though they did not always recognize their underlying causes. Although they were not above joining parochial ideologues like Inoue Tetsujirō in blaming "the West," as the progenitor and patron of "the modern," for the many ills that accompanied modernization's global spread—the rise of individualism, materialism, predatory capitalism, imperialism, racism and xenophobic nationalism—their international orientation also allowed them to acknowledge, to their fellow educators at least, that "modern Japan" was both a victim *and* a perpetrator of these ills. If Sawayanagi was less candid about this fact in his textbooks for Japanese middle schoolers or in his speeches before foreign audiences, it may have had less to do with national pride, imperial chauvinism, or international public relations than with a desperate, and misplaced, hope that the Japanese were uniquely positioned to resolve modernity's contradictions; which, paradoxically, both united the human race and turned human beings against one another. This, he vowed, would be Japan's long-overdue "contribution to the world."

NOTES

1. Motoyama, *Proliferating Talent*, p. 381; Ōi , *Nihon no "shin kyōiku shisō"*, pp. 8–17; Nakauchi Toshio, Tajima Hajime and Hashimoto Noriko, eds, *Kyōiku no Seikisha no sōgōteki kenkyū* (Tokyo: Ikkōsha, 1984), 82–87; Mark E. Lincicome, "Nationalism, Imperialism, and the International Education Movement in Early Twentieth-Century Japan," in *The Journal of Asian Studies* 58:2 (May 1999), 348.

2. Ōi, *Nihon no "shin kyōiku shisō,"* 37–50; Nakauchi et. al., eds, *Kyōiki no Seikisha no sōgōteki kenkyū*, 94–96.

3. For a discussion of relations between public and private education in modern Japan, see the following: Marshall, *Learning to be Modern*; and Richard Rubinger, "Education: From One Room to One System," in Marius B. Jansen and Gilbert Rozman, eds., *Japan in Transition: From Tokugawa to Meiji* (Princeton: Princeton University Press, 1986), 195–230.

4. Nitta Takayo, *Sawayanagi Masatarō: sono shōgai to gyōseki* (Tokyo: Seijō Gakuen Sawayanagi Kenkyū kai, 1971), 16–25. For more on the role of Nagano as a catalyst in the popularization and modernization of education in Japan, see Brian Platt, *Burning and Building: Schooling and State Formation in Japan, 1750–1890* (Cambridge, MA: Harvard University Asia Center, 2004). The role of the Tokyo Normal School and its laboratory elementary school in disseminating the developmental education doctrine and attendant pedagogical methods in early Meiji Japan is covered in Lincicome, *Principle, Praxis, and the Politics of Educational Reform.*

5. Hiroshi Mizuuchi, "Sawayanagi Masatarō," in Benjamin C. Duke, ed., *Ten Great Educators of Modern Japan* (Tokyo: University of Tokyo Press, 1990), 149–65; Nitta, *Sawayanagi Masatarō: sono shōgai to gyōseki*, 71–72. The Sawayanagi Incident was sparked by Sawayanagi's attempt to fire seven professors for undistinguished academic performance, a move that was criticized by the Faculty of Law as a violation of academic freedom.

6. Nitta, *Sawayanagi Masatarō: sono shōgai to gyōseki*, 141–46. Under Sawayanagi's direction, Seijō also established: a second middle school in 1922, offering a four-year curriculum that was incorporated into a seven-year higher school in 1926; a kindergarten in 1925; and a five-year higher school for girls in 1927. This comprehensive, private educational complex was renamed Seijō Gakuen in 1927, the same year that Sawayanagi died. Following the Asia-Pacific War, in accordance with educational reforms introduced during the Allied Occupation, the prewar middle school and higher school programs were abolished and replaced by co-educational middle and high schools. A university was added in 1950.

7. Nakano Akira, *Senkanki kyōiku e no shiteki sekkin* (Tokyo: EXP, 2000), 43–50, 64–69.

8. Ibid., 69–70.

9. Miura Tōsaku, "Hansei subeki Nihon Teikoku no ketten," in *Teikoku Kyōiku* 76 (December 1921), 21–32. According to Nakano Akira, Miura's criticisms of Hara, and the Diet as a whole, marked the Imperial Education Association's support for a more pervasive "movement to protect education" in the early 1920s, which inveighed against the government's support for military spending at the expense of funding for public education. See Nakano, *Senkanki kyōiku e no shiteki sekkin*, 77–82.

10. Noguchi Entarō, "Demokurashî shiten," in *Teikoku Kyōiku* 68 (August 1920), 21–38; Noguchi Entarō, "Kyōiku to demokurashî," in *Teikoku Kyōiku* 70 (November 1920), 60–67.

11. Sawayanagi Masatarō, "Kongo ni okeru kokumin no kakugo o ronjite kyōiku ni oyobu," in *Sawayanagi Masatarō zenshū*, vol. 8 (Tokyo: Kokudosha, 1976), 347–57.

12. Sawayanagi Masatarō, "Sengo no shakai jōtai to kyōiku," in Ibid., 376–83.

13. Sawayanagi Masatarō, "Sensō eikyō no ichikōsatsu," in Ibid., 384–90.

14. Sawayanagi Masatarō, "Zairai no sengo kyōikusaku o hihyō shite shin shugi o teishō su," in Ibid., 409–23; ""Tōashugi," in Ibid., vol. 9 (1977), 234–39; "Ajiashugi," in Ibid., vol. 9, 269–75.

15. Fujii Yūsuke states that the phrase "Greater East Asia Co-Prosperity Sphere" was concocted and made public on August 1, 1940 (as part of Prime Minister Konoe Fumimaro's "Outline of Fundamenal National Policy") to replace an earlier slogan, "East Asia Cultural Sphere" (*Tōa bunka kensetsu*). The reason had less to do with ideology than with international politics: Japan wanted to stake its own claim to territories in the southern part of the Asia-Pacific region prior to Germany's and Italy's anticipated victories in Europe, in order to discourage them from usurping the Asian colonies of their European opponents: Britain, France and the Netherlands. See his "Tōji no hihō: bunka kensetsu wa nanika?" in Ikeda Hiroshi, ed., *Dai Tōa kyōeiken no bunka kensetsu* (Tokyo: Jimbun Shoin, 2007), 38–39.

16. Barak Kushner, *The Thought War: Japanese Imperial Propaganda* (Honolulu: The University of Hawai'i Press, 2006), 11. For most Japanese, writes Kushner, the most effective wartime propaganda was not that which stimulated feelings about the emperor, but that which celebrated "Japan's modernity that they believed culminated in a beneficent empire. Wartime Japanese society envisioned the empire, with Japan at its pinnacle, as hygienic, progressive, scientific, the harbinger of civilization that Asia should strive to emulate" (10–11). This conviction is clearly evident in the writings of Sawayanagi and his Meiji-era contemporaries.

17. Ozawa Yūsaku, "Sawayanagi Masatarō no shokuminchi kyōiku kan," in *Sawayanagi Masatarō zenshū bekkan* (Tokyo: Kokudosha, 1979), 192–233. See also Nakano Akira, *Taishō demokurashī to kyōiku*, 42–54.

18. Sawayanagi Masatarō, "Waga kuni no kyōiku," in *Sawayanagi Masatarō zenshū*, vol. 9, 291–302.

19. Sawayanagi Masatarō, "Chōsen heigō shokan," in Ibid., 175–77.

20. Sawayanagi Masatarō, "Chōsen kyōiku wa Nihongo fukyū ni zenryoku o keichū subeshi," in Ibid., 178–81.

21. Ibid.

22. Sawayanagi assesses the educational policies of the Meiji government toward the Ainu, Ryūkyū natives, and Taiwanese in a 1909 essay, "Waga kuni no kyōiku," in *Sawayanagi Masatarō zenshū*, vol. 8, 282–302. For his views on the annexation of Korea and the relationship between Koreans and Japanese, see his 1910 essay, "Kankoku heigo shokan," in Ibid., 175–77, and another from the same year, "Chōsen kyōiku wa Nihongo fukyū ni zenryoku o keichū subeshi," in Ibid., 178–81.

23. Thomas Burkman's description of Nitobe as "a complex mixture of Japanism, social Darwinism, and Christian humanism" helps to account for Nitobe's "enthusiastic and effectual participation in Japan's colonial enterprise." Combining an evolutionary view of history that identified Japan as a superior civilization, a Christian-influenced view of colonization as a means to civilization and world peace, and a belief in hierarchies of race, Nitobe joined Sawayanagi in advocating educational policies that would rescue Japan's colonial subjects from their own primitive societies (the Ainu in Hokkaido and the aboriginal "headhunters" in Taiwan) and

aging civilizations (Korean and Chinese) through a gradual process of assimilation. Thomas W. Burkman, "Nationalist Actors in the Internationalist Theatre: Nitobe Inazō and Ishii Kikujirō and the League of Nations," in Stegewerns, ed., *Nationalism and Internationalism in Imperial Japan*, 102–04. See also Leo T.S. Ching, *Becoming "Japanese": Colonial Taiwan and the Politics of Identity Formation* (Berkeley: University of California Press, 2001), 158–60.

24. Cited in Ching, *Becoming "Japanese,"* 101.

25. E. Patricia Tsurumi, *Japanese Colonial Education in Taiwan, 1895–1945* (Cambridge, MA: Harvard University Press, 1977).

26. Ching, *Becoming "Japanese,"* 105.

27. Quoted in ibid., 4.

28. Tsurumi, *Japanese Colonial Education*, especially chapters 5 and 6; Miyata Setsuko, "Tennōsei kyōiku to kōminka seisaku," in Asada Kyōji, ed., *"Teikoku Nihon" to Ajia*, 152–72.

29. Iriye, *Cultural Internationalism and World Order*, 43–44.

30. Walter LaFeber, *The Clash: U.S.-Japanese Relations Throughout History* (New York: W. W. Norton and Company, 1997), 113–14; David Walker, *Anxious Nation: Australia and the Rise of Asia, 1850–1939* (St. Lucia: Queensland University Press, 1999), 168.

31. LaFeber, *The Clash*, 123–24; David Day, *Claiming a Continent: A New History of Australia* (Sydney: Harper Collins Publishers, 1996, 2005), 212–13.

32. Roger Daniels, *Coming to America: A History of Immigration and Ethnicity in American Life* (New York: Harper Collins Publishers, 1990), 113–14, 270–71.

33. Ibid., 250, 254–57, 271, 282–83; LaFeber, *The Clash*, 104–06.

34. Anders Stephanson, *Manifest Destiny: American Expansion and the Empire of Right* (New York: Hill and Wang, 1995), 66–97.

35. Reprinted in *The Annals of America*, vol. 12: *1895–1904, Populism, Imperialism, and Reform* (Chicago: Encyclopaedia Britannica, Inc., 1968), 336. The phrase "commercial supremacy of the world" is taken from an earlier campaign speech that Beveridge delivered on September 16, 1898. It is reprinted in the same volume, 198.

36. Raymond F. Betts, *Uncertain Dimensions: Western Overseas Empires in the Twentieth Century* (Minneapolis: University of Minnesota Press, 1985), chapter 2.

37. Ray Lyman Wilbur, "An Interpretation of America in Pacific Relations," in J. B. Condliffe, ed., *Problems of the Pacific: Proceedings of the Second Conference of the Institute of Pacific Relations, Honolulu, Hawaii, July 15 to 29, 1927* (Chicago: The University of Chicago Press, 1928), 64.

38. Sawayanagi Masatarō, *Ajia shugi* (Tokyo: Daitōkaku, 1919). Sawayanagi's lecture was edited for publication by the Kokumin Shisō Jiyō Kōshūkai; literally, the Lecture Society to Nurture Citizens' Thought. It was the first volume in an eclectic seven-part series, which also included the following titles: The Fundamentals of National Defense (Kokubō no hongi), Confucianism and Contemporary Thought (Jukyō to gendai shisō), The Beauty of the Japanese Polity (Nihon no kokutai bi), The Current State of Relief Work (Kyūgo jigyō no genjō), World Trends (Sekai no Taisei), and Buddhism and Ideal Civilization (Bukkyō to risōteki bunmei).

The problem of Japanese disdain for, and discrimination against, Chinese that

Sawayanagi refers to is evident from the July 1899 issue of *The Central Review* (*Chūō Kōron*), which carried an essay entitled, "The Problem of Chinese Mixed Residence." The author, Yamagata Tōkon, attempts to debunk various arguments that the Japanese media raised against removing government controls that were enacted during the Sino-Japanese War to restrict Chinese immigration to Japan and where Chinese residents were allowed to live. The media charged that Chinese residents in Japan were mostly uneducated, uncouth, unsanitary, unskilled laborers who, nevertheless, worked tirelessly for little pay. As such, they threatened the health of the Japanese public, the sanctity of Japanese customs, and the livelihoods of Japanese workers who refused to work as hard, or for so little pay. See Yamagata Tōkon, "Shinajin zakkyo mondai," *Chūō Kōron* (July 1899): 9–16.

39. Sawayanagi Masatarō, "Shisō no dōyō ni tsuite," in *Sawayanagi Masatarō zenshū*, vol. 8, 455–70. Sawayanagi elaborates upon Japan's failure to contribute to world culture in an April 1920 essay, which traces the problem to two sources: a lack of incentive to create ideas and doctrines beyond those that she could readily borrow from East and West; and her geographic isolation, which has kept the world ignorant of her creative achievements, such as the progressive educational ideas and methods developed by Tokugawa-era thinker Kaibara Ekken, whom Sawayanagi likens to John Locke. See "Nihon kokumin no bunkateki shimei," in Ibid., 482–90.

40. Sawayanagi Masatarō, "Sengo no kyōiku wa ikaga," in Ibid., 442–47.

41. Sawayanagi Masatarō, "Kokka kyōiku yori kokusai kyōiku e no katei." In *Sawayanagi Masatarō zenshū*, vol. 9, 523–29.

42. Obara Kunio and Kobayashi Kenzō, *Sawayanagi kyōiku: sono shōgai to shisō* (Tamagawa Daigaku, 1963), 74–91. Named after the high school in Dalton, Massachusetts where she began to perfect it in 1916, Parkhurst's Laboratory Plan bears the influences of contemporaries like Maria Montessori, with whom Parkhurst was affiliated between 1914 and 1918, and John Dewey. It envisions the school as a communal laboratory in which learning occurs through active personal investigation, rather than through teacher-centered instruction. The teacher develops assignments geared to the particular interests of each student, and then monitors each student's progress in acquiring and applying the knowledge needed to complete the assignment. Since it takes place in a communal environment, students are supposed to develop an attitude of respect for, and responsibility toward others at the same time as they learn to take responsibility for their own learning and their own actions. In Parkhurst's words:

> Children learn, if we would only believe it, just as men and women learn, by adjusting means to ends. What does a pupil do when given, as he is given by the Dalton Laboratory Plan, responsibility for the performance of such and such work? Instinctively he seeks the best way of achieving it. Then having decided, he proceeds to act upon that decision. Supposing his plan does not seem to fit his purpose, he discards it and tries another. Later on he may find it profitable to consult his fellow students engaged in a similar task. Discussion helps to clarify his ideas and also his plan of procedure. When he comes to the end the finished achievement takes on all the splendor of success. It embodies all he has thought and felt and lived during the time it has taken to complete. This is real experience.

It is culture acquired through individual development and through collective co-operation. It is no longer school—it is life.

Helen Parkhurst, *Education on the Dalton Plan* (New York: E. P. Dutton & Company, 1922), 23.

The Dalton School, founded by Parkhurst in New York City in 1919 under the name Children's University School, is still in operation, as are a number of other schools that subscribe to the Dalton Plan in Japan, Australia, England, Germany, the Netherlands and several other countries.

43. See Earl H. Kinmonth, *The Self-Made Man in Meiji Japanese Thought* (Berkeley: University of California Press, 1981).

44. Shimonaka Yasaburō Den Kankōkai, ed., *Shimonaka Yasaburō jiten* (Tokyo: Heibonsha, 1965), 429–35.

45. For additional biographical information on Shimonaka in English, see Nakano Akira, "Shimonaka Yasaburō" in Benjamin C. Duke, ed., *Ten Great Educators of Modern Japan: A Japanese Perspective* (Tokyo: University of Tokyo Press), 167–89.

46. Marshall, *Learning to be Modern*, 105–06.

47. *Shimonaka Yasaburō jiten*, 82.

48. Ibid. I have borrowed Kevin Doak's translation of *minzoku* ("ethnic nation"), which Taishō-era intellectuals had begun to privilege over terms like *kokumin* (political nation) and *kokka* (state), particularly in reference to Japan. See Kevin M. Doak, "Narrating China, Ordering East Asia: The Discourse on Nation and Ethnicity in Imperial Japan," in Kai-wing Chow, Kevin M. Doak, and Poshek Fu, eds., *Constructing Nationhood in Modern East Asia* (Ann Arbor: The University of Michigan Press, 2001), 85–113. For information on Shimonaka's Keimeikai in English, see the following: Benjamin C. Duke, *Japan's Militant Teachers: A History of the Left-Wing Teachers Movement* (Honolulu: University Press of Hawaii, 1973), 14–15; and Donald R. Thurston, *Teachers and Politics in Japan* (Princeton: Princeton University Press, 1973), 31–34.

49. See Nakauchi Toshio et. al., eds, *Kyōiku no Seikisha no sōgōteki kenkyū*, 625–27. See also: www.aim25.ac.uk/cgi-bin/search2?coll_id=2282&inst_id=5. The New Education Fellowship was renamed the World Education Fellowship in 1966.

50. "Kyōiku no Seikisha no kyōiku seishin," in *Kyōiku no seiki*, vol. 1, no. 1 (October 1923), p. 1. See also Nakauchi et. al., eds, *Kyōiku no Seikisha no sōgōteki kenkyū*, 628–33.

51. Nakano Akira, *Taishō demokurashī to kyōiku* (Tokyo: Shin Hyōron, 1990), 62–70.

52. Lincicome, "Nationalism, Imperialism, and the International Education Movement in Early Twentieth-Century Japan," 343–44.

53. Yamazaki Yūji, "Dai ichiji taisengo ni okeru 'kokusai kyōiku undo' no seiritsu to tenkai: Taishōki kyōiku kaizō undō no kokusaishugiteki sokumen," in *Kyōiku kenkyū* 30 (March 1986), (Tokyo: Aoyama Gakuin Daigaku Kyōiku Gakkai, March 1986), 71–74. See also Ogata, "The Role of Liberal Nongovernmental Organizations in Japan," 459–60.

54. The full text of this petition is reproduced in Nakano, *Taishō demokurashī*, 129–30.

55. Shimonaka signed the petition as Secretary of the Keimeikai, Noguchi as Secretary of the Federation of Educational Societies in Japan (Teikoku Rengō Kyōikukai), Sawayanagi as President of the Imperial Education Association, and Harada as Chief Editor of *The Educational Review*. The other signatories were: Baron Yoshirō Sakatani, President of the Japan Peace Society, Vice-President of the Society of League of Nations in Japan; Baroness T. Megata, President of the Japan Women's Peace Society; Dr. Masaji Anezaki, Professor of the Tokyo Imperial University; and Tomoji Ishida, Chief Editor of the *Bunka Undō*, Secretary of the Society of Culture Movement.

56. "Harada Minoru shi kyōikugaku," in Dai Nihon Gakujutsu Kyōkai, ed., *Nihon gendai kyōikugaku taikei* (Tokyo: Monasu, 1927), 314.

57. Yamazaki, "Dai ichiji taisengo," 78–80; Lincicome, "Nationalism, Imperialism, and the International Education Movement in Early Twentieth-Century Japan," 343–46.

58. Noguchi Entarō, "Kokusai Kyōiku Kyōkai no seiritsu," in *Teikoku Kyōiku* 77 (February 1922), 6–7.

59. Shimonaka Yasaburō, *Kyōiku Saizō* (Tokyo: Keimeikai, 1920), Preface.

60. Ibid., 11–18. I have borrowed the phrase "popular nationalism" from Dick Stegewerns to translate *kokuminshugi*, which he defines as "the nationalism in which the claims of the nation (in the sense of 'the people') are favored over the claims of the state," as opposed to "*kokkashugi*. . . a concept of nationalism where the claims of the state are favored over the claims of the people." See Dick Stegewerns, "The Dilemma of Nationalism and Internationalism in Modern Japan: National Interest, Asian Brotherhood, International Cooperation or World Citizenship?" in Stegewerns, ed., *Nationalism and Internationalism in Imperial Japan*, 12.

61. Ibid., 18–40, 55–61.

62. Ibid., 41–44.

63. Ibid., 48–54.

64. Yamazaki, "Dai ichiji taisengo," p. 81. Joining the International Education Society of Japan in establishing the Japan League for Peace were: the League of Nations Association; the Society of Supporters of Arms Reduction (Gunbi Shukushō Doshikai); the Women's Peace Society (Fujin Heiwa Kyōkai); the Women's Temperance Society (Fujin Kyōfukai); the Christian Women's Youth Alliance (Kirisutokyō Joshi Seinen Dōmei); the Christian Youth Alliance (Kirisutokyō Seinen Dōmei); and the Christian World League (Kirisutokyō Sekai Renmei).

65. Noguchi Entarō, "Jo," in *Kokusai kyōiku no riron oyobi jissai* (Tokyo: Kokusai Kyōiku Kyōkai, 1923).

66. Asada Kyōji, *Nihon Shokuminchi kenkyū shiron* (Tokyo: Miraisha, 1990), 306–14.

67. Izumi Tetsu, "Rikken kokumin to kokusai kyōiku," in *Kokusai kyōiku no riron oyobi jissai*, 37–41.

68. Noguchi Entarō, "Kokusai kyōiku kaigi oyobi sono mokuteki," in Ibid., 309–27.

69. Harada Minoru, "Kyōiku sekaika no genri," in Ibid., 141–48.

70. The stated objectives of the San Francisco conference were: (1) "To promote friendship, justice, and good will among the nations of the earth"; (2) "To bring about

a world-wide tolerance of the rights and privileges of all nations regardless of race or creed"; (3) "To develop an appreciation of the value and the inherited gifts of nationality through centuries of development and progress"; (4) To secure more accurate and satisfying information and more adequate statements in the textbooks used in the schools of the various countries"; (5) To foster a national comradeship and confidence which will produce a more sympathetic appreciation among all nations"; (6) To inculcate into the minds and hearts of the rising generation those spiritual values necessary to carry forward the principles emphasized in the Conference on Limitation of Armaments"; (7) Finally, throughout the world, in all schools, to emphasize the essential unity of mankind upon the evils of war and upon the absolute necessity of universal peace." *World-Wide Education for Peace: Report of the World Conference on Education, Held in San Francisco, June 28–July 5, 1923.* Educational Series, Pamphlet III (Washington, DC: National Council for the Prevention of War), 5.

71. Shimonaka Yasaburō, "Zenjinrui ai ni tettei seyo: hirakaruru kokusai kyōiku kaigi no sho mondai," in *Kokusai kyōiku no riron oyobi jissai*, 173–88.

72. Inoue Tetsujirō, "Kokumin dōtoku to kokusai kyōiku," in Ibid., 53–73.

73. *World-Wide Education for Peace*, 4.

74. Sawayanagi Masatarō, "Sekai no taisei to kokusai kyōiku," in *Kokusai kyōiku no riron oyobi jissai*, 5–8.

75. Nitta, *Sawayanagi Masatarō: sono shōgai to gyōseki*, 229–30.

76. *World-Wide Education for Peace*, 5–9.

77. Ibid., 9–10.

78. Ibid., 6. The Imperial Education Association was one of seven charter members of the World Federation of Education Associations, and it remained the only Japanese member organization when the World Federation held its second international meeting in 1927, in Toronto. See *Proceedings of the Second Biennial Conference* (Augusta, Maine: The World Federation of Education Associations, 1927), 771–72.

79. Nitta, *Sawayanagi Masatarō: sono shōgai to gyōseki* , 221.

80. According to official conference proceedings, Sawayanagi was joined in Toronto by five other Japanese delegates: H. Aizawa, who had worked with Sawayanagi in the Association for the Promotion of National Education; Katayama Noboru, President of Fukuyama Normal College; Itō Chōshichi, Principal of the Tokyo Prefectural Fifth Middle School; Mizobuchi Susumu, Director of the Fifth Government Higher School in Kumamoto; and S. Tsuchida of Tokyo. See *Proceedings of the Second Biennial Conference.* Sawayanagi missed the first international meeting of the World Federation of Educational Associations, held in Edinburgh, Scotland, in 1925, due to illness. See Obara and Kobayashi, *Sawayanagi kyōiku: sono shogai to shisō*, 231.

81. The Japanese delegation to the 1925 IPR conference numbered 19, including three non-Japanese, while the 1927 conference delegation numbered 18. A majority were educators, but business, labor, journalism, and the non-profit sector (Y.M.C.A. and Y.W.C.A.) were also represented. Those who joined Sawayanagi at both conferences were: Ishii Akira, former Vice President of the Nippon Yūsen Kaisha Steamship Company; Saito Sōichi, General Secretary of the Y.M.C.A. in Tokyo; Takaki Yasaka, Professor of Law at Tokyo Imperial University; Takeyanagi Kenzō, Professor of Law

at Tokyo Imperial University; Takeyanagi's wife; and author Tsurumi Yūsuke and his wife. See: *Institute of Pacific Relations: Honolulu Session* (Honolulu: Institute of Pacific Relations, 1925), 35–40; and J. B. Condliffe, ed., *Problems of the Pacific: Proceedings of the Second Conference of the Institute of Pacific Relations* (Chicago: University of Chicago Press, 1928), 599.

82. Tomoko Akami, *Internationalizing the Pacific: The United States, Japan and the Institute of Pacific Relations in War and Peace, 1919–1945* (London and New York: Routledge, 2002), 105.

83. Ibid., 65–70.

84. Sawayanagi Masatarō, "The General Features of Pacific Relations as Viewed by Japan," in Condliffe, ed., *Problems of the Pacific*, 32.

85. *Proceedings of the Second Biennial Conference*, 16–17.

86. Ibid., 17.

87. Ibid., 18.

88. Ibid.

89. By 1932, the Assocation's membership roster also included 556 women, for whom an auxiliary organization had been established two years earlier. The organization also supported branch associations in 16 prefectures, led by local political and business leaders. See Ogata, "The Role of Liberal Nongovernmental Organizations in Japan," 462–63; and Nish, *Japan's Struggle with Internationalism*, 11–12.

90. On public attitudes toward the League and the political divide that separated supporters and opponents of Japan's membership in the League, see the following: Naoko Shimazu, *Japan, Race and Equality: The Racial Equality Proposal of 1919* (London: Routledge, 1998); and Barbara J. Brooks, *Japan's Imperial Diplomacy: Consuls, Treaty Ports, and War in China* (Honolulu: University of Hawai'i Press, 2000). Sawayanagi was not immune from the political pressures directed at defenders of the League, having been appointed to the House of Peers, in the Imperial Diet.

91. Sawayanagi Masatarō, "Nihonjin," in *Chūgaku shūshinsho*, vol. 2 (Tokyo: Dobunkan, 1909), 94–100.

92. Sawayanagi Masatarō, "Nihonjin no menmoku," in *Kaitei chūgaku shūshinsho*, vol. 2 (Tokyo: Dobunkan, 1923), 78–81.

93. Sawayanagi, "Meiji shodai no chūtō kokumin," in *Chūgaku shūshinsho*, vol. 4, 104–09.

94. Sawayanagi, "Kyōiku aru kokumin no ninmu," in *Kaitei chūgaku shūshinsho*, vol. 4, 63–65.

95. Ibid., vol. 1, 62–65.

96. "Kyōzon to kyōei," in Ibid., vol. 4, 94–98.

97. "Sekai ni okeru waga kuni no ichi," in Ibid., vol. 5, 92–96.

98. "Kokusai renmei to kokusai seishin," in Ibid., 108–14.

Original cover of the magazine Sekai no Nihon.
Used by permission of the Meiji Shinbun Zasshi Bunko at Tokyo University.

Sawayanagi Masatarō, his family and acquaintances host Helen Parkhurst and her personal secretary at Sawayanagi's home in Tokyo in April 1924.
Used by permission of Seijō Gakuen Kyōiku Kenkyūjo.

Sawayanagi Masatarō with students from Seijō Gakuen.
Used by permission of Seijō Gakuen Kyōiku Kenkyūjo.

(From left to right) Konishi Shigenao, Sawayanagi Masatarō, Nagata Arata, Shimomura Juichi and Itō Jinkichi in Egypt in 1922. Used by permission of Seijō Gakuen Kyōiku Kenkyūjo.

Sawayanagi Masatarō and other Japanese delegates in San Francisco to attend the International Education Conference in 1923. Used by permission of Seijō Gakuen Kyōiku Kenkyūjo.

*Sawayanagi Masatarō and other Japanese delegates to the
1923 International Education Conference sightseeing in Yosemite National Park.
Used by permission of Seijō Gakuen Kyōiku Kenkyūjo.*

*Sawayanagi Masatarō and other delegates in Hawai'i to attend
the inaugural conference of the Institute of Pacific Relations in 1925.
Used by permission of Seijō Gakuen Kyōiku Kenkyūjo.*

Noguchi Entarō. Used by permission of Heibonsha.

Ceremony in July 1936 marking the dissolution of the Jidō no Mura Shōgakkō. Used by permission of Heibonsha.

テキノ　タマガ、雨ノ　ヤウニ
トンデ　來ル　中ヲ、日本グンハ、
イキホヒヨク　ススミマシタ。
テキノ　シロニ、日ノマルノ
ハタガ　タカク　ヒルガヘリ
マシタ。
「バンザイ。
バンザイ。」
バンザイ。
勇マシイ　コエガ
ヒビキワタリ・
マシタ。

Excerpt from Yoi kodomo, *a 1941 second-grade reader, celebrating the bravery of flag waving Japanese soldiers lining the walls of a captured Chinese fortress.*

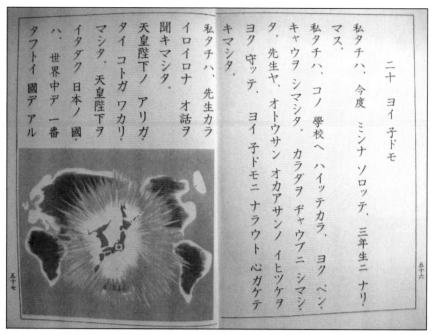

二十　ヨイ子ドモ

私タチハ、今度　ミンナ　ソロッテ、三年生ニ　ナリ・マス。

私タチハ、コノ　學校へ　ハイッテカラ、ヨク　ベン・キャウヲ　シマシタ。カラダヲ　ヂャウブニ　シマシ・タ。先生ヤ、オトウサン　オカアサンノ　イヒツケヲ　ヨク　守ッテ、ヨイ　子ドモニ　ナラウト　心ガケテ　キマシタ。

私タチハ、先生カラ　イロイロナ　オ話ヲ　聞キマシタ。天皇陛下ノ　アリガ・タイ　コトガ　ワカリ・マシタ。天皇陛下ヲ　イタダク　日本ノ　國・ハ、世界中デ　一番　タフトイ　國デアル・

Excerpt from Yoi kodomo, a 1941 second-grade reader, depicting Imperial Japan as the "Light of the World" and reminding children of the blessings bestowed by the Emperor, who is the leader of the world's most noble and sacred country.

Excerpt from Kōdansha no ehon (June 1941): Japanese children play happily with local children in the warm waters of the South Seas. From the Collection of the Department Library, Graduate School of Education, Tokyo University.

Excerpt from Kōdansha no ehon (June 1941): Japanese tourists watch South Seas beauties perform a traditional dance. From the Collection of the Department Library, Graduate School of Education, Tokyo University.

Excerpt from Kōdansha no ehon (June 1941): Vast quantities of oil from the South Seas are transported in tankers to foreign countries. From the Collection of the Department Library, Graduate School of Education, Tokyo University.

Shomonaka Yasaburō addressing the World Education Conference in Tokyo in October 1957. Photo used by permission of Heibonsha.

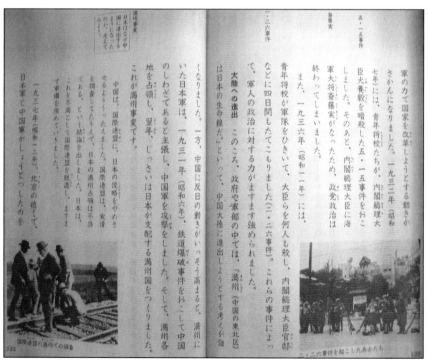

Excerpt from Shōgakkō shakai (1976 edition of sixth-grade social studies textbook) illustrating late 1970s expanded coverage of Japan's "road to war" (1936 Incident, Manchurian Incident, Japan's "invasion" of China and resignation from League of Nations). Used by permission of the Kokuritsu Kyōiku Seisaku Kenkyūjo.

世界へのびる日本

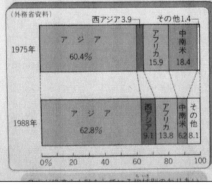

日本は、世界でも有数な経済大国になりました。日本の企業は、アメリカ合衆国やアジアをはじめとして、世界じゅうに進出するようになり、日本の国際社会の中での役わりも大きくなってきました。

現在、日本は、アジアを中心とした発展途上国に、毎年多くの資金をえん助し、国の発展に協力しています。

さらに日本は、外国から多くの研修生を受け入れ、農業や工業の技術の指導者を育成しています。また、日本からも毎年多くの技術専門家を外国に送り、産業の発展に協力しています。

国によっては、失業者を少なくするためや、進んだ技術を求めるために、日本の企業の進出を積極的に受け入れているところもあります。

国際社会の一員として、日本はどんな役わりを果たさなければならないのだろう。

Excerpt from Shōgakkō shakai (1992 edition of sixth-grade social studies textbook) touting contemporary Japan's active membership in, and contributions to, the international community. Used by permission of the Kokuritsu Kyōiku Seisaku Kenkyūjo.

世界につくす日本

日本は，発展途上国へ，技術や技能をもった青年を，青年海外協力隊員としてはけんしています。隊員は，相手国の人々と生活や労働をともにしながら，土木・建築，保健・衛生，教育・文化・スポーツなどの発展に協力しています。隊員のはけん数も年々ふえ，1989(平成元)年には，約40か国に2000人をこす隊員を送りました。特に，アジアやアフリカの国々の新しい国づくりや発展に大きなこうけんをしています。

現在，世界には，日本だけでは解決できない多くの問題があります。その1つが環境問題で，海洋汚染・森林破壊・酸性雨やオゾン層の破壊などが年々深刻となり，その対策の必要性が世界の国々からさけばれています。日本は，進んだ研究や技術を生かし，国連を通じて世界の国々と協力しながら，環境問題にも取り組んでいかなければなりません。

世界につくす日本の役わりが，これからますます期待されているのです。

青年海外協力隊のパンフレット(左)と活やくのようす(右)

Excerpt from Shōgakkō shakai (1992 edition of sixth-grade social studies textbook) touting contemporary Japan's active membership in, and contributions to, the international community. Used by permission of the Kokuritsu Kyōiku Seisaku Kenkyūjo.

⊕満州をせめる日本軍

⊕満州の土地の開拓

⊕ナンキン（南京）城を占領する日本軍

中国との戦争が広がる

日本が中国で行った戦争は，どのような戦争だったのだろうか。

「山田さんのおじいさんは，戦争のためにどこへ行ったのですか。」

わたしは，中国大陸で中国軍と戦いました。わたしたちは，広くアジアの人々のためを考えているのに，中国はそれを理解しようとしないと教えられ，わたしもそうですが，多くの人がそれを信じていました。

それなのに，日本軍は，中国の村や町を破かいし，多くの中国人の命をうばったのです。いっぽうで，日本人も大勢戦死しました。

中国の人たちは，日本のことをどう思っているのだろうか。

韓国を植民地にしたのち，日本は，中国大陸へも勢力を広げるようになり，満州（中国東北部）で持ってきた日本の権利や利益を守らなければ，日本の国

100

Excerpt from Shintei atarashii shakai *(2000 "corrected" edition of sixth-grade social studies textbook) covering Japan's "invasion" and occupation of Manchuria and China, Nanjing Massacre and Chinese resistance.*

凡例（地図）
■ 1941年以前の戦場
■ 1942年以後の戦場
← 日本軍の進路

ソ連
モンゴル
満州国
北京（ペキン）
朝鮮
中国
南京（ナンキン）
日本
重慶（チョンチン）
香港（ホンコン）

0　1000km

🔴日中戦争の広がり　日本軍の占領地は、都市とその交通路をおさえただけというのが実態でした。

🔴破かいされた中国の都市

12月13日に日本軍が城内を占領すると、建物が焼かれ、銃声が難民区内にまで聞こえてきた。あとで知ったことだが、郭さんたちが住んでいた町一帯の1000戸の家はすべて焼き払われ、残っていた住民たちはほとんど殺されてしまった。もちろん、郭さんの家も焼かれ、家財道具はいっさい失われていた。

🔴南京事件と日本軍

がほろびると考える人々が出てきました。

　1931年(昭和6年)、満州にいた日本軍が、中国を侵略する満州事変をおこして満州を占領し、翌年には満州国として中国から切りはなして実権をにぎりました。

　そして、1937年ごろから戦いは中国の各地に広げられ、全面的な日中戦争となりました。

　日本軍は、首都ナンキン(南京)の占領を進めたとき、武器をすてた兵士や、女性や子どもをふくむひじょうに多くの中国人を市の内外で殺害し、諸外国からきびしい非難を受けました。しかし、日本の国民には、その事実は知らされませんでした。

　このような日本の侵略に対し、中国の人々は国の独立を守ろうとねばり強く戦い、戦争は、日本の予想をこえて長びいていったのです。

🔴戦争へ行くお父さん　おばあさん、お父さん、お母さん、子どもは、それぞれ何を思っているのでしょうか。

101

Excerpt from Shintei atarashii shakai *(2000 "corrected" edition of sixth-grade social studies textbook) covering Japan's "invasion" and occupation of Manchuria and China, Nanjing Massacre and Chinese resistance.*

Excerpt from Shinpen atarashii shakai *(2004 "revised" edition of sixth-grade social studies textbook) illustrating Japan's transformation into a peaceful country, in which the authors juxtapose (on facing pages) a black and white photo of Japanese university students marching off to war with a color photo of Japanese athletes marching at the opening ceremony of the 1964 Tokyo Olympics.*

神武天皇の東征伝承

●大和朝廷のおこり●

一つの政治勢力が登場し，しだいに影響力を拡大して，やがて大きな力を備えた統一政権に成長するまでには，ふつう長い年月を必要とする。大和朝廷のもとになった勢力が，いつ，どこで始まったかを記す同時代のたしかな記録は，日本にも中国にもない。しかし，わが国で最も古い歴史書である『古事記』や『日本書紀』には，大和朝廷のおこりについての伝承が残っている。それは，初代天皇とされる神武天皇をめぐる物語である。

⇒p.44

●神武天皇の東征●

『日本書紀』に収める神武天皇の物語は，次のようなあらすじである。

天照大神の直系である神日本磐余彦尊（のちの神武天皇）は，国内を治めるにふさわしい土地を求めて，政治の場をそれまでの日向（宮崎県）の高千穂から東方の大和（奈良県）に移す決心をする。そこで，さっそく水軍を率いて瀬戸内海ぞいに東へ進んだ。

大阪湾から上陸しようとしたが，手ごわい長髄彦の抵抗を受け，兄の一人が流れ矢で戦死してしまう。苦戦の末，軍勢は熊野（和歌山県）に上陸し，大和をめざす。険しい山道を踏み迷うさなか，天照大神のお告げがあり，巨大なカラスが道案内をしてくれる。

尊は，抵抗する豪族を討ちほろぼし，服従させて目的地にせまった。ふたたび長髄彦が進路をはばむ。氷雨が降り，戦いが困難をきわめたちょうどそのとき，どこからか金色に輝く一羽のトビが飛んできて，尊の弓にとまった。トビは稲光のように光って，敵軍の目をくらました。

こうして，尊は大和の国を平定して，畝傍山の東南にある橿原の地に立派な宮殿をつくり，初代天皇の位についた。これが大和朝廷のおこりであると伝えられている。

●歴史の中の神武天皇像●

大和朝廷がつくられるころに，すぐれた指導者がいたことは，たしかである。その人物像について，古代の日本人が理想をこめてえがきあげたのが，神武天皇の物語だったと考えられる。だから，それがそのまま歴史上の事実ではなかったとしても，古代の人々が国家や天皇についてもっていた思想を知る大切な手がかりになる。

■2月11日の建国記念の日は，神武天皇が即位した日として『日本書紀』に出てくる日付を，太陽暦に換算したものである。

●神武天皇の東征（野田九浦 作 神宮徴古館農業館蔵）弓の先に金色のトビがとまっている。後世の想像図。

30

●日本サッカー協会のシンボルマーク この伝承に登場するカラスがデザインされている。足が3本えがかれている。

Excerpt from Atarashii rekishi kyōkasho (2005 "revised commercial edition" of Fujioka Nobukatsu's controversial middle school history textbook) recounting Emperor Jinmu's pacification of the realm.

昭和天皇
（しょうわてんのう）

●お人がら●

昭和天皇は，1901（明治34）年4月29日，皇太子（のちの大正天皇）の第一子として誕生した。御名は迪宮裕仁。幼少のころから，きわめてまじめで誠実なお人がらだった。

即位ののち，1931（昭和6）年11月，九州の鹿児島から軍艦に乗って帰京されるとき，天皇が夜になって暗くなった海に向かって一人挙手の礼をされているのを，お付きの者が見つけ不思議に思った。そこで海のほうを見ると，遠く暗い薩摩半島の海岸に，天皇の軍艦をお見送りするために住民たちが焚いたと思われるかがり火の列が見えた。天皇はそれに向けて答礼をされていたのである。

●昭和天皇とその時代●

昭和天皇が即位された時期，日本は大きな危機をむかえていた。天皇は各国との友好と親善を心から願っていたが，時代はそれとは異なる方向に進んでいった。しかし，天皇は，たとえ意に反する場合でも，政府や軍の指導者が決定したことは認めるという，立憲君主としての立場を貫かれた。

ただ，天皇がご自身の考えを強く表明し，事態を収めたことが2度あった。一つは，1936（昭和11）年の二・二六事件のときで，も⇐p.198う一つは，1945（昭和20）年8月，終戦のとき⇐p.211であった。どちらも君主としての強い自覚によってなされた行動だった。

●国民とともに歩む●

終戦直後，天皇と初めて会見したマッカーサーは，天皇が命乞いをするためにやって来たと思った。ところが，天皇の口から語られた言葉は，「私は，国民が戦争遂行にあたって行ったすべての決定と行動に対する全責任を負う者として，私自身をあなたの代表する諸国の裁決にゆだねるためお訪ねした」というものだった。

マッカーサーは，「私は大きい感動にゆすぶられた。死をもともなうほどの責任，明らかに天皇に帰すべきではない責任を引き受けようとする，この勇気に満ちた態度は，私の骨の髄までもゆり動かした」（『マッカーサー回想記』）と書いている。

敗戦後，天皇は日本各地を巡幸され，復興にはげむ人々と親しく言葉をかわし，はげまされた。激動する昭和という時代を，一貫して国民とともに歩まれた生涯だった。

↑天皇巡幸（福岡県三池鉱業所）

225

3

Japan's Imperial Internationalism

UNIVERSALISM AND PARTICULARISM
IN INTERWAR TEXTBOOKS

The conspicuous addition of commentary on "coexistence and co-prosperity," on cultivating an "international spirit," and on the League of Nations in the fourth edition of Sawayanagi's middle school textbook was neither a fluke nor an anomaly. In her roundtable presentation at the 1927 IPR Conference, "How Japan is Trying to Develop the International Mind in Her Young People," Hoshino Aiko, Acting President of Tsuda Women's College, was at pains to point out that

> the [secondary school] textbooks on Morals that are being taught in all these schools, contain as a rule a good deal of international material. Going over carefully the several series of text books on Morals written by different authors and recommended by the Department of Education as most widely used in Japan, I have found that every kind contains one or more chapters exclusively devoted to the teaching of International Affairs.[1]

This was no exaggeration. Yumoto Genichi was another author who included several such chapters in the commercial edition (*toshi yō*) of his 1926 *New Civics Textbook* (*Shinsei kōmin kyōhon*). Indeed, his treatment of the origins and aims of the League of Nations is more detailed than Sawayanagi's. In a chapter entitled, "International Relations," Yumoto provides an account of the birth of the League, including an excerpt from the Versailles Peace Treaty authorizing its creation, followed by a summary of the League's major activities. His readers also learn that the League is but one of many initiatives that countries have been pursuing in the name of international understanding, cooperation and justice. Other examples that he touches upon include: the 1921 Washington Conference; the annual International Labor Conference, launched in 1919; the International Institute of Agriculture; and various international exhibitions. Yumoto concludes this chapter by charging individual citizens with the responsibility for maintaining world peace, since history shows that most wars stem from animosity between citizens of different countries. Citizens in every country must "train themselves to be international" (*kaku kokumin wa kokusaiteki ni jibun o kunren senebanaranai*). At the same time, they must cultivate "international morality" (*kokusai dōtoku*), which is rooted in individual morality (*kojin dōtoku*).[2]

However, Yumoto's celebration of a new era in international cooperation, and his charge to Japanese citizens to "be international" by doing their part for world peace, stand in uneasy juxtaposition to his subsequent analysis of Japan's international position, set forth in the final chapter of his textbook, "Japan and the World." In a throwback to the original (1909) edition of Sawayanagi's textbook, Yumoto proclaims that Japan is unique among nations of the world, being the only country blessed with an unbroken line of emperors stretching back more than 2500 years, and the only country never to suffer foreign invasion, whose people retain a vigor and prosperity that belie the country's age and defy the typical fate of European and other nations throughout history. These facts demonstrate that the Japanese national character (*waga kokuminsei*) has special strong points, and that the Japanese empire has been blessed with a special providence (*tokubetsu na tenyo*) and a special mission (*tokubetsu na shimei*).

Following the Meiji Renovation, Yumoto continues, Japanese interacted widely with the countries of the world, assimilating their culture, engaging in wars when there was no alternative, and in the process, gaining grudging respect from Caucasians who were surprised by Japan's amazing progress. However, Japan is surrounded by countries that are victims of competition between the Western Powers: India, Annam and Burma have been colonized, while the Republic of China, Japan's closest acquaintance, has lost control over its own affairs. The collapse of China would leave Japan as the only independent country in the Orient (*Tōyō*), and would cede the world to Caucasians. That would complicate its position, so Japanese must cultivate the practical ability (*jitsuryoku*) to contend with those difficulties.

In the past, he laments, the sovereign territories of the Orient (*Tōyō no kokudo*) belonged to Orientals, but now nearly all of them are occupied by Westerners who have also trampled on Oriental culture, which was once the equal of Western culture. Only Imperial Japan is in a position to reverse the decline of the Orient, restore Orientals' former prosperity, and point the way to a bright future. At minimum, only Japan has the power to preserve peace in the Orient. One other important responsibility that Japanese bear is to draw upon their experience of assimilating, and improving upon, the cultures of the Orient and the Occident to give humanity a more perfect culture.

Yumoto concludes by warning his young readers that while the advanced countries have invested the League of Nations with real power for the sake of maintaining world peace, popular nationalism (*kokuminshugi*) is again on the rise, and tensions between them have not been erased. Even if they manage to avoid becoming entangled in another war, economic warfare will intensify, so Japanese must prepare to face competition with the advanced countries, whatever form it takes. Among other things, Japanese should not blindly follow every new idea from the West. Rather, they should cultivate the traditional national character that they inherited from their ancestors.[3] These statements by Yumoto about "Japan and the World" cast some doubt on the assurance which Hoshino gave to the IPR conference delegates in 1927: that in the case of Japan's middle school morals textbooks, "generally speaking, narrow patriotism is guarded against and international cooperation for the good of all is upheld as desirable and necessary."[4]

Ikeoka Naotaka, another educator whose *Middle School Civics Textbook* (*Chūtō kōmin kyōkasho*) also appeared in 1926, echoes many of Yumoto's ideas and accompanying terminology in his own commentary on international affairs, which occupies the final three chapters, beginning with "International Relations." The increasing frequency and complexity of international relations, Ikeoka writes, place a premium on universal respect for international morality (*kokusai no dōtoku*) and international law (*kokusai hō*). International morality is necessary to sustain an international spirit (*kokusai seishin*), to respect the sovereign rights of each country, and to advance world peace and the welfare of humanity. International law manages the practical aspects of international relations through negotiated treaties, the exchange of ambassadors and consuls general, and so forth. Ikeoka reminds his readers at the end of this chapter that, whereas in the past, international relations were conducted in secret by diplomats, under a constitutional system of government international relations have entered the public domain, conducted in accordance with public opinion. Consequently, citizens have a responsibility to exercise care as they carry on healthy discussions about international relations. Furthermore, since good relations between countries are rooted in friendly relations between their citizens, Japanese must act respectfully and discreetly in their personal interactions with foreigners.[5]

Ikeoka's description of the origins, aims, and structure of the League of Nations is also reminiscent of Yumoto's textbook, although Ikeoka provides even more factual information. After recounting the failure of two earlier international peace conferences, held at the Hague in 1899 and 1907, to try and prevent the outbreak of the Great War in Europe, he explains that the

League was founded at the same time as the peace treaty was concluded at Versailles. To promote world peace and the welfare of humanity, he writes, the League is guided by 26 statutes mandating such initiatives as: arms reduction; respecting sovereign territory and political independence; establishing a court of arbitration and a court of international law; addressing human rights issues (labor problems, trafficking in women and children, drug trafficking, vaccination programs, etc.); and establishing volunteer Red Cross agencies. It is noteworthy that Ikeoka also concludes his remarks on the League with the same admonition as Sawayanagi: do not expect miracles from the League, and give it more time to reach its full potential.[6]

Ikeoka's commentary in his final chapter, "Japan in the World," is noticeably less inflammatory than Yumoto's chapter of the same title: there is no mention of race—white or yellow; no reference to Western colonialism in Asia; and no discussion of economic competition as a prime threat to Japan and its neighbors. Indeed, initially Ikeoka is content to refer to humankind in the singular: praising its emergence from a primitive state of nature to a species that has mastered the laws of nature through the evolution of human intellect. At the same time, the development of human thought has also made it possible to govern human society through philosophy, morality, religion, technology, politics, law and economics. The culmination of this process is the social formation known as the nation-state (*kokka*), without which human beings would be like fish out of water; unable to secure their existence, prosper, or achieve their full potential.

But if Ikeoka managed to avoid the essentialist discourse on race that preoccupied many of his contemporaries, among them Sawayanagi and Yumoto, "culture" was another matter. His comments on *bunka* strike a familiar chord, centering on the broad division between Orient and Occident; although, in contrast to Yumoto, Ikeoka asserts that while Eastern culture only developed a spiritual/philosophical dimension (Confucianism courtesy of China, Buddhism courtesy of India), Western culture managed to develop *both* a spiritual/philosophical dimension (courtesy of Greece and Rome) and a material dimension (through the advent of science after the Middle Ages). Ikeoka then invokes the common refrain that Japan stands alone in the world, due to its unique national polity (*kokutai*)—emanating from the divine land, the imperial family, and the special sentiments of the Yamato ethnic nation (loyalty, filial piety, patriotism)—and to its unrivaled ability to create a more perfect human culture through the selective adoption of elements of both Oriental and Occidental cultures. Predictably, this leads him to the same conclusion as Sawayanagi and Yumoto: Japan has a special mission to repay its debt to Oriental and Occidental societies alike, by sharing this more perfect culture with the entire world.[7]

Turning from Japanese middle school textbooks to those used in the primary schools, Hoshino candidly admitted to the IPR conference delegates in 1927 that her examination of the Readers used by teachers of Japanese language found no mention of "the peace of the World, or the existence of the League of Nations," although she did come across one chapter on international relations in the final volume of the MOE's primary school ethics textbook, which introduces the League of Nations and remarks on the League's importance to the peace of the world. But in other respects, she concludes, Japanese primary school textbooks "have a strong tendency both in their tone and material toward international friendship and peace. They have nothing that will produce ill-will against any foreign country or people, nor anything that will encourage our children toward love of war, or race-prejudice, or narrow patriotism."[8]

The reasons for this disparity between the primary and middle school grades regarding their coverage of the world beyond Japan, and of Japan's place in it, date back to the pedagogical theories that were introduced into Japan and contended for legitimacy during the 1870s and 1880s. First, the child-centered developmental education doctrine (*kaihatsushugi*), which enjoyed widespread support at teacher training institutions and filtered down to the primary schools until the mid-1880s, argued that early education should respect the "natural" progression of the child's recognition of the world he or she inhabits, which begins with the child's immediate surroundings (home, neighborhood, village) and then gradually expands to encompass one's country and, finally, the world. Ironically, this theory also found support among critics of developmental education beginning in the mid-1880s, who complained that developmental education's emphasis on self-discovery and individualized instruction neglected the pressing need for standardized instruction designed to produce loyal, patriotic imperial subjects who should learn to identify themselves as members of the Japanese ethnic nation *before* they learn to become citizens of the world. Accordingly, by the late 1880s Herbartian educational theory (*Herubarutoshugi*), which promised to remedy this oversight, had begun to find favor among educators at the imperial universities and normal schools, and among MOE bureaucrats.[9]

A second reason why middle school teachers were expected to provide more coverage of international affairs in their classrooms than their counterparts in the primary schools is rooted in the relationship between education, politics, and social class. The Meiji government, in 1872, became the first in Asia to make primary schooling compulsory, for boys as well as girls, because basic education was deemed vital to the intellectual, moral and spiritual preparation of loyal, dedicated imperial subjects who, as adults, would apply their basic knowledge of the three R's to the goal of national wealth and power in a variety of blue-collar occupations: from farmer, to factory laborer, to soldier. Middle school education, which only became compulsory under the influence of the Allied Occupation following the Asia-Pacific War, was another matter, however. Its principal function was to identify the members of Japan's future elite, and to arm them with the broader knowledge and more refined cognitive and socials skills necessary to manage Japan's increasingly complex domestic and international affairs: as white-collar diplomats, bureaucrats, educators, and businessmen. This correlation between education, occupation and social class began to weaken after the Meiji Period, as more graduates of primary school sought entry into middle schools, higher schools and universities, but it was still a factor influencing the compilation of school textbooks in the 1920s.

While this disparity between primary and middle school textbooks published in the 1920s is very conspicuous, it was not as extreme as Hoshino's assessment at the 1927 IPR conference suggests. The chapter on international relations that she singled out for comment gives repeated examples of the imperial family's support for peace between nations: beginning with a declaration by the Meiji Emperor in 1908; followed by another from the Taishō Emperor on January 1, 1920 to commemorate the signing of the Versailles Peace Treaty and the birth of the League of Nations; followed by Prince Hirohito's half-year tour of various European capitals, where he was warmly welcomed. The chapter concludes by admonishing primary school pupils to never forget the importance of international relations, to make a concerted effort to learn about international affairs, and to strive to increase the spirit of friendship and harmony in their personal interactions with foreigners.[10]

A more abstract endorsement of the humanitarian spirit, aimed at primary school pupils, is found elsewhere in volume five of the same ethics primer, titled simply "Humanitarianism." It recounts the story of a small crew of Japanese sailors during the Tokugawa period who were rescued by an American whaling ship when their coastal transport was blown out to sea. Months later, after the whaler completed its expedition, her captain and crew took the castaways to Hong Kong, where they were taken in by a Japanese innkeeper who, in turn, arranged transport for them to Shanghai aboard a French ship. From there, through the intercession of the Chinese government, they were finally repatriated to Japan, some three years after their ordeal began. The moral of the story, "Exhibiting love to acquaintances and strangers alike is the Way of Humanity (*ningen no michi*)" is underscored by referring to the famous story of how Captain Kamimura rescued six hundred Russian sailors from drowning, after he had attacked and disabled their ship during the Russo-Japanese War.[11]

Hoshino also overlooked the final chapter in a widely used primary school history textbook that recounts Japan's cooperation with the Allied Powers during the Great War. After describing the circumstances that compelled Japan to "honor her alliance with England and to preserve peace in the Orient" by declaring war against Germany, and following a summary of Japan's major contributions to the war effort, the text turns to the armistice, the Paris Peace Conference and the Versailles Treaty, and the establishment of the League of Nations. While encouraging students to take pride in Japan's elevation to Great Power status and to dedicate themselves to the country's continued advancement, the chapter also urges them to devote themselves to the advancement of world peace, and thus contribute even greater luster to the country's history.[12]

In a country where the government, through the MOE, has been scrutinizing and shaping the content of school textbooks since the 1880s, the attention that these primary and middle school textbooks devote to international affairs could not have occurred without official acquiescence. That the MOE was more than just a bystander in the interwar discourse on international education is evidenced not only by the fact that it was responsible for compiling and editing the primary school textbooks mentioned above, but also by a collection of essays that it compiled and published in 1925 under the title, *International Education* (*Kokusai kyōiku*). These essays were based on lectures that their authors delivered during a special International Education Symposium (*kokusai kyōiku kōshūkai*), convened by the MOE in June 1924 in order to "disseminate knowledge of international affairs (*kokusai chishiki*), and to provide a resource for national education (*kokumin kyōiku*)."[13] Unlike *Theory and Practice of International Education* (the 1923 publication by the International Education of Society of Japan that was analyzed in chapter 2), the essays contained in the MOE's *International Education* exhibit greater uniformity in their respective treatments of this topic. Several of these essays—notably, those by Sakatani Yoshirō, Morioka Tsunezō, and, of course, Sawayanagi—also bear strong resemblances to those chapters on international relations, the League of Nations, and Japan's "mission" in the world that were featured in the middle school textbooks analyzed above.[14]

THE ASSAULT ON "LIBERAL INTERNATIONALISM"

However, the mid-1920s turned out to be the high-water mark for reformers who had rallied under the banners of liberal education, new education and international education during the preceding nine or ten years. As early as 1924, the minister of education began to criticize advocates of new education, prompting its slow retreat from the public school sector.[15] While the Century of Education Society managed to sustain the movement's momentum in the private sector until the mid-1930s, financial problems and other factors forced it to close the Children's Hamlet Primary School in 1936, cease publication of its journal, and finally disband.[16] Shimonaka's teachers' union was an early victim of government censorship and harassment, and was forced to disband after only a few short years. It was succeeded in 1929 by a communist-led teachers association, which was also forced to disband the very next year, after forty-five of its members were arrested under the 1925 Peace Preservation Law. A third union that was established with a proletarian platform in 1930 suffered a similar fate. Indeed, between 1926 and 1935, the government arrested 748 teachers on ideological grounds and punished 649 of them. The only teachers' association to survive this period was the Imperial Education Association, but at the cost of the relative autonomy from government interference that Noguchi and Sawayanagi had secured for it.[17] Sawayanagi himself may have anticipated this shift in the ideological winds, judging from a rare moment of candor in his July 1925 speech at the first conference of the IPR in Honolulu, entitled "Some Suggestions for Internationalizing Education." Commenting on the number and popularity of college and university branches of the League of Nations Association in Japan, he remarks that "It is an interesting fact that at our universities and colleges the professors and students are most[ly] radicals. In this respect there is a wide difference between our higher institutions of learning and those of other lands; so much so, that some people complain there is too much internationalism in our academic circles."[18]

The International Education Society of Japan, too, became moribund after the mid-1920s, although Noguchi and Sawayanagi continued to pursue its agenda under the aegis of the Imperial Education Association until the latter's death in 1927. The Society's premature demise was surely hastened by the failure of its leaders to raise its public profile or to recruit a broad-based membership.[19] But equal weight should be given to the changing ideological and political climate, both at home and abroad, which put Japanese supporters of liberal education, peace education, and the League of Nations increasingly on the defensive, at a time when more radical reformers in the socialist, communist and labor movements were being subjected to arrest and censorship.

This ideological shift is further illustrated by contrasting the MOE's 1924 symposium and resulting publication, *International Education*, with another symposium for teachers that it sponsored five years later, which focused on education for working-class Japanese preparing to emigrate abroad (*ishoku-min kyōiku*). The slogans that punctuated many of the lectures delivered at the 1924 meeting—"education for international understanding," "international morality," "humanitarianism," "democracy," "equality"—were conspicuously absent from those delivered at the 1929 symposium. Education for outbound Japanese was treated as an extension of vocational training: tellingly, a majority of the symposium participants were teachers at agricultural and other vocational schools, while most of the featured lecturers were chosen for their expertise in overseas development in specific regions targeted by the Japanese government, notably Manchuria, the "South Seas" (Nanyō), and South America. The speakers included: Shirakami Yukichi and Moriya Shigeo, administrators from the Overseas Association (Kaigai Kyōkai); Ōhashi Chūichi, an official from the Ministry of Foreign Affairs; Nakamura Yoshinori from the South Manchurian Railway Company; Iizumi Ryōzō from the South Seas Association (Nanyō Kyōkai); Akamatsu Yoshiyuki, former consul general in Sao Paulo; and Fukuhara Hachirō, president of the South America Colonization Company (Nanbei Takushoku Kaisha).

Shirakami's lead essay in the published proceedings of the symposium strikes a pessimistic tone that conveys none of the hope for achieving "mutual prosperity and peaceful coexistence" which accompanied the signing of the Versailles Treaty and the establishment of the League of Nations at the beginning of the decade. He speaks of war not only in the past tense but as a distinct possibility in the future; a war that would pit Japan against the United States and Britain in a bid for economic survival. Should it occur, he says, Japan's prospects for victory are, at present, grim. Japan's highly touted elevation to Great Power status following the Great War is a chimera; due less to Japanese military, economic, scientific and technological prowess than to the dramatic loss of Great Power status by those who ended up on the losing side in that war. Shirakami recites a host of facts and figures to illustrate Japan's inferiority to Britain and the US in every major category: from GNP to per capita automobile ownership; from the number of naval ships (regulated by the 5-5-3 formula in the 1922 Washington Treaty) and the number of men in military uniform to the number of miles of train track per capita; from the extent of their natural resources to their agricultural productivity. That is why emigration is vital to Japan's survival: as a foreign source of income, raw materials and foodstuffs.

Therefore, he continues, the education of would-be emigrants must begin by explaining these geo-political facts to the Japanese people, who are so gullible and susceptible to the utopian allure of radical Western ideologies like communism that they no longer understand what it means to sacrifice for the sake of the nation, and who thus are not keen to emigrate. Japanese educators must reflect on these conditions, and they must do a better job of teaching Japanese youth—tomorrow's leaders, and the generation most attracted to radical Western ideas—how to dispassionately analyze the social and economic origins of those ideas and their long-term consequences.[20]

Eschewing Shirakami's dire talk of war, Ōhashi, the Foreign Ministry official, uses his speech to explain how the Japanese government supports emigrants, and how emigration advances the national interest in an era of peace, when old-fashioned imperialism and coercion are no longer countenanced by the international community. The government offers financial and logistical assistance to departing emigrants; provides various support services such as schooling to overseas Japanese communities; and has relaxed its citizenship laws to encourage overseas Japanese and their offspring to acquire citizenship in their adopted country. In return, Japanese who settle abroad create markets for Japanese companies that provide emigrants needed services such as shipping; they help to expand the overseas market for Japanese products like soy sauce and works of art by introducing them to foreign consumers; and they remit significant sums of money to their relatives back in Japan. Regrettably, however, their reluctance to assimilate to the culture, climate, and way of life of the host country has also fanned anti-Japanese sentiment abroad, which creates diplomatic problems for Japan. Education exacerbates this situation in two ways. First, education in Japan does not do enough to educate pupils about foreign countries and prepare them to live abroad. Second, rather than entrust their offspring to the education practiced in the host country, Japanese living abroad insist upon opening their own schools, where they replicate the outdated forms of education which they recall from their own childhood back in Japan: complete with Japanese textbooks and Japanese teachers who spend inordinate amounts of time teaching mathematics and difficult Chinese characters (*kanji*). While it speaks well of Japanese dedication to learning, such education is of limited value because it is divorced from the host society and out of step with the times.[21]

The most extensive treatment of emigrant education was provided by the only professional educator on the symposium program: Nagata Chū, principal of the Overseas Colonists' School (Kaigai Shokumin Gakkō). In six hours of lectures over a two-day period, Nagata's remarks ranged from a novel theory of overseas development to an equally novel proposal for a new subject in the Japanese school curriculum, which he calls simply, Emigrants (*ishokumin*). Nagata's theory divides human activity into vertical and horizontal dimensions. For much of their history down to the present, Japanese have concentrated on vertical activity: below the earth's surface (botany, agriculture, fishing, mineralogy) and above it (philosophy, religion). Meanwhile, they have largely avoided the horizontal dimension; that is, outward expansion and development (*kaitaku*) across the earth's surface, which they ceded to other countries. Japanese can no longer afford to neglect the horizontal dimension: the fundamental spirit underlying human progress is none other than the spirit of development (*kaitaku no seishin*).

However, warns Nagata, the government cannot be counted on to support policies favorable to outward development, including colonization and emigration, whose popularity is subject to changing political winds. This is why it is important to cultivate this spirit in Japanese youth through education: beginning in the home, where parents can pique their children's imagination and sense of foreign adventure by reciting the folk tales of Momotarō and Urashima Tarō; and continuing in the classrooms of primary schools, middle schools, vocational (agricultural, commercial, industrial) schools, and supplemental schools (*hoshū gakkō*) by establishing a new subject in the curriculum, called Emigrants. This subject could be taught using appropriate sections of existing textbooks compiled for other subjects—morals, history, geography, and so forth—by teachers who have given careful thought to this matter. Those who would benefit most from this preparation for a life overseas are the 25 to 50 percent of middle school graduates who lack the ability, motivation or resources to continue their schooling, and who lack good job prospects at home. The opportunity to make something of themselves by going overseas could be just what they need to find a direction and a sense of purpose in their lives.[22]

IDEOLOGICAL CONTRADICTIONS
AND POLITICAL COMPROMISE

It is common for historians of Japanese education to ask whether these ominous changes in the ideological and political climate, which have been implicated in the *tenkō* (ideological conversion) phenomenon that decimated the communist movement at this time, produced a similar effect among the community of middle class educational reformers inhabited by Noguchi, Shimonaka and Harada. Did they renounce their commitment to liberalism and humanism, which informed their new education and international education platforms, and summarily "convert" to the sort of chauvinistic ultranationalism that they had decried in their earlier writings?

Just such an accusation was leveled against Noguchi by his own contemporaries, judging from a defense he mounts in his 1938 book, *Reform Education First: A Message to the Japanese People*, which was published by Shimonaka's company, Heibonsha. Noguchi responds directly to criticisms that he has changed since his early days as an advocate of liberal, individualized education, by insisting that his fundamental views have not changed. Rather, it is the world around him that continues to change, and he is merely adjusting to it. Such external change is both natural and inevitable, he insists, as is man's adaptation to it.[23]

Noguchi's protestations notwithstanding, a closer look at this text helps to explain why most postwar historians of Japanese education have rendered a verdict similar to Noguchi's contemporary critics. The opening chapter, "Ideals of the Japanese Ethnic Nation," could easily be interpreted as a thinly disguised defense of Japanese imperialism in Asia, blatantly contradicting Noguchi's earlier espousal of equality, liberty, democracy and humanitarianism. Like Sawayanagi in his speech at the second conference of the IPR eleven years earlier (see chapter 2), Noguchi contends that Japan is a victim of its own successful drive to modernize its economy, society and culture. Modernization enhances productivity and economic growth, which not only stimulates population growth and a demand for natural resources, but depends upon them. Being a small, resource poor country, however, Japan has no choice but to look beyond its narrow borders for new sources of natural resources, new markets for its goods, and new outlets for its burgeoning population. Exercising its right to survive and develop as a nation, yet thwarted by the restrictive laws limiting Japanese emigration to, and free trade with, Western countries like the United States, Canada, and Australia, Japan has naturally turned to neighboring China and Manchuria to satisfy its needs.[24]

From Noguchi's perspective, however, this defense of Japan's foreign policy toward the continent does not mark a radical departure from his earlier humanism or a *conversion* to imperialism, so much as a pragmatic *convergence* between his unchanging principles and historical contingency. He goes on to explain that Japan's need for China's assistance is accompanied by Japan's desire to assist China in its own modernization, and to repay Japan's historical debt to Chinese civilization. At the same time, Japan would be helping China to stave off the threat of communist exploitation posed by the Soviet Union, and to resist imperialist exploitation at the hands of Great Britain.[25]

Likewise, in his second chapter, "Our National Character as Observed through [Our] National Way of Life," Noguchi finds new purpose in the argument he presented in his 1923 essay on behalf of international education, that is, that when each country's distinctive national character is respected and allowed to develop, then each can make its own distinctive contribution to humanity. Among the three great Asian peoples—the practical (*jikkōteki*) Japanese, the artistic (*geijutsuteki*) Chinese, and the meditative (*meisōteki*) Indians—only the practical Japanese have yet to make any lasting contribution to world culture. Hence, Japan's current mission is not only to uplift Asia, but to contribute to world culture (*sekai no bunka*) and world peace (*sekai heiwa*) at the same time.[26]

Another example of intellectual convergence between the "new education" reforms Noguchi had once advocated and those he deemed necessary in 1938 can be discerned in the fourth chapter of his book. The difference here is that his arguments appear less clear and confident, suggesting that even Noguchi may have sensed their inherent contradictions, while trying to keep the spirit of "new education" alive amid the shroud of militarism that was enveloping Japan. At one point, for example, he praises the success of Japanese primary and middle schools in thoroughly disseminating the spirit of loyalty to the national polity (*kokutai*), and obedience and sacrifice to the Japanese emperor, while he castigates officials and professors in Japanese universities for failing to take this task seriously. If the latter refuse to police themselves, he warns, then the government has no choice but to restrict discussion of unorthodox ideas that constitute a clear and present danger to the national polity or that might cause students to waiver in their commitment to defend it. The next moment, however, Noguchi takes pains to distinguish between a professor's public pronouncements in the classroom and his private scholarship, warning that to completely restrict Japanese intellectuals from contact with new and unorthodox ideas would risk exposing the nation to a different sort of danger.[27]

Noguchi also renews his earlier appeal for education that respects the particular abilities, interests, and personality of each individual, but again with a difference. This time he makes no mention of cultivating those individual traits for the sake of the individual. Instead, he emphasizes the value to society of educating individuals who can meet the demand for a diversified workforce.[28]

Lastly, Noguchi revisits the issue of "liberty versus control" (*jiyū to tōsei*) that lay at the heart of the "new education" reform movement and other manifestations of the Taishō Democracy phenomenon. Once again, we find a convergence between his longstanding advocacy of liberty and the prevailing trend toward totalitarianism. One cannot debate the merits of liberty versus control in terms of absolutes, he writes. Whether one is speaking of politics, economics, or education, circumstances sometimes favor greater liberty and less control, and at other times they favor the opposite. In terms of education, even Rousseau, the most ardent proponent of a natural, unfettered approach to learning, recognized that the child's natural teachers — parents — must intervene to guide the child's development in the proper direction. When it comes to education on a national scale, the government should set certain standards that can be empirically measured through exams. But responsibility for determining the school curriculum and teaching methods should rest with local communities.[29]

Like Noguchi, Harada's writings after the mid-1920s also illustrate how the process of ideological convergence led proponents of liberal education, international education, and peace education in the 1920s to become apologists for Japan's Greater East Asian War by the late 1930s. Harada never renounces the arguments that he presented in his 1923 essay, "Principles of the Globalization of Education," which was analyzed in chapter 2. On the contrary, he repeats them almost verbatim on more than one occasion. He is most adamant about reiterating that "society" is a product of historical change: gone are the days of the feudal era, when society was confined to the isolated, self-contained village community like the one depicted by the Meiji-era novelist Higuchi Ichiyō in her novella, *Takekurabe*.[30] Thanks to the development of transportation and communications technology, and the attendant expansion of transnational economic, intellectual, political and cultural exchange, society has now breached the borders of the modern nation-state (*kokka*), which must follow suit by becoming a global state (*sekai no kokka*), or an international state (*kokusaiteki kokka*), just as Japan has become a global Japan (*sekaiteki Nihon*). From this, he says, it follows naturally that citizens should be educated to extend their patriotic love of country (*aikokushin*) to embrace the entire world (*aisekaishin*) and all of humanity (*aijinruishin*).[31]

However, with the onset of war, what had been an admonition to citizens of Japan to become responsible, caring citizens of the world, instead became a justification for Japan to serve the world and to save humanity by awakening the various ethnic nations throughout the world (*sekai no shō minzoku*) to true culture (*tadashii bunka*), and by guiding them to construct a new world order (*shin sekai chitsujo kensetsu*).[32]

Accompanying this shift in Harada's discourse on globalism are important changes in his depiction of the emperor, and in his views regarding the role of politics in determining educational policy. As late as 1930, in an essay analyzing Japan's educational development since the Meiji period, Harada rebukes a parade of conservative ideologues and bureaucrats who manipulated education for political ends. They include nativists who tried to push through educational policies that contravened the reformist spirit of the Imperial Charter Oath of 1868; Inoue Tetsujirō and other nationalists who distorted the intent of the 1890 Imperial Rescript on Education in order to disparage Christianity; as well as bureaucrats who also found the Rescript a convenient excuse to replace developmental education doctrine (*kaihatsushugi*) with a formulaic version of Herbartianism, as part of a calculated "educational policy of ideological moral patriotism" (*kannenteki na dōtokuteki aikokushugi no kyōiku hōshin*) designed to discourage political activism among students. Fortunately, he writes, the Sino-Japanese War and the Russo-Japanese War imparted to the Japanese people a more sophisticated understanding of their country's position in Asia and the world, along with a more enlightened patriotism that values peaceful coexistence over martial conflict. War also demonstrated that survival of the human species demands objective study of human experience and behavior, leading to the introduction into Japan of a host of new educational theories and approaches: from social education, civics education, and experimental psychology, to vocational and labor education.[33]

In this narrative, the emperor looms as a farsighted, benevolent leader who defends reason and impartiality in the face of threats from ideological and political extremists.

By 1941, however, this tension has been resolved; or, at least, removed from public view. Writing for an audience of teachers about their role in preparing Japanese youth to carry on the country's crusade (*seisen*) to serve— and save—the world, Harada cites sources ranging from the eighth-century *Nihon Shoki*, to the Meiji and Shōwa emperors, to Prime Minister Konoe Fumimaro, to Foreign Minister Matsuoka Yōsuke, all in order to justify Japan's pursuit of a New Order in East Asia (*shin Tōa no kensetsu*) and, ultimately, a new world order (*sekai shin chitsujo kensetsu*). In so doing, Harada does not simply dissolve the earlier tension between education and politics, and between the emperor and politics, which he decried eleven years earlier; in effect, he effaces that tension from history altogether by tracing the origins of Japan's holy crusade all the way back to the mythical First Emperor, Jinmu, through his proclamation to "cover the earth with an eight-fold roof" (*hakkō ichiu*).[34]

Nevertheless, Harada's writings during these years hint that he was a reluctant apologist for the war, and that he sought to defend his earlier educational beliefs by discreetly weaving them into his remarks on wartime educational policy. In 1944, for example, he opens an essay entitled, "Educational Policy in the Greater East Asia Co-Prosperity Sphere," by professing support for the government's decision three years earlier to scrap the prewar Primary School Law (Shōgakkō Rei) and replace it with a new National School Law (Kokumin Gakkō Rei), which regarded the schools—not to mention pupils and teachers—as little more than instruments in the war effort.[35] But whereas the new law champions the collective conscious over individuality, conformity over creativity, and moral over intellectual education, Harada insists on the need to preserve some balance between these extremes.[36]

Evidence of conversion from an interwar discourse on liberal internationalism, to a wartime discourse on what I call "Japanese imperial internationalism," is most pronounced in the writings and actions of Shimonaka. His strident justification of wartime policies before an audience of skeptical educators is all the more poignant in light of the government's crackdown on his teachers union. Following the Manchurian Incident, Shimonaka assumed prominent roles in a number of short-lived organizations dedicated to liberating the masses—both at home and abroad—from economic, political, social and cultural oppression. They included: the Greater East Asia Society (Dai Ajia Kyōkai), which was founded in 1933 to promote Japan's righteous mission to reunite the ethnic nations of Asia through an alliance led by Japan, which would liberate Asia from Western political control and economic exploitation and establish a new order in its place; the Renovation Discussion Group (Ishin Konwa Kai), established by Shimonaka in 1934, which condemned party governments beholden to special interests, and which backed Konoe Fumimaro to head the government and make it more responsive to the plight of poor Japanese at home and to mounting threats abroad; and the World Renovation Education Association (Sekai Ishin Kyōiku Kyōkai), established in 1938 to harness the energies of educators to liberate the ethnic nations of Asia and Africa from Western oppression.[37]

Shimonaka held fast to this doctrine throughout the ensuing Asia-Pacific War, culminating in his 1944 polemic, *Disquisition on Ideological Warfare* (*Shisōsen o kataru*). In the preface he states that the purpose of this tract is to clarify the nucleus or focal point of Japan's ideological war: protecting and manifesting the imperial national polity (*kōkoku kokutai*). To this end, he purports to analyze the character of the enemies of that nucleus—the Allied Powers—and offers advice on how to resist their ideological warfare by conducting Japan's own.[38]

Ideological warfare, he writes, is both one facet of total war and that which defines the basis for total war. It serves two purposes simultaneously: to weaken the spirit of the enemy while buttressing the spirit of Japanese troops, the Japanese people at home, and the people living in occupied territories. Making frequent references to passages from the eighth-century *Kojiki* and *Nihon Shoki* by way of illustration, Shimonaka declares ideological warfare to be the very essence of Japanese imperial warfare: it can be summed up as war for world renovation through *hakkō ichiu*; to spread justice (*taigi*) throughout the "eight corners of the world."[39]

The enemy is Western civilization and its fundamental motivating principle: the primacy of the individual. Individualism does not ignore the whole, but it regards the whole in terms of actualizing the individual. The economic manifestation of this principle is capitalism, its political manifestation is democracy, and its cultural manifestation is liberalism that advocates absolute freedom for the individual. Recognizing the failure of this principle, Germany and Italy have each embarked on their own distinctive totalitarian remedy, but only Japan possesses an ideal totalitarianism, passed on since ancient times through its unbroken line of divine emperors. This is the source of Japan's strength, and it can become the nucleus around which the people of Asia and throughout the world can unite.[40]

The conclusion that Shimonaka underwent a voluntary conversion to ultra-nationalism by the early 1930s is even more tempting when one notes the uncanny similarities between these statements and the memorandum that communist leaders Sano Manabu and Nabeyama Sadachika addressed to their lawyers and friends from prison in 1933, and which historians credit with precipitating a wave of *tenkō* among other communist party members:

> There are common characteristics among Asian peoples in language, culture, race, and religion. There is spiritual solidarity among them in their confrontation with Western capitalism. . . . The struggle against Western capitalism, which will develop into a war, will be a progressive step for the peoples of Asia. Japan should be the leader of Pan-Asianism and should unite the peoples of the East on a class basis into one great nation. The West, reorganized by the proletariat, and the East, reconstructed through Pan-Asianism, will ultimately become one.[41]

However, such a conclusion ignores the continuities between Shimonaka's strident calls for *hakkō ichiu* during the Asia-Pacific War and his Taishō Democracy-era world view and reform agenda, which: proclaimed support for Japan's ethnic nationhood based on its emperor-centered *kokutai*; condemned the economic, political and cultural inequalities and conflict produced by capitalism, and called upon the ruling classes in the most advanced countries (including Japan) to rectify them; advocated world peace and universal human happiness by equalizing the level of cultural development of people everywhere; and thought in terms of a world state (*sekaiteki kokka*) based on humanitarian principles and an alliance among people rather than between governments. In short, Shimonaka, like Noguchi and Harada, did not see himself as abandoning one ideology or set of principles for another, but as adjusting to the reality of historical change. If world reconstruction could not succeed through peaceful means under the terms of the New World Order established by the Western powers after the Great War, then it would have to proceed in tandem with a war that would destroy the old order and make way for a new order foreordained by the heavenly founders of Japan.

Sandra Wilson observes that the Manchurian Crisis—which was precipitated in September 1931 when the Japanese Kwantung Army staged a clandestine attack on the South Manchurian Railway as a ruse to occupy Manchuria and "liberate" it from Chinese control—was a "defining moment" for a variety of moderate and progressive reformers in Japan, who thereafter "showed themselves to be committed at a profound level to the 'national interest'. . . . A willingness to cooperate with the state, or not openly go against it, had often been implied in their earlier behavior. Events of the period 1931–1933, however, forced them to define their position more clearly than before."[42] However, whether they see it as a process of ideological "conversion" or a less dramatic "convergence," scholars continue to debate whether it came about by choice or by coercion.

If Shimonaka sounds more passionate, more committed, and less equivocal than Harada in his support for Japanese imperial internationalism—which would first save Asia and then proceed to save the world by enveloping the whole under an "eightfold roof"—his writings during the early 1940s suggest that not all of his fellow educators shared his conviction. It is striking that in the two years preceding publication of his *Disquisition on Ideological Warfare*, Shimonaka was at pains to explain to Japanese educators why the country was at war, why they should support the war effort, and the special role that education must play in Japan's grand scheme. Consecutive essays in the 1942 and 1943 editions of the magazine *Japanese Education* (*Nihon kyōiku*) repeat the same mantra: Japan's string of victories since the Manchurian Incident, and especially since the well-planned and executed attack on Pearl Harbor, have made a mockery of skeptics—Japanese and foreign alike—who doubted that the country was capable of carrying out an unprecedented quest to save Asia and the world. It is a quest that differs from the West's two-hundred-year-old imperialist drive to control Asia: both because it seeks to save the world rather than to exploit it for Japan's own gain, and because it follows a calculated plan first employed by the gods when they created the "eight islands" of Japan. The role that educators have in this endeavor is twofold. First, they must "reconstruct Japan from within" (*Nihon kokunai no saisetsu de ari*): by eradicating the "European Japan" (*Yōroppa Nihon*) that has made Japan a slave to European influence ever since the Meiji Renovation; and by reviving the native Japan, whose heart still beats in the breasts of Japanese farmers and laborers. They should manipulate every means at their disposal: not just social and educational institutions—including the school curriculum, teaching materials, and textbooks—but also literature, the arts, and popular customs. A new generation of Japanese, so educated, will then be prepared to undertake the second phase by going abroad, situating themselves within other ethnic nations, and directing first an "Asia-Pacific Renovation" (*Ajia Taiheiyō ishin*), followed by a "World Renovation" (*sekai ishin*).[43]

JAPAN AND THE
INTERNATIONAL EDUCATION COMMUNITY

What did this gradual but unmistakable shift from liberal internationalism to Japanese imperial internationalism mean for Japan's position in the international education community, which men like Sawayanagi and Noguchi had done so much to reach out to in the early 1920s through their petitions to the League of Nations, their support for the San Francisco conference, Sawayanagi's participation in the WFEA and the IPR, and Noguchi's involvement in the International New Education Fellowship? Was there an educational equivalent to Japan's diplomatic rebuke of, and abrupt withdrawal from, the League of Nations in 1933?

Formal relations between Japanese educators and their counterparts abroad persisted through the mid-1930s, only gradually succumbing to political and ideological strains in the run-up to the Asia-Pacific War. One sign of stagnation is the number of delegates that Japan sent to international education conferences. For example, whereas Sawayanagi was joined by five other Japanese representatives at the WFEA's second biennial conference in Toronto in August 1927, only three Japanese delegates appear on the program of the association's Pacific Regional Conference, held in Honolulu in July 1932, where special attention was given to educational development and future challenges in the very region where Japan expected to play a leading role.[44]

On the other hand, there is little to suggest that Japan's participation in these educational conferences sparked the kind of confrontation like the one recorded in the proceedings of the 1929 conference of the IPR in Kyoto, when one Japanese delegate "rose to protest and to demand the right to answer the 'charge'" from the Chinese delegation that the Japanese government was responsible for the murder of Chang Tso-lin.[45] This does not imply greater civility on the part of international educators compared to the more diverse membership of the IPR, or that the issues discussed among the WFEA conferees were any less important or urgent. Rather, it suggests that Japanese and foreign educators continued to find common ground at this time, as hopes for the dawn of a new stage in the evolution of society and enthusiasm for "new education" following the Great War were tempered by disturbing signs of social anomie.

It is not difficult to imagine the Japanese delegates to the 1932 Pacific Regional Conference of the WFEA nodding in agreement as they listened to the Association President, Columbia University Professor Paul Munro, speak metaphorically about "educational deflation and inflation" against the backdrop of the Great Depression. By "deflation" Munro means the lamentable "decrease in the common valuation of all the things which education may do for society and for the individual," and the resulting reduction of support for education among political and educational authorities. A major factor contributing to this deflation was the nineteenth-century philosophy propounded by the likes of Herbert Spencer, John Stuart Mill, and Thomas Jefferson, along with educational reformers like Rousseau, Pestalozzi and Froebel, which "posited as its major premise that the individual in following his own self-interest would inevitably attain the status best for society as a whole." This gave rise to "the correlated thought . . . that society had the obligation to offer the opportunities for individuals to obtain such an education as would further their efforts to attain these individualistic goals." This theory, says

Munro, "perhaps coincided with reality during the nineteenth century when they were throwing off the shackles of political oppression," but it is proving detrimental in the twentieth: "We now talk much about social planning, when our accepted theories of education held for generations have been all against such a belief."[46]

Munro unwittingly lends further credibility to opponents of liberal education in Japan as he describes a second type of educational deflation, "found in the view that education is the natural and uncontrolled development of the child's interests and the unthwarted development of the child's attitude and choice—what used to be called the child's will," which has adversely affected the present generation:

> There has grown up a disregard for restraint, a disrespect for law, a hostility to group control, and in education a distrust of discipline in social life, a disregard for authority which now results in a distinct menace to our civilization. This distrust concerns not alone our individualistic system, which is usually called a capitalistic system; it has undermined in many respects our traditional system of morals, has changed the character of family life, is producing a generation that rejects any external control in favor of a complete response to the individual interest or desire. This concerns the American people more than any other peoples. For above all other peoples, the American is an individualist and above all other peoples is now showing this disregard for traditional moral standards and for government and law.[47]

Munro's prescription for "an inflation in education" includes "the use of education in the development of nationalism and internationalism." Seeking a balance between the two, he states, "Without denying the need of nationalism, the righteousness of patriotism, we can all admit the evils of the excesses and the means that have been used to the development of . . . excessive nationalism. Nor does it mean that the schools must be used to develop an internationalism opposed to or dangerous to nationalism," nor that it is necessary "to urge membership in a Society or League of Nations until that organization becomes better understood."[48]

> Why study formulae of a League of Nations or histories of war or build up an emotional patriotism when a factual analysis of our present-day paralyzed and dangerous state of affairs carries with it its own lessons?[49]

Japanese educators also found common ground with their American counterparts on the question of assimilation policy in the colonies. As early as 1925, at the inaugural conference of the IPR in Honolulu, Arthur L. Dean criticized Oriental language schools in Hawaii as a barrier to the successful assimilation of Asian immigrants. Four years before Foreign Ministry official

Ōhashi issued a similar warning to Japanese attendees at the Ministry of Education's aforementioned symposium on emigrant education, Dean complains that the "Language Schools were conducted entirely in the Japanese language and there are probably no more than half a dozen white men in Hawaii who can understand it; there were reasons to believe that children were turned in the direction of Japan instead of America." Accordingly, the territorial government stepped in to regulate these schools:

> The law requires that no child shall go to a Foreign Language School for more than one hour a day, and that hour must be after public school. Teachers must have a license, and must be able to read, write and speak the English language; they must know American history and the principles of democracy; the text books must be approved by the Department of Public Instruction. The fundamental educational value of these schools is to enable the children born here to translate from English to a foreign language and from a foreign language into English. It is an asset if they can do that sort of thing.[50]

WARTIME PEDAGOGY AND TEXTBOOKS:
THE ILLUSION OF COHERENCE

Having condemned individualism as the bane of Western civilization, the writings of Shimonaka, Harada, Noguchi and other educators who professed varying degrees of support for the Asia-Pacific War increasingly resorted to a stable of hackneyed, politically correct (in the literal sense of the term) phrases and contorted arguments in their attempts to explain what Japanese were fighting and dying for. The language, imagery and logic they employed conformed closely to official wartime educational discourse, which was initiated by the MOE when it convened a Committee to Investigate the Problem of Student Thought (Gakusei Shisō Mondai Chōsa Iinkai) in July 1931, just two months before the Manchurian Incident. The Committee compiled a laundry list of troubling social conditions—unrest among laborers and farmers, growing economic hardship for the middle class, poor job prospects for graduates, dissatisfaction with domestic politics and the conduct of political parties, public ignorance about constitutional self-government, creeping materialism—for causing more and more students to gravitate to radical ideologies like Marxism, socialism and communism. Similar committees were established by the prefectures, in order to educate teachers about this problem and to come up with appropriate measures to "clarify the concept of the national polity" (*kokutai kannen no meichō*) to students, teachers, and the public at large. This culminated in two publications by the MOE,[51] which effectively circumscribed educational discourse until Japan's defeat in 1945: *Fundamental Principles of the National Polity* (*Kokutai no hongi*), published in May 1937, and a companion work, *The Way of the Subject* (*Shinmin no michi*), published in July 1941. The former leaves no doubt about the state's official verdict on Japan's earlier engagement with liberal internationalism: it condemns Occidental theories of the state because they

> do not view the State as being a nuclear existence that gives birth to individual beings, which it transcends, but as an expedient for the benefit, protection, and enhancement of the welfare of individual persons. . . . Hence, wherever this individualism and its accompanying abstract concepts have developed, concrete and historical national life became lost in the shadow of abstract theories; all states and peoples were looked upon alike as nations in general and as individuals in general; *such things as an international community comprising the entire world and universal theories common to the entire world were given importance rather than concrete nations and their characteristic qualities*; so that in the end *there even arose the mistaken idea that international law constituted a higher norm than national laws*, that it stood higher in value, and that national laws were, if anything, subordinate to it.[52]

Translating these *principles* of Japan's *kokutai* into pedagogical *practice* was not to be left to chance, or entrusted to individual teachers. Consider, for example, a volume of essays compiled by teachers on the faculty of the Hiroshima Higher Normal School and its affiliated primary school, and published in July 1940 under the title, *Japanese Education for a Prosperous Asia* (*Kōa Nihon no kyōiku*).[53] Seventeen essays make up the "Theory" (*riron*) section of the volume; most were written by university professors and bear such titles as, "[Increasing] Citizens' Awareness of Current Conditions," "Aims of the Japanese Ethnic Nation," and "Education 'Today' for Tomorrow." The "Praxis" (*jissai*) section of the book contains twelve more essays: each one written by a teacher at the primary school affiliated with the Hiroshima Higher Normal School, and each one dedicated to a specific subject in the curriculum (morals, Japanese language, mathematics, Japanese history, science, drawing, music, physical education, and manual training).

Typical of the "theoretical" essays is "State, Citizens, Ethnic Nation and Education," which highlights problems related to the teaching of Japanese language and morals. The author, university professor Shinmi Yoshiharu, laments that the Sino-Japanese terms *kokka*, *kokumin*, and *minzoku*. along with derivative terms like *kokkashugi*, *kokuminshugi*, *minzokushugi*, and *kokuminsei*, have been conflated and carelessly equated with English terms like "nation," "nationalism," and "state," or German terms like "volk." This linguistic imprecision is not merely annoying; to the extent that the Japanese people fail to grasp the unique meaning and essence of Japan's *kokutai*, centering on the emperor and his relationship to his subjects, then both the *kokutai* and the very future of Japan are at risk.[54]

To highlight the uniqueness and superiority of Japan's *kokutai*, Shinmi, like other writers before him, draws a distinction between Western and Japanese conceptions of race and ethnicity. Racial prejudice, he writes, has long been a conspicuous trait of Western civilization: witness Western colonizers' treatment of colored peoples under their control; or white Americans' treatment of Negroes, not to mention Orientals; or the exclusionary brand of totalitarianism (*zentaishugi*) practiced by Germans and Italians, based on a narrow conception of ethnic nationhood that denies citizenship to people of foreign bloodlines, notably Jews. Japan, on the other hand, has never advocated racial prejudice. The imperial family has always set a magnanimous example of inclusiveness toward all peoples, whatever their race or origin. In the distant past, Ezo people from the north and Hayato people from the south were admitted into the imperial court. Immigrants from abroad were assimilated and even their blood was intermixed. Shinmi concedes that there have been momentary lapses of judgment: at the time of the Meiji Renovation, for example, some Japanese called for "expelling foreigners" (*jōi*) and persecuted them; and later, during the Sino-Japanese War, some zealous Japanese derided the Chinese enemy with derogatory taunts of "chan chan bōzu." But the fact that Japanese after the Meiji Renovation quickly came to admire Westerners and Western culture, and that the most recent incident with China has not provoked anti-Chinese sentiment or brought any harm to Chinese residents in Japan, attest to the educational advancement of the Japanese people. In the future, Japanese education should be nationalistic education that promotes the imperial fortunes (*kōun hōyoku no kokkashugi kyōiku*), and not be guided by a narrow ethnic nationalism (*semai minzokushugi*). It should aim to produce subjects loyal to the emperor, not subjects who abhor mixing with the bloodlines of other races and ethnic groups. The New Order in East Asia should not prepare for conflict between racial and ethnic groups, but should plan for an end to racial and ethnic discrimination.[55]

However, the goal of uniting Japan, Manchuria and China into one large family brings Shinmi back to the problem of language and language education. Historically, the incorporation of Chinese characters into the Japanese and Korean languages has made it difficult to standardize these languages and to eliminate semantic imprecision. This fact has put these languages at a particular disadvantage relative to Western nations in the modern era, which treat language as an inherent trait of ethnic nationhood, and which subject language to a process of purification and standardization. The problem of language is further complicated by the goal of establishing a New Order in East Asia that transcends the borders of the ethnic nations of Japan, Korea, Taiwan, Manchuria, and China. Shinmi's solution to this problem is to advocate the adoption of a standardized version of Japanese as the lingua franca of the New Order in East Asia—just as Latin was the common language of Europe during the Middle Ages—inasmuch as the Japanese people are responsible for directing the efforts of their non-Japanese brethren in the construction of this New Order.[56]

It was left to teachers of Japanese language and morals at the Hiroshima Higher Normal School to translate Shinmi's "theory" into classroom "praxis"; predictably, the lack of substance in the former is reflected in the latter. In his essay on the practice of moral education, for example, the only advice that Horinouchi Tsuneo offers his readers is to make Japanese pupils understand: (1) that building a New Order in East Asia demands cooperation between Japanese, Manchus, and Chinese; which, in turn, requires that Japanese stop demeaning other Asians and show them more respect; (2) that the goal of building a New Order in East Asia is not simply a pragmatic product of government policymakers responding to the needs of the Japanese state, but an epoch-making crusade unparalleled in world history.[57] And Satō Tokuichi, writing on Japanese language education, argues that in the aftermath of the Manchurian and China Incidents, which launched Japan on its historic mission in Asia, it is no longer enough for the Japanese people to simply revert back to the Japanese spirit of old. Rather, they must further develop that spirit in light of current conditions. Japan's history of borrowing attributes from other cultures and assimilating them into her own culture without doing violence to her national polity means that she is uniquely qualified to undertake this mission in Asia. In contrast to moral education, he continues, the role of Japanese language education in developing the Japanese spirit is broader, touching upon every facet of daily life. To that end, language teachers should: (1) incorporate literature in their classroom materials; (2) introduce their students to Japanese mythology, including new myths reflective of contemporary Japanese culture; (3) incorporate a new generation of children's stories and songs in their classes that reflect Asian themes, rather than exclusively Japanese themes.[58]

With so little truly practical advice available on how to tailor their classroom instruction to a distinctly Japanese doctrine of imperial internationalism that authorized world war in the name of world peace, Japanese teachers had little choice but to fall back on wartime school textbooks for direction about what to teach. The irony, of course, is that these textbooks exhibit all of the characteristics which Sawayanagi, Noguchi, and Hoshino, not to mention the World Federation of Educational Associations, had condemned during the 1920s as antithetical to international education: sanctimonious, self-serving historical narratives, myths, and morality tales that were carefully compiled to justify Japan's wartime policies and glorify its wartime actions in the Asia Pacific, promote the values enshrined in the Imperial Rescript on Education (loyalty to the emperor, patriotism and sacrifice in defense of the nation, filial piety), and breed animosity toward Japan's foreign enemies. Such were the contradictory faces of Japanese imperial internationalism.

This initiative began in the early primary grades, with short textbooks like *Good Children* (*Yoi kodomo*): a 1941 second-grade reader comprised of short chapters written mostly in *katakana* and liberally illustrated with large, colorful drawings. One chapter features a drawing of Japanese soldiers standing shoulder to shoulder atop the walls of a Chinese fortification with arms, rifles and Japanese flags raised in a jubilant *banzai* salute to the emperor. The text reads: "Japanese soldiers advanced swiftly amid the enemy's bullets, which fell like rain. The Hinomaru flag fluttered high over the enemy's fort. Booming voices resounded, 'Banzai! Banzai! Banzai!'"[59] A later chapter, bearing the same title as the book, features a drawing of the Japanese Empire and the Hinomaru flag radiating light over the dark continents of Europe, Africa, Asia, and North and South America. The text reads in part, "Since entering this school, we have studied hard. . . . We heard various stories from our teachers. We learned gratitude toward the emperor. We came to know that Japan, blessed with the emperor, is the most respected country in the world. Together we must be loyal to the emperor, and strive to make this good country an even better country."[60]

In its primary school history textbook published in 1943, the MOE opens its chapter on "International Developments" (*sekai no ugoki*) between the Meiji and Taishō periods by highlighting the dramatic increase in America's "desire for East Asia" (*Beikoku no Tōa ni taisuru yokubō*) following its annexation of Hawaii and the Philippines. The Russo-Japanese War is mentioned chiefly in the context of Japan's tenuous relations with America and Britain, and as a segue to Japan's development of its colonies on Sakhalin (Karafuto) and the Liaodong Peninsula (Kantō Shū), as well as its "efforts to protect Korea in order to maintain stability in East Asia." The motivation to unite Japan and Korea is attributed to the Korean people—who were impressed by Japanese efforts to protect Korea from foreign meddling and guide the reform of the Korean government, and who concluded that this union was important for maintaining peace in East Asia—and also to the Korean monarch, who prevailed upon the Emperor Meiji to grant a union of the two countries.

After devoting one quarter of this chapter to the death of the Meiji emperor and empress, the suicides of General Nogi and his wife, and the establishment of the Meiji Shrine in Tokyo in memory of the emperor and empress, the textbook then takes up Japan's decision to enter the Great War "in order to protect East Asia once again," and to uphold the Anglo-Japanese Alliance it signed in 1902. The most conspicuous departure from the prewar school textbooks that were analyzed previously occurs in the MOE's treatment of the Versailles Treaty, the League of Nations, and the Washington Conference. America and Britain are accused of manipulating these covenants in order to advance their national interests in the Asia-Pacific at the expense of Japan, which bargained in good faith, only to be rewarded with a ban on Japanese immigration to the United States, and with the United States and Britain working to undermine relations between Japan and China.[61]

The most explicit statement of Japanese imperial internationalism at the compulsory level of schooling appears in the MOE's 1943 primary school textbook for moral education in a chapter entitled, "A New World." It declares that ever since the Greater East Asian War began in 1941, a huge, bright hope has taken shape. Together with the like-minded countries of Germany and Italy, which are carrying on the fight against Britain and America in Europe, the Mediterranean, Africa, and the Atlantic, we Japanese are beginning to destroy the old world that was built upon the crude desire to dominate it. There is no doubt that other countries have come to believe it is possible to build a proper new world in place of the old: Manchuria is already the scene of tremendous development; the national government in China is establishing a firm foundation; Thailand and Indochina have developed intimate mutual relations with Japan and are cooperating to build a Greater East Asia. Echoes of that construction can also be heard farther south: in Malaya, Singapore, Burma, the Philippines, and Indonesia. Japan has opened its arms and is beckoning the masses in East Asia. Japan continues to serve at the head of the Greater East Asia project, determined to bring genuine peace to the world.[62]

A more measured tone is adopted by Tokyo Imperial University Professor Toda Teizō, the author of a middle school civics textbook that was published in 1937 and underwent four revisions until 1943, in his lengthy chapter, "National Defense and International Relations." Even so, his message to middle school students is unambiguous: while mankind aspires to the ideal of universal peace and prosperity, history demonstrates that war will be an unavoidable fact of life for the foreseeable future, because as civilization progresses international relations become more complex and competition more fierce, which creates more opportunities for misunderstanding and conflict. Countries thus need a dedicated citizenry and a strong military capable of preserving their independence, before they can pursue friendly relations and negotiate effective treaties with other countries that will contribute to world peace and the welfare of mankind. Japan's national defense is vital if she is to forever advance according to the imperial doctrine of *hakkō ichiu*, propagate the Imperial Way (*ōdō*) across the four seas, and achieve stability in East Asia and peace throughout the world. The remainder of the chapter devotes as much attention to the organization and roles of Japan's military and reserve forces as it does to the duties of the foreign minister, ambassadors, consuls general, and the diplomatic tools at their disposal: bilateral treaties, multilateral treaties and organizations, and international law. The League of Nations is mentioned as the most ambitious multilateral treaty organization, but one whose goals of world peace and international cooperation were not pursued in good faith, as evidenced by the League's rejection of Japan's legitimate actions in establishing Manchukuo.[63]

The final chapter in Toda's textbook, "Our National Mission," begins by declaring that Western countries (England, Germany, Italy, the Soviet Union, and the United States are singled out for special mention) believe themselves to be the material, technological and cultural masters of the entire world. They have used their advances in the physical and natural sciences to assert their military, economic and cultural influence over vast territories stretching from the Atlantic to the Orient. Japan's position as the only country in the Orient to retain its independence from Western control gives it a unique mission: to construct a New Order in East Asia that will establish a strong and secure Orient for the Orientals; to secure a permanent peace for East Asia and the world; and to share with the world the superior culture which the Japanese have created by synthesizing the best attributes of Oriental and Occidental cultures.[64]

It is important to note that official publications like school textbooks were not the only ones that propagated Japanese imperial internationalism to the public. Commercial publishers like Kōdansha found that patriotism and profit could go hand in hand, as can be seen in *Kōdansha's Pictorial* (*Kōdansha no Ehon*): a lavishly illustrated children's magazine published four times each month. For example, the February 1, 1940 issue, billed as a "National History Picture Scroll Commemorating the 2600th Anniversary of the Imperial Reign," features a number of episodes chosen to highlight the country's longstanding global aspirations and significance. They include: Toyotomi Hideyoshi's defeat of the Ming forces in order to "radiate Japan's influence (*ikō*) throughout the world"; Yamada Nagamasa, who, determined to make a name for himself, traveled to Siam and gained the favor of its king by quelling the king's enemy from a neighboring country; Mamiya Rinzō, who "protected Japan's northern frontier," surveyed the island of Karafuto (Sakhalin), and even explored Siberia during the Tokugawa period; the Sino-Japanese War, when Japan awed the world with its victory over the Chinese navy in the Yellow Sea; General Nogi Maresuke's lengthy siege of Port Arthur, and Admiral Tōgō Heihachirō's sinking of the Baltic Fleet during the Russo-Japanese War; Japan's pacification of the South Seas during the Great War; and Japanese troops' defense of the Foreign Settle-

ment in Shanghai at the time of the China Incident. One other entry in the
same issue features a drawing of children from Japan, China and Manchuria
(identifiable from their clothing and from the national flags they carry)
mingling happily together. The accompanying caption tells the magazine's
young readers to be kind and helpful to our neighbors—the people of China
and Manchuria—and to look forward to the day when China abandons its
wrongheaded ideas and mends fences with Japan, allowing this region to
become the finest in the world.[65]

The following year, another issue of the magazine showcased the exotic
peoples, cultures, customs, and natural features of the South Seas, along with
Japan's munificent assistance to the natives. In the Introduction, the editors
explain the purpose of this feature issue of the magazine:

> The South Seas is a very good place. It has surprising amounts of oil, rubber,
> coffee, lumber, rice and such, which is why it is known as the treasure islands.
> But for all of its treasures, the South Seas has barely been opened up. If one
> ventures into the interior, it is just as if no one lives there, so it is Japan's job to
> open it up and make it into something wonderful.
>
> As the neighborhood leader (*kumichō*), Japan has taken countries like Man-
> chukuo, China and Thailand by the hand and brought them together to form a
> big neighborhood association (*tonarigumi*) called the Greater East Asia Co-
> Prosperity Sphere. So, from now on Japan and the South Seas will become
> friendlier and will help one another, and all of you must learn as much as you
> can about the South Seas. That is why this picture book has been made. Please
> pay attention not only to what is rare and interesting about the South Seas, but
> also to what makes the South Seas so valuable to Japan.[66]

To reinforce this image of the South Seas, the magazine is filled with drawings of smiling natives: riding a water buffalo along a path lined with palm
trees; waving Japanese flags as a large passenger seaplane passes low over the
beach; gazing at a procession of floats taking part in a flower festival in Thailand; swimming happily in the surf alongside their lighter-skinned Japanese
counterparts; riding elephants; carrying baskets of fruit on their heads; and
selling songbirds in the market. Omnipresent Japan is also featured in drawings of: a Japanese Shinto shrine honoring Amaterasu Ōmikami; a classroom
of Japanese pupils and their teacher; a loyal Japanese family conducting the
daily morning ritual of bowing reverently in the direction of the Japanese
homeland while the Hinomaru flag flies overhead; a small crowd of Japanese
tourists dressed in Western clothing, gazing at a performance of traditional
dance by South Seas maidens wearing native costumes; two Japanese children enjoying cups of coffee made from beans harvested by basket-carrying

natives; and Japanese cargo ships and tankers docked in a South Seas port where dozens of oil wells dot the horizon.[67]

CONCLUSION

Historians have long criticized Japan's political and military leadership for putting national interests ahead of multi-lateral ones in their decision to honor the Anglo-Japanese Alliance and support Britain and her allies in the Great War against Germany in 1914. Which is to say that Japan acted in the same manner as every other party to that conflict; the major difference is that Japan's rewards in return for her investment in the war effort were proportionately greater. Indeed, historians routinely characterize Japan as the real victor in that war, noting that in its aftermath Japan emerged as the leading power in East Asia. According to this narrative, in return for minimal direct involvement in the fighting and a modest supporting role helping to keep the sea lanes open in the Indian Ocean, Japan acquired jurisdiction over strategically important territories captured from the Germans in northeast China (the Shandong Peninsula) and the South Pacific (the Caroline, Mariana and Marshall Islands), captured foreign markets for its own exports which had previously been dominated by other parties to the conflict, and made a handsome profit by supplying war materiel and other vital commodities to its allies.

And yet, there is no denying that most of the Japanese public was relieved to see the Great War come to end; none more than the educators who have been profiled in this study. Nor is there any denying the sincerity of the peace movement that reached its apex in Japan during the decade following that conflict. As noted earlier, the movement found it strongest advocates among Japan's increasingly well educated, urban members of a new middle class, and also found various forms of expression ranging from the League of Nations Association of Japan to the international education movement. As Harada explained in several of his essays, these people often found greater support for this cause among their well-educated middle class counterparts abroad than with their working class brethren in Japan; not because the latter were opposed to world peace, but because they had other battles to fight at home: against rapacious landlords, exploitative business owners, and elected politicians and career officials who seemed more interested in pursuing power than in serving their constituents.

Like their counterparts abroad, with whom they gathered at international meetings of organizations such as the World Federation of Educational Associations and the Institute for Pacific Relations, Japanese representatives of the peace and international education movements usually found it easier

to criticize other countries, or to accuse "governments" in general, of undermining the peace movement than to publicly criticize their own. To be
sure, the movement for liberal internationalism following the Great War
was rife with contradictions that understandably prompted many Japanese
to question Western nations' commitment to this cause, and to contemplate
ulterior motives. The examples most frequently cited by Japanese skeptics
were: Australia's successful gambit to reject the insertion of Japan's so-called
Racial Equality Clause into the Versailles Treaty; America's failure to join the
League of Nations; passage of the 1924 Immigration Act by the US Congress,
which barred further Japanese immigration into the US; the Five Power Naval
Treaty of 1922, which appeared to the Japanese public to place unfair limits
upon Japanese military naval tonnage vis-à-vis the US and Britain; and the
continued exploitation of their overseas colonies in Asia and Africa by the
Western powers, including the US, while paying lip service to the fifth of
Woodrow Wilson's famous Fourteen Points.[68]

Notwithstanding this litany of complaints against Western governments'
hollow support for liberal internationalism, it is debatable whether educators
like Noguchi, Harada, or even Shimonaka would have shifted their support to
what I call "Japanese imperial internationalism" without the added incentive
provided by their own government, beginning with passage of the Peace Preservation Law in 1925. That law made it illegal to criticize the bedrock principle of capitalism—ownership of private property—and more importantly,
Japan's *kokutai*; meaning, in this case, the system of government enshrined in
the Meiji Constitution, which vested absolute sovereignty in an emperor who
was officially declared "sacred and divine." Furthermore, as noted earlier in
this chapter, the Peace Preservation Law was soon backed up with massive
arrests of communists and anyone else—teachers included—whom the government deemed a threat to social order and to its own power.

Under the circumstances, what had been reluctance on the part of educators
like Noguchi and Harada to air Japan's own dirty laundry when it came to abid-
ing by the ideals of liberal internationalism, thereafter became official policy:
reinforced following the Manchurian Incident, Japan's resignation from the
League of Nations, and its growing imbroglio on the Asian continent by the
MOE's publication of *Fundamental Principles of the National Polity* and *The
Way of the Subject*, as well as its continued control over Japanese school textbooks. With "individualism"—including the practice of free speech—now
condemned as the root of Western decadence, the contradictions inherent in
Japanese imperial internationalism devolved into absurdities. The ever more
strident claims that Japanese internationalism—centered on the proclamation
of *hakkō ichiu* by a mythical emperor—was somehow free of the racial and
ethnic discrimination, naked exploitation, and violent coercion which marked

the West's relations with the rest of the world could only be sustained by a combination of government censorship and self-censorship.

This study readily acknowledges that the political, economic, social and educational views espoused by Noguchi, Harada and Shimonaka underwent important shifts between the era of Taishō Democracy and the era following the Manchurian Incident; shifts that reveal certain contradictions which these men were either unwilling or unable to acknowledge. It does, however, stop short of interpreting these changes as evidence of an abrupt or dramatic "conversion" (*tenkō*) from a liberal, democratic ideology to an antipodal fascist, totalitarian ideology.

This assessment is based on the fact that many of those contradictions were present in their thought and action throughout their careers, predating the Taishō Democracy era and persisting into the era of ultra nationalism. On one hand, even during the height of the Taishō Democracy phenomenon, most middle class writers and educators—including Noguchi, Harada and Shimonaka—who criticized excessive government control, bureaucratization, militarism, and statism (*kokkashugi*), and who advocated greater individual freedom and political power at home and peaceful coexistence abroad, also maintained that sovereignty rested with the Japanese emperor; that one purpose for developing the individual's inborn talents and capacity for "self-government" (*jichi*) should be to promote the welfare of the nation; and that since Japanese imperialism was intimately related to Western imperialism, then the best way to eliminate the former was to argue for a collective strategy that would end the scourge of imperialism altogether. On the other hand, even at the height of the Asia-Pacific War, they adopted the position that war was a historic necessity to achieve the longstanding aims which they had lobbied for, without success, during the brief era of world peace that followed World War One; an era whose potential for genuine economic, political, and cultural "reconstruction" (*saizō*) had been undermined by the continued domination of Western imperialism.

It is these contradictions, transcending the seemingly great divide between Taishō Democracy and Shōwa ultra nationalism, which the standard treatment of *tenkō* fails to discern. As well, it fails to discern important ideological differences that distinguished contemporaries like Noguchi, Harada and Shimonaka from one another. While all three appear, on the surface, to have "converted" from liberalism to ultra nationalism, and while all three resorted to similar rhetoric at similar times in their writing, they also retained some fundamental differences. Noguchi never subscribed to the kind of utopianism that was a consistent component of Harada's and Shimonaka's world views; and Noguchi and Harada never resorted to the race-based categories that led Shimonaka to condemn all forms of Western cultural contamination during the Asia-Pacific War.[69]

NOTES

1. Aiko Hoshino, "How Japan is Trying to Develop the International Mind in Her Young People." Typewritten text of speech delivered at the Institute of Pacific Relations Conference, Second Session, July 20, 1927. Seijō Gakuen Kyōiku Kenkyūjo, Item Number 110-006.

2. Yumoto Genichi, "Kokkō," in *Shinsei kōmin kyōhon, toshi yō,* vol. 2 (Tokyo: Tokyo Kaiseikan, 1926), 112–18.

3. Yumoto, "Sekai to Nihon," in Ibid., vol. 2, 127–32.

4. Hoshino, "How Japan is Trying to Develop the International Mind in Her Young People."

5. Ikeoka Naotaka, "Kokkō,", in *Chūtō kōmin kyōkasho,* vol. 2 (Tokyo: Kōdōkan, 1926), 184–86.

6. Ikeoka, "Kokusai renmei," in Ibid., 186–90.

7. Ikeoka, "Sekai to Nihon," in Ibid., 190–94.

8. Hoshino, "How Japan is Trying to Develop the International Mind in Her Young People."

9. See Lincicome, *Principle, Praxis, and the Politics of Educational Reform in Meiji Japan.*

10. "Kokko," in Monbushō, ed., *Jinjō Shōgaku Shūshinsho,* vol. 5 (Tokyo: 1922), 11–13.

11. "Hakuai," in Ibid., vol. 5, 68–71.

12. "Ōshū no taisen to wagakuni," in Monbushō, ed., *Jinjō shōgaku rekishi,* vol. 2 (Tokyo: 1921), 147–53.

13. Monbushō Futsūgakumukyoku, ed., *Kokusai kyōiku* (Tokyo: 1925), 1.

14. Sakatani Yoshirō, "Kokka to kokusai undō," 3–37; Sawayanagi Masatarō, "Kokusai kyōiku," 41–80; Morioka Tsunezō, "Kokusai kyōiku no hōshin," 83–121, in Ibid.

15. Nakauchi et al., eds., *Kyōiku no Seikisha,* 632; Ōi, *Nihon no "shin kyōiku" shisō,* 174–75.

16. *Shimonaka Yasaburō jiten,* 67.

17. Duke, *Japan's Militant Teachers,* 14–16, 20, 25–26.

18. Sawayanagi Masatarō, "Some Suggestions for Internationalizing Education." Typewritten draft of speech dated July 7, 1925. Seijō Gakuen Kyōiku Kenkyūjo.

19. Yamazaki, "Dai ichiji taisengo," 83.

20. Shirakami Yukichi, "Wagakuni no genjō to ishokumin mondai," in Monbushō Jitsugyō Gakumukyoku, ed., *Ishokumin kyōiku* (Tokyo: Monbushō, 1929), 7–38.

21. Ōhashi Chūichi, Waga kuni imin seisaku," in Ibid., 41–60.

22. Nagata Chū, "Kaigai Tōkōhō" in Ibid., 257–75.

23. Cited in Ōi, *Nihon no "shin kyōiku" shisō,* 140.

24. Noguchi Entarō, *Mazu kyōiku o kakushin seyo: Nihon kokumin ni tsugu* (Tokyo: Heibonsha, 1938), 1–79.

25. Ibid.

26. Ibid., 86–93.

27. Ibid., 233–42.

28. Ibid., 268–75.

29. Ibid., 275–79.

30. An English translation of Higuchi's novella, titled "Child's Play, is included in Robert Lyons Danly's book, *In the Shade of Spring Leaves: The Life and Writings of Higuchi Ichiyō, a Woman of Letters in Meiji Japan* (W. W. Norton & Company, 1981, 1992), 254–87.

31. Harada Minoru, "Kokusaiteki seishin no zensei to sono kyōkun," reprinted in *Nihon kyōiku no shiteki shin shiya* (Tokyo: Meiji Tosho Kabushikigaisha, 1937), 141–52. See also Harada Minoru, *Nihon no kyōiku o kangaeru* (Tokyo: Jinbun Shobō, 1929), 5–9.

32. Harada Minoru, *Shin taiseika no kyōshi* (Tokyo: Shōgakkan, 1941), 1–2.

33. Harada Minoru, "Meiji Taishō Shōwa Nihon kyōiku taikan," in *Nihon kyōiku no shiteki shin shiya*, 1–32.

34. Harada, *Shin taiseika no kyōshi*, 12–22.

35. One teacher recalls that "As a young teacher at a National School (*kokumin gakkō*), I legitimized the war, promoted the ideals of the Greater East Asia Co-Prosperity Sphere, and advocated the destruction of America and England. While guiding pupils' character development, I worked hard to inspire their determination to continue the war. The classroom was dyed in military overtones: the walls were always decorated with posters that beautified the war; I marked the battlefields on a map and spoke about the superiority of Japanese soldiers; pupils practiced writing slogans like 'Certain Victory' (*hisshō*), while other slogans like 'Thank you, honorable soldiers. We, too, will persevere!' were put on display." Quoted in Tsubouchi Hirokiyo, *Kokumin gakkō no kodomotachi: senjika no 'kami no kuni' kyōiku* (Tokyo: Sairyūsha, 2003), 64–65.

36. Harada Minoru, "Dai Tōa Kyōeiken no kyōiku seisaku," in Sekai Seiji Kenkyūkai, ed., *Dai Tōa sensō to sekai* (Tokyo: Chūō Kōronsha, 1944), 211–36.

37. *Shimonaka Yasaburō jiten*, 10–11, 192–93, 242–49.

38. Shimonaka Yasaburō, *Shisōsen o kataru* (Tokyo: Izumi Shobō, 1944), preface.

39. Ibid., 1–3.

40. Ibid., 3–5.

41. Quoted in Beckmann and Ōkubo, *The Japanese Communist Party*, 248.

42. Sandra Wilson, *The Manchurian Crisis and Japanese Society, 1931–1933* (London: Routledge, 2002), 218–129.

43. Shimonaka Yasaburō, "Dai Tōa kyōeiken seiji taiseiron," in *Nihon kyōiku* (Kokumin Kyōiku Tosho Kabushikigaisha), July 1942, reprinted in *Kokumin gakkō sōgō zasshi "Nihon kyōiku,"* edited by Shimomura Tetsuo (Tokyo: Emutei Shuppan, 1991), vol. 2, 22–32; Shimonaka Yasaburō, "Ajia minzoku no sho mondai," in *Nihon kyōiku*, February 1943, reprinted in *Kokumin gakkō sōgō zasshi "Nihon kyōiku,"* vol. 4, 16–21.

44. *Pacific Regional Conference of the World Federation of Education Associations* (Honolulu, 1932).

45. Chester H. Rowell, "The Kyoto Conference of the Institute of Pacific Relations," in *International Conciliation: Documents for the Year 1930* (New York: Carnegie Endowment for International Peace, 1930), 242.

46. Paul Munro, "Educational Deflation and Inflation," in *Pacific Regional Conference*, 43–44.

47. Ibid., 45.

48. Ibid., 49.

49. Ibid., 50.

50. Arthur L. Dean, "Assimilation in Hawaii," in *Institute of Pacific Relations: Honolulu Session*, 117–18.

51. Kindai Nihon Kyōiku Seido Shiryō Hensankai , ed., *Kindai Nihon kyōiku seido shiryō*, Vol. 7 (Tokyo: Dai Nihon Yūbenkai Kōdansha, 1956), 299–304. Both the *Kokutai no hongi* and the *Shinmin no michi* are reprinted in this volume. The former was translated into English by John Owen Gauntlett, edited by Robert King Hall, and published in 1949 by Harvard University Press (Cambridge, Massachusetts) under the title, *Kokutai no Hongi: Cardinal Principles of the National Entity of Japan*.

52. John Owen Gauntlett, trans., *Kokutai no Hongi: Cardinal Principles of the National Entity of Japan*, reprint edition (Newton, MA: Crofton Publishing Company, 1974), 180–81. Emphasis added.

53. As explained in a Forward, these essays originally appeared in April 1940, in an expanded edition of the journal *School Education* (*Gakkō kyōiku*). See Hiroshima Kōtō Shihan Gakkō Fuzoku Shōgakkō, Gakkō Kyōiku Kenkyūkai, ed., *Kōa Nihon no kyōiku* (Tokyo: Kabushikigaisha Jitsubunkan, 1940), 2–3.

54. Shinmi Yoshiharu, "Kokka, kokumin, minzoku to kyōiku," in Ibid., 20–23.

55. Ibid., 24–25.

56. Ibid., 25–28.

57. Horinouchi Tsuneo, "Kōa Nihon no shūshin kyōiku," in Ibid., 179–89.

58. Satō Tokuichi, "Kōa Nihon no kokugo kyōiku," in Ibid., 190–97.

59. Monbushō, *Yoi kodomo*, vol. 1 (Tokyo: Nihon Shoseki Kabushikigaisha, 1941), 38–39.

60. Ibid., vol. 2, 56–59.

61. Monbushō, *Shotōka rekishi*, vol. 2 (Tokyo: Tokyo Shoseki Kabushikigaisha, 1943), 145–64.

62. Monbushō, *Shotōka shūshin*, vol. 4 (Tokyo: Nihon Shoseki Kabushikigaisha, 1943), 118–23.

63. Toda Teizō, *Shinsei chūgaku kōmin kyōkasho* (Tokyo: Chūtō Gakkō Kyōkasho Kabushikigaisha, 1937, 1943), 167–86.

64. Ibid., 187–202.

65. *Kōdansha no ehon* (Tokyo: Kōdansha), February 1, 1940.

66. *Kōdansha no ehon* (Tokyo: Kōdansha), June 5, 1941.

67. Ibid.

68. "A free, open-minded, and absolutely impartial adjustment of all colonial claims, based upon a strict observance of the principle that in determining all such questions of sovereignty the interests of the populations concerned must have equal weight with the equitable claims of the government whose title is to be determined."

69. Nakauchi et. al., *Kyōiku no Seikisha no sōgōteki kenkyū*, 754–56.

4

Educating
"Japanese Citizens of the World"
and the Problem of History since 1945

The aim of this chapter is to revisit the discourse on internationalizing Japanese education that developed in the decades following the Asia-Pacific War, in light of what previous chapters have revealed about prewar and wartime precursors to that discourse. The foregoing analysis of educational thought, policy debates, and curriculum content in Japan has demonstrated that sixty years before Prime Minister Nakasone's Ad Hoc Council on Education coined the phrase "coping with internationalization" and designated it a key component of its reform agenda, an earlier generation of educational reformers had already identified the major issues and devised most of the terminology that the Council would adopt as its own. In the face of domestic political resistance, the interwar movement for international education questioned prevailing ideas about the nation, individual versus national identity, relations between the individual and the state, and relations between nations and states. It also authorized a new purpose for national education that tied the goals of *national* unity, power and prosperity to those of an *international community*, such that even apologists for the Asia-Pacific War were obliged to justify that conflict as Japan's alternative to the failed doctrine of liberal internationalism associated with Versailles and the League of Nations.

However, the willingness among leaders of the interwar movement to transfer their support to the official doctrine of Japanese imperial internationalism, as the 1920s gave way to the 1930s, was due as much to ideological and political contradictions imbedded in their "liberal" interwar discourse as it was to the state's blatant use of propaganda, censorship and repression. Thus, one of the major questions to be taken up in this chapter is whether the contradictions which bedeviled that earlier generation of reformers—notably, their failure to hold Japan accountable to the very "international laws" and universal standards of "international morality" which were supposed to govern relations between *all* states and peoples—have their counterparts in the postwar debates on internationalizing Japanese education.

So much media attention was devoted to the Ad Hoc Council's proposals to "cope with internationalization" during the mid-1980s, and to the specific reform policies that ensued over the next decade, that it is easy to forget the extent to which this issue figured in earlier debates and conflicts over educational policy and content that took place between the 1950s and the 1970s. Occupation-era political and educational policies established the parameters of those early debates along lines that would have looked familiar to the Taishō-era reformers and their critics who were profiled in chapters 2 and 3. Those policies resurrected terminology that had already found its way into Japanese educational discourse by the Taishō period—liberty, individual personality, creativity, democracy, peace, culture—but invested these terms with the sort of legitimacy which had eluded them earlier by incorporating them into the 1946 Constitution, the 1947 Fundamental Education Law, and the 1947 School Education Law. Nor do the similarities end there: these changes to domestic policy occurred against the international backdrop of the founding of the United Nations—which resurrected the same cautious hopes for world peace that greeted the League of Nations a quarter of a century earlier—and the onset of the Cold War, which, in turn, recalled the failure of the League to fulfill those hopes.

DÉJÀ VU

Who can say how men like Sawayanagi Masatarō, who died in 1927, or Noguchi Entarō, who died in 1941, would have reacted to this altered political, ideological and educational landscape in postwar Japan? Fortunately, in the case of Shimonaka Yasaburō, there is some empirical evidence available. Shimonaka survived the war (although his second son was a war casualty in the Philippines), only to become ensnared in the Occupation's purge in 1947 on account of his earlier association with various "extreme nationalist organizations." As a result, he was forced to resign as head of Heibonsha, the publishing company he founded thirty years earlier.[1] However, this setback did not deter the indefatigable Shimonaka, who threw himself into a number of early postwar organizations and activities in the name of world peace, nuclear disarmament, and the liberation of colonized peoples in Asia and Africa, until his death in 1961.

Coming on the heels of his very public support for the Asia-Pacific War, Shimonaka's postwar résumé has been described by some critics as another example of his susceptibility to ideological conversion (*tenkō*), and by others as another example of opportunism by a man whose views changed with the political winds.[2] However, recent studies on internationalism in Japan question both of these conclusions. Jessamyn Abel Reich and Konrad M. Lawson have each identified various wartime politicians, professors, journalists and other supporters of what Reich terms "imperialist internationalism," Lawson terms "transnational idealism," and I have labeled "Japanese imperial internationalism," who, like Shimonaka, responded to Japan's defeat by attempting to reorient their ideas about internationalism to the new realities facing Japan.[3]

Although Lawson does not mention Shimonaka, one of the examples he cites is the All Japan League for World Federation (Sekai Renpō Zen Nihon Renmei). The All-Japan League traces its origins to two parent organizations: the World Peace Association (Sekai Heiwa Kyōkai), founded by Christian writer and activist Kagawa Toyohiko in September 1945; and the World Movement for World Federal Government (WMWFG). The WMWFG was established by representatives from 23 countries meeting in Montreux, Switzerland in August 1947, in response to concerns that the young United Nations lacked the power to carry out its mandate, as shown by its inability to control the proliferation of nuclear weapons. Kagawa chose August 6, 1948 — the third anniversary of the atomic bombing of Hiroshima — to launch the All-Japan League, which from its inception was formally affiliated with the WMWFG; it even sent a Japanese representative to attend the second international meeting of the WMWFG, held in Luxembourg in 1948. Shimonaka, along with veteran politician Ozaki Yukio, became central figures in the All-Japan League around 1952; in 1959, Shimonaka, who was serving concurrently as a director of both the All-Japan League and the WMWFG at the time, even attended the latter's ninth annual meeting in St. Petersburg.[4]

The All-Japan League subscribed to a modified version of the WMWFG's 1947 Montreux Declaration, which was reprinted in Japanese in each issue of the journal *World Federation* (*Sekai Renpō*):

1. All of the peoples (*minzoku*) and nations (*kokka*) of the world can participate.
2. National sovereignty will be limited, and all legislative, executive and judicial powers related to world affairs will be transferred to the World Federation.
3. World law will be enforced for all individuals no matter who they might be, within the jurisdiction of the World Federation. The World Federation will guarantee human rights and will protect the security of the federation.
4. A supranational military force, capable of guaranteeing the security of the world federal government and of its member states will be created.

Member nations must disarm their militaries and retain only that which
is necessary for internal policing.

5. The World Federation will control the development of atomic technology and any other scientific discoveries capable of mass destruction.
6. The World Federation will have the power to raise taxes directly and
   independently of individual national budgets.[5]

However, it would be a mistake to take this as evidence that the All-Japan
League represented the sum total of Japanese interest in the concept of a
world government, or that Japanese were dependent upon their counterparts
abroad for inspiration and intellectual leadership. As Lawson observes when
discussing the writings of some of Shimonaka's contemporaries in the early
postwar years, "The movement for establishing a world government in Japan
. . . cannot simply be seen as a derivative movement inspired by the developments towards federalism in the United States or Europe."[6] Shimonaka himself is proof of that, as he worked through the All-Japan League to resurrect
his prewar vision for world peace, which was predicated on the achievement
of Asian political freedom, economic development, and pan-Asian unity.
Under the auspices of the All-Japan League, Shimonaka took a leading role
in organizing a World Federation Asia Conference, which convened in Hiroshima in 1952, bringing together representatives from eight Asian countries
and fourteen Western countries to push for the abolition of nuclear weapons
and other weapons of war, and an end to racial and ethnic discrimination. He
also helped the All-Japan League to sponsor additional conferences in Japan
in 1954, 1957, and 1960.[7]

Shimonaka's postwar internationalism also found other outlets beyond
the All-Japan League. In October 1957 he helped to organize a three-
day meeting of the International New Education Association (Kokusai
Shin Kyōiku Kyōkai), which brought together 531 Japanese and foreign
representatives (among them, Harada Minoru) to discuss topics such as
"A New World View and Moral Education," "Intellectual, Scientific and
Technical Education," "Mass Media and Education," and "Education for
International Understanding."[8] He was also involved in the short-lived
World Brotherhood, which began in the United States and then developed
chapters in countries throughout the world. Its original aim was to end
religious bigotry and promote religious tolerance, but the Japanese
affiliate, which was established in Tokyo in 1957 and soon had branches
in other major Japanese cities, turned its attention to educational, labor,
and communications issues, in addition to religion.[9] Finally, Shimonaka is
recognized as the founder of the Seven-Person Committee Appealing for
World Peace (Sekai Heiwa Apīru Shichinin Iinkai), whose efforts to press

the UN and world leaders to abolish nuclear weapons and reduce their military forces continued for more than a decade after his death.[10] Common to all of these examples is the same radical idealism that marked Shimonaka's writings and organizational activities throughout his career; an idealism that combined elements of nationalism, liberal internationalism, imperial internationalism, and utopian globalism.

OCCUPATION POLICIES AND THE POLITICS OF EDUCATION

Yet, as in the case of Japan in the first half of the twentieth century, so, too, in the second half. The idealism that allowed educators like Shimonaka, on both sides of the August 1945 divide, to imagine a world governed by a new set of relationships among individuals, nations and states invariably came into conflict with the politics of education when they attempted to apply that idealism to the reform of curriculum content. This is certainly true with respect to internationalizing Japanese education, although the intensity of that conflict has waxed and waned in the decades since the Occupation.

Actually, Occupation policies helped set the stage for this conflict, as recent scholarship has shown. The governing principle underlying the original mission of the Supreme Command for the Allied Powers (SCAP) and its Civil Information and Education Section (CIE)—imposing democracy from above—emboldened progressives and conservatives alike, albeit for different reasons. On one side of the divide, educators who escaped the purge were emboldened by the Occupation's early steps to democratize and decentralize Japanese education, and to harness the schools to the goal enunciated in the preamble to the Fundamental Law of Education (which was drafted and adopted at the behest of the Occupation authorities in place of the 1890 Imperial Rescript on Education): "contribute to the peace of the world and welfare of humanity by building a democratic and cultural state." They were soon organizing labor unions to bargain for better wages and professional autonomy; leveraging their collective influence in the political area by harnessing their unions to the nascent socialist political parties; and running union candidates for open seats on the newly created local school boards. On the other side, MOE bureaucrats could point to the active intervention of the CIE in shaping postwar education policies as justification for continued MOE intervention in the future. As Byron Marshall observes, "Although central control over the educational system might have been seen originally as a temporary accommodation to the requisites of carrying out revolutionary change, nevertheless SCAP in effect sowed the seeds of the resurgence of the Education Ministry in Tokyo."[11]

Before long, MOE bureaucrats and conservative politicians found additional encouragement in SCAP's so-called "reverse course," which undercut some of its original educational and political reforms. This included: the Occupation's push for Japan to rearm, in contravention of Article Nine of the new "Peace Constitution"; prohibition of a nationwide general strike which the teachers unions and other labor unions had planned for February 1, 1947; recognition of the Japanese government's claim that as public servants, teachers should be prohibited from joining unions and bargaining collectively; and a systematic purge of leftist teachers with alleged ties to the Japan Communist Party.[12]

One way to gauge the effects of this conflict upon curriculum content generally, and its international dimension in particular, is by examining postwar policies governing school textbooks, and by comparing successive versions of MOE curriculum guidelines (*gakkō shidō yōryō*) and textbooks that were approved for classroom use. Japan's textbook screening process itself became an international issue beginning in 1982—ironically, on the eve of Nakasone's decision to form his Ad Hoc Council on Education—when the press alleged that the MOE had abused its authority to screen textbooks by requiring that textbook authors alter or delete certain passages for partisan political reasons. In the most famous example, the MOE allegedly objected to passages describing Japan's "invasion" (*shinryaku*) of China during the Asia-Pacific War, and it "requested" that the verb "advance" (*shinshutsu*) be used instead. However, Laura Hein and Mark Selden report that "The Japanese government also ordered authors to sanitize their discussions of colonial policy in Korea and Taiwan, the Nanjing massacre, and the treatment of the military comfort women," all of which prompted formal protests from various Asian governments, as well as critical scrutiny from Japanese and foreign journalists and scholars, who have continued to report on the volatile "textbook issue" ever since.[13]

Before examining the merits of these allegations of historical revisionism against the MOE, it is important to acknowledge an accompanying irony that reveals much about the impact of defeat in 1945 and the postwar Occupation upon Japan's attempts to reinvent its national and international identities in the decades since. Whereas Sawayanagi, Hoshino and other Japanese delegates to international conferences sponsored by the World Federation of Educational Associations and the Institute of Pacific Relations during the 1920s were obliged to address allegations that Japanese textbooks glorified war and promoted a martial spirit, today's MOE officials and conservative politicians have been obliged to address allegations of deemphasizing war and Japan's military history in textbooks published after 1945. Meanwhile, according to Mark Selden, the United States, which came under international criticism during the 1910s and 1930s for its isolationist policies at the onset of both world wars, has been feeding American school children a diet of war-inspired patriotism ever since its triumph in "The Good War":

> The textbooks of nearly all nations bristle with nationalism. There are, nevertheless, differences and gradations that differentiate nations over time. Many American textbooks, far more than their Japanese or German counterparts, for example, invoke national pride in the nation's history, reaching an apogee in the treatment of wars, notably the American revolution and World War II. This pride is manifest in such titles as: "The American Pageant," "Our American Heritage," "The Great Republic," "The Enduring Vision," and, perhaps the most lyrical, "America: The Glorious Republic."[14]

Understandably, most of the investigations of MOE curriculum policies have concentrated on policy changes dating from the infamous 1982 incident and their influence upon the accounts of Japan's wartime actions published in subsequent editions of junior high and senior high school history textbooks (*rekishi kyōkasho*). Less attention has been paid to MOE policies governing curriculum and textbooks prior to the 1980s; or to the MOE's positions on other topics of a conspicuously "international" nature; or to the treatment of those topics at the primary school level.

To address this lacunae, I turn now to the official MOE Course of Study guides (*gakushū shidō yōryō*) and sample textbooks that were published in conformity with the Course of Study[15] between 1959 and 2001 for use in teaching social studies (*shakaika*); a new subject inspired by American practice that stirred controversy both inside and outside the MOE when it was introduced into the curriculum in 1947. As Nozaki Yoshiko explains, many historians at the time complained that social studies—which would integrate the subjects of morals, civics, geography and history into one course and explore topics in relation to students' personal experiences—would preclude teaching history in the traditional chronological manner. Defenders of the chronological approach within the MOE quickly took steps to preserve it,[16] and thus influenced how the social studies curriculum and textbooks for the primary grades came to be organized. That is, topics pertaining to civics (political values, government laws and institutions, citizen rights and responsibilities), geography and economics are covered in grades one through five; grade six serves up a chronological account of Japanese history from prehistoric times to the present, and concludes with a discussion of current international relations and their implications for Japan. Social studies textbooks are used in grades three through six, and all textbook publishers produce complete series of textbooks spanning all four grades. The following analysis is limited to sixth grade textbooks, since they are devoted to Japanese history and international relations.

Even before SCAP began its early assault on Japanese wartime textbooks as part of its overall program of "demilitarization and democratization," Japanese authorities took some preemptive measures of their own. On August 22, 1945, days before the first American military personnel arrived in Japan to begin formal occupation, the cabinet ordered an end to military training in the schools and the removal of militaristic sections from textbooks.[17] The MOE followed up with its own directive on September 20, ordering schools to blot out offending passages in those textbooks. The purpose, according to Nozaki Yoshiko and Inokuchi Hiromatsu, was to "keep militaristic content from the sight of occupation officials or to create a favorable impression on them." However, its order "left intact those passages that celebrated the imperial nationhood and morality," and stopped short of specifying those to be deleted; a task which thus devolved to local school officials and teachers.[18]

By late December, SCAP ordered that instruction in morals, Japanese history and geography be suspended; that textbooks and teachers' guides in these subjects be withdrawn; and that new history textbooks be prepared. Pressure from SCAP also effectively ended the MOE's direct involvement in writing textbooks, but not its role in screening and approving textbooks, which was shared with the Civil Information and Education Section (CIE) of SCAP.[19]

However, the ensuing era of liberal reform—with respect to both textbook content and the screening process—was ephemeral. As Occupation policy shifted from nurturing a peaceful, democratic nation to nurturing a remilitarized ally on the front line of the Cold War, the MOE found in SCAP a willing ally in its goal to "revise the narrative of a new, peaceful, democratic Japan that was fostered during the early postwar years and promoted by teachers."[20]

Thus began what Caroline Rose calls the first of three "textbook offensives" that have taken place in Japan since the end of the war. Significantly, each of these offensives was mounted at a moment when political conservatives in the Diet, in bureaucracies like the MOE, and in the business community experienced a resurgence of influence following a period of relative weakness.[21] As well, each textbook offensive was accompanied by other assaults on the educational front. During the first offensive, in the mid-1950s, new laws were passed: giving the minister of education full authority to screen textbooks; limiting the political activities of teachers; and making the composition of local school boards (introduced during the Occupation) subject to government appointment rather than local elections. At the same time, a young Nakasone Yasuhiro pressed for a more centralized textbook publishing and adoption system, in order to remedy what he and other conservatives decried as bias and a lack of patriotic tone in the existing crop of textbooks.[22]

INTERNATIONALIZING THE SOCIAL STUDIES CURRICULUM

Evidence of a conservative political agenda informing the (re-)writing of an official narrative of Japanese history and society during this period is subtle— topics glossed over or excluded from that narrative are as significant as those singled out for emphasis—and is not uniformly distributed in the Revised Course of Study for Primary Schools that the MOE issued in October 1958. Before turning to the chapter on social studies, it is worth noting that twenty-five years before Nakasone's Ad Hoc Council on Education recommended that "education for international understanding" be incorporated throughout the school curriculum, the MOE had already endorsed this approach in its curriculum policy. Of course, the idea was not exactly new to the postwar period: earlier chapters in this book have documented that textbooks published between the 1920s and the end of the Asia-Pacific War for subjects like morals, civics, and history all made room for descriptions of prevailing international conditions, their implications for Japan and Asia, and Japan's "mission" to pursue justice and world peace along with its own national security, power and prestige. The major difference is that in 1958 the MOE accepted the 1947 Fundamental Law of Education and the School Education Law as the bases for conducting education for international understanding in the primary schools. Thus, the 1958 Course of Study describes the aims of moral education (*dōtoku kyōiku*) by paraphrasing the Preamble of the Fundamental Education Law, including the phrase "we have shown our resolution to contribute to the peace of the world and welfare of humanity by building a democratic and cultural state." Even the chapter on Japanese language instruction includes among the list of aims, "impart an understanding of the world's climate, natural features and cultures, and contribute to the cultivation of a spirit of international cooperation and a global perspective."[23]

The latent tension between education to cultivate a Japanese national identity and patriotic spirit, versus education to cultivate an international identity and a spirit of international cooperation, surfaces early in the chapter devoted to the social studies course. Although the phrase "cultivate a spirit of international cooperation" is included in the list of aims, the MOE is more forthright about the aim of cultivating "an attitude of respect for the achievements of our forefathers and rich cultural heritage, and an attitude to strive for the advancement of the state (*kokka*) and society that incorporates a proper self-awareness of national identity (*tadashii kokuminteki jikaku*)." What this means in practice becomes clearer in the detailed advice given to sixth grade teachers: impress upon pupils Japan's dependence on other countries for its survival, and pay special attention to the present-day economies of those countries with which Japan has vital trade relations. As for Japanese history, social studies teachers should highlight: the distinctive political and cultural advancements which the country's forefathers have made down through the ages; Japan's deepening ties with other countries; and the creation of a unique Japanese culture that has benefited from amalgamating carefully chosen foreign influences. So, for instance, when teaching about the "opening of the country" and developments following the Meiji Renovation, teachers should highlight evidence of Japan's successful drive to modernize, which was led by the government and various prominent individuals: the adoption of Western culture; the creation of a constitution, which opened the way to representative government; and the growth of modern industry. Modern Japan's military past is barely mentioned, although hints remain of the triumphal narrative that figured so prominently in school textbooks before August 1945: the first Sino-Japanese War and the Russo-Japanese War are cited in the same sentence as revision of the unequal treaties, as events that contributed to the elevation of Japan's international standing. World War One merits no mention at all, and World War II is described simply as the occasion when "Japan was defeated, domestic conditions changed, and the country undertook a new [stage of] development as a democratic state." The 1958 MOE guidelines say nothing at all about Japanese colonialism, Japanese aggression, or about the effect of Japan's actions upon the countries she colonized, invaded or fought against. Nor, for that matter, do they mention the destruction visited upon Japanese cities by American conventional and nuclear bombs.[24]

Turning from history to contemporary international relations and Japan's role in the world, these MOE guidelines also remind us of the narratives we encountered in Sawayanagi's, Yumoto's and Ikeoka's middle school ethics and civics textbooks from the 1920s. Their summary descriptions of the workings of the League of Nations, and their expressions of hope that the League might pave the way to world peace, find their counterparts in the 1958 Course of Study, which states that pupils should learn that the United Nations was established after World War II in order to promote cooperation among member countries in the pursuit of world peace and the welfare of humanity, and they should appreciate the "important role" that Japan is playing as a member nation.[25]

Another characteristic refrain from the 1920s that resurfaces in this Course of Study is the realization that the world has grown smaller. Children need to understand that "the lives of people in the various regions of the world are tightly bound by the advanced networks of transportation, communication and information"; that Japan is heavily involved in "economic and cultural interchange" with foreign countries; and that "people's appeals for peace grow more urgent in today's atomic age," which promises a "frightening result" if countries persist in turning to war to settle international disputes.[26]

If Japan's role as aggressor in the Sino-Japanese War, the Russo-Japanese War, and the Asia-Pacific War is missing from the outline for history education fashioned by the MOE for social studies teachers in 1958, so, too, is the figure of the emperor (*tennō*), in whose name those wars were fought. In fact, the emperor makes only one appearance in the guidelines for the sixth grade social studies curriculum, when teachers are advised that pupils need to learn that "the ideals of the state, the position of the emperor (*tennō no chi'i*), the important rights and duties of citizens, and so forth are determined under the Constitution of Japan."[27] In place of the word *tennō*, the Course of Study refers to the Yamato court (*Yamato chōtei*) in the section recounting the origins of the nation:

> In our country, the emergence of agriculture gradually raised the people's standard of living; the Yamato court unified the nation, carried out political reform, and the cities of Nara and Kyoto thrived as capitals, governed by the nobility serving the court; at this time, continental culture was introduced and a unique Japanese culture was created.[28]

However, the MOE has no such reservations about mentioning "our national flag," which it does in a way that is reminiscent of Sawayanagi's 1923 middle school ethics textbook, analyzed in chapter 2. Like Sawayanagi, the MOE expects teachers to take steps "to get the children to deepen their concern about the national flag of Japan and to improve their attitude of respecting it, and to get the children to adopt an attitude of respect for the national flags of foreign nations." The MOE describes this as yet another way to cultivate a spirit of international understanding and international cooperation.[29]

As noted earlier, the MOE's Course of Study is designed as a "guide" for textbook writers as well as classroom teachers, although neither had any choice in the matter: in 1958 the MOE made compliance with its guidelines mandatory for textbook writers. And, as we have seen in the case of the MOE's obscure references to Japan's modern military past in the 1958 Course of Study, there would seem to be considerable room for interpretation between textbook writers and those who screen and approve—or reject—those textbooks under the authority of the MOE. However, 1958 was a particularly harsh year for textbook writers, when the MOE rejected 33 percent of the manuscripts submitted.[30] Let us turn, then, to *New Society* (*Atarashii Shakai*)—a social studies textbook assembled under the direction of Tokyo University Professor Kaigo Tokiomi, in conformity with the 1958 Course of Study, and approved by the MOE screeners—in order to discern what the MOE deemed acceptable during this first "textbook offensive."

After a quick geography lesson covering the locations of the major continents and how to use maps and globes to chart their locations, the

opening chapter in the sixth grade volume turns immediately to an over-
view of "Asian countries with which Japan has close ties." Topping the list
is China: no distinction is made between the People's Republic of China
and the Republic of China on Taiwan, although it soon becomes apparent
that the focus is on the PRC. The irony here is that in 1958 Japan, bowing to American pressure, did not formally recognize the PRC and was
discouraged from doing business with it. Most of the information concerns
the kinds of crops that are grown, the kinds of minerals that are mined,
and the kinds of industries that are being developed by the world's largest
population, in a country twenty times the size of Japan.[31] Reflecting a desire among many politicians, bureaucrats, and the general public to resume
trade and cultural exchange with China, it paints a picture of a dynamic
country that is making rapid progress in education and the development
of its infrastructure (railroads, bridges, ports, hydroelectric dams). There
is no mention here of Japan's relations with China, past or present, and
needless to say, no mention of Japan's "advance into China" (or was it an
"invasion"?) during the Asia-Pacific War.

The same treatment is given to Korea. While the textbook notes, "Korea
has had close relations with Japan for centuries," the nature of those contacts
is not described at all; neither cultural exchange, nor economic exploitation or
colonial occupation. In fact, the only reference to colonialism in this chapter
is to British control of India. In compliance with the MOE's Course of Study,
the textbook pays little attention to those countries deemed marginal to Japanese economic interests. Pakistan is dismissed in two sentences: "Pakistan
gained independence from India. It is known for growing rice and wheat."
The Philippines is summed up in one sentence: "The Philippines is an agricultural country, which is famous for Manila Hemp (*Manila asa*)." Iran and
Iraq are nothing more than "countries that produce a lot of oil."[32]

By comparison, the very next chapter has a great deal to say about Japanese foreign trade and industry, highlighted with detailed graphs and charts.
It even offers some historical perspective: describing, for example, how
foreign trade grew with the opening of Japan in the nineteenth century; how
early exports of agricultural products and handmade crafts were eventually
outstripped by the output of government-subsidized factories producing silk
and cotton fiber; and how a succession of wars benefited Japan by increasing
demand for goods at home and abroad, but also made her more dependent
on foreign suppliers of raw materials. This sense of national vulnerability
runs throughout the whole chapter, which asks pupils to ponder the same two
dilemmas that preoccupied Japanese nationalists and internationalists alike in
the 1920s and 1930s: (1) "Being a country poor in natural resources, Japan
will never become prosperous unless it expands its foreign trade"; (2) "Japan

cannot grow enough to feed its growing population, so foodstuffs make up a sizeable portion of its imports."[33]

The next chapter strikes a more positive tone as it segues into a discussion of international cultural and scientific exchange, beginning with Japan's long history of cultural borrowing: first from Asia (rice cultivation and early tools, Chinese script, Buddhism and Confucianism), and then from the West (guns, Christianity, science). Science, in turn, provides another segue to illustrate how learning is cumulative and transnational, advancing through incremental discoveries made by scientists in different countries, such as Japanese bacteriologist Kitasato Shibasaburō and Yukawa Hideki, Japan's first Nobel laureate. The textbook even cites Yukawa's work in theoretical physics for advancing research on nuclear energy, whose peaceful uses promise to be a boon to mankind. UNESCO's role in promoting international research in science and education is also noted as a way to "enhance culture in underdeveloped regions."[34]

A separate section of *New Society* is devoted to presenting a chronological account of Japan's political history (*seiji no rekishi*). In accordance with the MOE Course of Study, it combines synchronic descriptions of Japanese politics during specific time periods (Nara, Heian, Muromachi, etc.) into a diachronic narrative designed to show how, in the words of the MOE, Japan's "current politics and citizens' livelihoods have resulted from our ancestors' political adjustments, their assimilation of foreign cultures, and their efforts to advance state and society."[35] If one is looking for evidence of conservative influence upon Japanese history education in the 1950s, one could start with the following brief passage from this chapter's explanation of the origins of the Japanese nation:

> About 1500 years ago, the Yamato court gathered together the smaller kingdoms (*kuni*) around it and expanded the [Yamato] kingdom. The leaders of these small kingdoms remained powerful, but they proceeded to offer tribute to the Yamato court. It is said that the first emperor (*tennō*) of the Yamato court was Emperor Jinmu.[36]

The problem with this passage is that it does not distinguish between imperial myth and empirical fact in naming the legendary Jinmu as the first emperor of Japan. Furthermore, mention of Jinmu here recalls his earlier appearance in wartime textbooks as the progenitor of the doctrine of *hakkō ichiu*, which foretold Japan's creation of a co-prosperity sphere that would eventually "cover the world under one roof."

More troubling than this sin of commission, however, is the sin of omission that mark's this chapter's coverage of Japan's foreign relations in the decades after the Meiji Renovation. Adhering to the MOE's Course of Study, the textbook dispenses with the Sino-Japanese War and the Russo-Japanese War in a single sentence:

> From the early Meiji period, Japan successfully pursued a policy of enriching the country through the development of industry and increasing its power by strengthening the military. Thereafter, Japan fought China over the matter of Korea, and eventually fought Russia in Manchuria.[37]

There is no discussion of the wars' origins; no mention of their costs in lives and economic treasure; no mention of the spoils of war that transformed Japan into a colonial power in Taiwan, the Pescadore Islands, Korea and southern Sakhalin.

Although the Course of Study never even acknowledged World War One, the textbook does, at least, mention it, while staying within the carefully prescribed parameters that the Course of Study applied to the earlier wars: "During World War One, Japan joined the Allied Powers. From this point on, Japanese industry and trade developed extensively. As a result, Japan was counted among the Great Powers."[38]

Turning to the causes underlying the Asia-Pacific War, the textbook adheres to the explanation that was favored not only by Japan's political conservatives, but also by SCAP, which had its own reasons to exonerate the general population of responsibility for the war and pronounce it an aberration. Specifically, the "road to war" (*sensō e no ayumi*) begins with public anger toward Japan's political parties for putting their own partisan interests ahead of the nation's, even as the people faced growing hardships triggered by the Great Depression. According to the textbook, this situation prompted some in the military to conclude that "a path could be opened for Japan" by provoking war on the continent. "These people dealt harshly with those who disagreed with their views, and people's liberty was largely sacrificed." This war "dragged on with no end, until the whole world was enveloped in the Asia-Pacific War (*Taiheiyō sensō*). Ultimately, [Japan] was defeated and forced to surrender to America, England, the Soviet Union, China and the other Allied Powers."[39]

The final chapter of the textbook, "World Peace," revisits the Asia-Pacific War in a similarly oblique fashion, again in careful compliance with the MOE's Course of Study. It opens by observing that in spite of the fact that Japanese, and people everywhere, desire a peaceful world in which to lead comfortable and pleasant lives, countries have repeatedly resorted to arms to settle disputes, which arise because people do not think alike, because of economic disparities, and so forth. However, the destruction resulting from World War II was so great that people resolved to try and avoid wars in the future, resulting in the establishment of the United Nations. The body of the chapter dwells at length on the workings of the UN and other peace-oriented organizations (the Junior Red Cross, International Pen Pal Club, Olympics, Nobel Peace Prize), but steers clear of any discussion of the specific causes of World War II: as the MOE phrased it in its Course of Study, the war simply "happened."[40]

On the other hand, the textbook devotes considerable space to describing the sufferings of those caught up in the conflict, beginning with the Japanese. The text builds upon a photograph of the Cenotaph for Atomic Bomb Victims in the Hiroshima Peace Park and its controversial inscription: viewing the Cenotaph "would cause anyone to think, 'Let that evil not be repeated.'" What follows is a literal "textbook case" of what John Dower aptly terms the "tragic narrative"[41] of Japan's victimization: a grim description of the deaths of over 200,000 Hiroshima victims, "many of whose bodies and shadows disappeared in an instant, in what was truly Hell on Earth"; the addition of more A-Bomb victims (*hibakusha*) in Nagasaki three days later, many of whom "suffered excruciating deaths"; and the endless suffering of other Japanese over eight years of fighting (1937–1945), who lost fathers and sons in battle, their livelihoods back home, and their own lives from conventional bombings, which also destroyed homes, factories and railroads. Defeat, when it came on August 15, was both a source of sadness (*kanashii koto*) and a source of great happiness (*ōkina yorokobi*). "Bells of peace echoed through the air in Nagasaki. As they listened, people felt that they had returned to the living as they emerged from bomb shelters and barracks."[42]

Those who accuse the MOE of manipulating the textbook screening system for the sake of historical revisionism often cite this "tragic narrative" as proof of its determination to downplay Japan's role as a victimizer. For its part, the MOE maintains that this approach personalizes the war for Japanese students, and helps them to grasp the broader problem of world peace as something real and immediate, and not as an abstract idea. Indeed, its Course of Study frequently advises social studies teachers in all grades to employ teaching methods and appropriate supplementary materials in order to stimulate student interest in the topic at hand. However, the MOE defies its own logic when it tries to water down statements about Japan's role in precipitating the war, and the suffering that others endured because of its conduct during the war. What better way to personalize the event for Japanese students? What better way to prepare their generation to avoid "repeating that evil?"

The MOE revised its Course of Study for primary education two more times—in 1968 and 1978—before Nakasone's Ad Hoc Council on Education published its recommendations for reform in the mid-1980s. The 1968 edition did not correspond to a "textbook offensive." Of course, this does not mean that it was free from ideological and political considerations. With respect to the sixth grade social studies curriculum, the principal difference from its predecessor is a greater emphasis on deepening students' "understanding and love of our country's history and traditions, and fostering a feeling of belonging to the nation (*kokuminteki shinjō*). Thus, in the unit covering Japanese history following the Meiji Renovation, teachers are advised to emphasize how "our country, having secured its independence within a severe international environment, trod the path to modernization by avidly adopting Western systems and culture, while maintaining its age-old traditions."[43]

The emperor also receives more attention than before:

> Concerning the emperor, use easy-to-understand, concrete examples to illustrate the functions of the emperor in national affairs, as determined by the Constitution; drawing upon their study of history, it is necessary to deepen [students'] understanding, affection and esteem (*keiai*) for the emperor.[44]

One other change signaled a major shift in the way that the MOE approached the task of selecting and packaging information about foreign countries to promote "international understanding." Whereas the 1958 Course of Study stipulated that social studies teachers should focus students' attention on those foreign countries deemed vital to the Japanese economy, the 1968 version pressed teachers to better inform students about the entire world, using concrete examples to illustrate the diversity of natural and human environments, and the complex relationship between the human and natural worlds.[45]

That said, the 1968 Course of Study did not constitute a radical departure from its predecessor. Textbooks were another matter, however. The 1968 edition of *New Society* for sixth-graders, which Professor Kaigo and his editorial team revised in conformity with the MOE's 1968 Course of Study, differs markedly from its predecessor, featuring more expansive coverage of Japanese history and international relations. Its account of Japan's earliest history relies on archeological evidence to illustrate the social organization and livelihoods of communities in the Jōmon and Yayoi periods. The Yamato clan is still identified as the progenitor of the imperial family, but its path to political conquest over its rivals is told in more detail, and the emperor's elevation to a position of supremacy is described as a tactical decision, involving a lengthy process that met with resistance. The story of Emperor Jinmu's unification of the country is described as myth (*shinwa*) rather than as fact, along with the legends of Ōkuninushi and Yamato Takeru. The *Kojiki* and *Nihongi* are mentioned as sources of myths and legends recounting the origins of the nation, while the early Chinese histories are cited as sources of insights about prehistoric Japan. Japan's indebtedness to continental cultural influences from Korea and China is described in more detail: the textbook even alludes to Japan's invasion of Korea in the fourth century; euphemistically described as Japan's "extension of its power to the Korean Peninsula" which "served to promote contacts with China and Korea."[46]

The textbook's narrative of Japanese history and international relations after the Meiji Renovation is also more revealing, and some previously taboo items are now acknowledged, if only barely. Most conspicuous is the coverage devoted to military matters. The conscription system, inaugurated in 1873, is briefly described and attributed to the Meiji government's doctrine of "rich country, strong military." A map is employed to illustrate the vast expanse of Western colonialism throughout Asia, and to explain Meiji Japan's preoccupation with national security and sovereignty. The Sino-Japanese War is described as a conflict over Korean independence from Chinese suzerainty, leading to victorious Japan's receipt of an indemnity and the territories of Taiwan and the Liaodong Peninsula; the latter provoking the Triple Intervention by Russia, France and Germany. Russian encroachment into Manchuria and Russian interest in Korea are cited as catalysts for the Anglo-Japanese Alliance and, ultimately, the Russo-Japanese War, which brought Japan the South Manchurian Railway and southern Sakhalin, and also paved the way for the annexation of Korea. Like the textbooks of the 1920s that were examined in chapters 2 and 3, the devastation from World War One is cited as the inspiration for the establishment of the League of Nations:

> The League of Nations was established at the urging of the American President, Wilson. Forty-two countries participated, with the goal of cooperating to preserve peace. Japan was chosen to serve in the Secretariat.

The economic boom and bust that Japan experienced as a result of the war is also described in more detail, and cited as a factor contributing to public disenchantment with the political parties and the rise of militarism (*gunkokushugi*).

The 1968 edition of *New Society* adheres to the 1958 version of the rise of militarism, which continues to be blamed on a segment of the military which concluded that Japan's future should be secured by using the military's power to reform domestic politics and "extend Japan's power onto the Asian continent" (*Ajia tairiku ni Nihon no seiryoku o nobashi*). However, rather than segue immediately into a discussion of the Manchurian Incident as the point of no return, the textbook offers some historical background to this violent clash between Chinese and Japanese forces; making oblique reference to the Twenty-One Demands and the resulting Chinese boycott of Japanese goods. It also explains that Japan resigned from the League of Nations in 1933, after the League refused to accept Japan's "occupation" (*senryō*) of Manchuria and its creation of the state of Manchukuo.

The China Incident of 1937 is also described briefly, following which "fighting spread throughout China," while back home Japan geared up for a long war and "the people had to sacrifice their livelihoods for the sake of victory."

The Asia-Pacific War is referred to throughout this chapter as World War II, and the narrative begins with events in Europe, leading to Japan's alliance with Germany and Italy and her "advance into Southeast Asia" (*Tōnan Ajia e shinshutsu shimashita*) from southern China. The "tragic narrative" that was so conspicuous in 1958 is still present in 1968, although coverage of the A-Bomb attacks is scaled back, in order to summarize the details of the Potsdam Declaration, presaging Japan's future of foreign occupation, abandonment of militarism, and embrace of democracy.[47]

The story of Japan's postwar rehabilitation and revival concludes with a slogan we first encountered in the Meiji Period: "Japan in the World" (*Sekai no naka no Nihon*). In a world that continues to strive for peace even as wars persist, and in an era marked by scientific and technological progress and space exploration, it is important to think carefully about what kind of issues Japan faces and work hard to make Japan a superb country and to bring peace and happiness to the world.[48]

Scholars who have studied revisions to the narrative of Japanese history as it appears in Japanese textbooks published since the Occupation credit the late Ienaga Saburō—who challenged the constitutionality of the MOE's screening system through a series of celebrated lawsuits—with pressuring the MOE to approve more candid, empirical treatments of modern Japan's military past, such as the one that we have just encountered in portions of the 1968 edition of *New Society*. While Ienaga's influence should not be discounted, was it the only factor? Ienaga did not file his first lawsuit until 1965, and details of the case were not widely known by the time that the MOE granted approval, in April 1967, to publish the new edition of *New Society*. Furthermore, no rulings were made in any of Ienaga's lawsuits before 1970.[49]

Coverage of Japanese history in social studies textbooks during the 1970s did, indeed, continue along the "liberal" trajectory that marked portions of the 1968 edition of *New Society*. But so did the "conservative" trajectory of the MOE's Course of Study, Ienaga's lawsuits notwithstanding. It is the 1977 Course of Study that sheds light on the MOE's greater tolerance for social studies textbooks that did not strictly toe its conservative line. Authors of the 1977 Course of Study acknowledge that their work was motivated by widespread criticism that education in postwar Japan catered to the country's demand for a skilled workforce, while sacrificing the "spirit of respect for humanity" (*ningen sonchō no seishin*):

Previous revisions [to the Course of Study] were closely related to contemporary social developments. For example, the 1958 revisions arose from the expectation that honing school education to make it suited to the affairs of an independent Japan would lead to rapid economic and social progress. The 1968-1969 revisions aimed at making education modern and scientific, in support of science and technology, high-speed economic growth, and society.[50]

Restoring the "spirit of humanity" to Japanese education in 1977 required that schools and teachers be given more leeway to interpret and apply MOE guidelines, in order to personalize education for each student, and to make education more reflective of, and responsive to, rapidly changing social conditions:

> The current revisions are based on a thorough examination of the fundamental way of thinking about the curriculum, with the Course of Study indicating only the aims and core content of each subject, thereby allowing each school and each teacher to implement the Course of Study based on plans which they devise themselves. In other words, by using the Course of Study flexibly, each school can exhibit greater independence.[51]

The inspiration for this reform of the school curriculum in 1977 can be traced back to a report entitled, *Basic Guidelines for the Reform of Education*, which was prepared by the Central Council for Education (CCE)—an advisory body to the MOE—and published in 1970.[52] This is the same report that, as noted in the Introduction to this book, was also cited by Nakasone's Ad Hoc Council for Education as the inspiration for its reform proposals in the mid-1980s. The CCE report warns that the quickening pace of social change has created problems that the existing system of education has failed to address. They include: "a gap between nature and man" due to "scientific and technological progress and a high rate of economic growth"; challenges to spiritual and mental health, social solidarity, and public morality due to urbanization and population growth; changes in family structure and kinship relations; and a growing number of elderly people, who could lead richer and more productive lives with the provision of "life-long learning opportunities."[53] Complicating this domestic agenda is the added challenge that Nakasone's Ad Hoc Council would later dub "coping with internationalization":

> Due to expanding international exchange and the development of mass media, events which are going on all over the world in different cultures are giving new stimulus to our daily lives. This international stimulus contributes instability to our value systems. Furthermore, many of our people have [a] confused attitude towards the nation because of our defeat in the war. In consequence, there is much ambiguity in our society concerning the basis of nationhood, and much

conflict with respect to the meaning of democracy. This setting is unprecedented in the history of our society, and yet it is within this setting that we must succeed in the difficult task of human development.[54]

This particular passage in the CCE report is significant to our examination of the complicated interplay between nationalism and internationalism in the discourse on Japanese education, for several reasons. To begin with, we now know to be false the CCE's claim that "this setting is unprecedented in the history of our society." In fact, there are remarkably close—and troubling— parallels between the CCE's characterization of international events as threats to Japanese values and national identity, and the characterizations made by earlier generations of educational reformers, dating back to the Meiji period. Second, the statement that "many of our people have a confused attitude towards the nation because of our defeat in the war" is proof that conservatives in postwar Japan's political, business and educational establishments discerned the volatile relationship between historical memory and internationalism long before the MOE's textbook screening system first attracted international scrutiny and criticism in 1982. Third, this passage resurrects the same dilemma that has dogged conservative advocates of internationalizing Japanese education from the 1920s down to the present: how to produce creative, independent, self-reliant, democratic, peace-loving citizens of the world who are ever mindful of their patriotic duty to exercise their creativity, independence, democratic values and desire for peace as "*Japanese* citizens of the world" (*sekai no naka no Nihonjin*)?

This dilemma helps to explain why, from time to time, the MOE textbook screeners have approved comparatively "liberal" textbooks that push the politically conservative boundaries of the MOE's official Course of Study. It reveals the dynamic, controversial, and often contradictory discourse between bureaucrats, textbook writers, teachers, and the media regarding what it means to be a "*Japanese* citizen of the world," and what combination of empirical knowledge, practical skills, and social values those citizens should possess. Repeated proposals, counterproposals, policy initiatives and policy revisions that have appeared throughout the twentieth century in the name of internationalizing Japanese education show how much is at stake. So it is that the 1977 Course of Study advises teachers—and textbook writers—that

> It is not easy to get sixth graders to recognize they are Japanese citizens of the world. There is no guarantee that this consciousness or realization will dawn upon children as a result of spending a certain number of hours learning about international trade or about the United Nations. What is the best way to proceed so that children do not simply end up amassing a body of facts and figures in those fields? The issue boils down to the teacher's ability, and to the way that individual schools structure their guidance plans, select teaching materials, and conduct lessons.[55]

The MOE's greater tolerance for critical historical discourse is evident in the 1979 edition of *Primary School Social Studies* (*Shōgakkō shakai*), whose section on Japanese history sets out to personalize, and problematize, history for its sixth-grade readers by explaining why it is important to study history:

> Compared to the childhoods of our parents and grandparents, we are blessed in many ways. Compared to our grandparents and their parents, we have grown up in a world marked by great advances. However, in each era progress is accompanied by new problems, which those people have to make efforts to solve.
>
> So, who causes history to evolve? There are politicians and so-called great men who have changed history, but they are not the only ones. The incessant efforts of many nameless people—our ancestors—have caused history to evolve.
>
> We study history in order to understand the real power responsible for the evolution of history, so that we ourselves will become the main actors (*shujinkō*) who solve the problems facing Japan.[56]

The textbook is also quick to highlight the value of empirical science for the study of history. The opening chapter explains how the chance discovery of the Ōmori Shell Mounds by American Edward S. Morse in 1877 helped to advance knowledge of Japan's earliest inhabitants, whose lives during the Jōmon and Yayoi periods are then described while referring to further archeological discoveries. For instance, the authors cite the discovery of ten arrows buried amid skeletal remains uncovered in Yamaguchi Prefecture in order to explain how military technology introduced into ancient Japan from the Asian continent sparked more violent battles between villages, leading to their gradual consolidation through brute force into larger kingdoms (*kuni*) governed by powerful rulers (*kimi*). Citing the early Chinese histories, the authors go on to describe the harsh lives of the "1,000 slaves" and other inhabitants of the kingdom of Yamatai, during the reign of Queen Himiko around the first century A.D.[57]

The grim realities of modern Japanese history also receive more candid coverage than before. For example, the authors note that while the Meiji government's early policy of direct investment in, and construction of, new factories served to increase productivity and Japanese exports, the principal beneficiaries were the large merchant houses like Mitsui, Iwasaki (Mitsubishi) and Furusawa, which took advantage of their close ties to the government to assume ownership of these factories at rock bottom prices. Similarly, the authors explain that while the government's policy to open up the Hokkaido wilderness to American-style large-scale farming created opportunities for unemployed lower samurai and poor farmers to battle hardship and Nature in development schemes with minimal government support, the main victims were the indigenous Ainu people, who were unable to make a living and suffered a decline in population due to inadequate government protection.[58]

When these authors turn their attention to international relations, the resulting picture of an aggressive Japan, scheming to advance the national interest
at the expense of its regional neighbors, stands in sharp contrast to earlier
textbook versions of this story. The Sino-Japanese War is described as the
culmination of a long series of measures taken by the Meiji government to
"open up Korea and extend Japan's influence" against the wishes of both the
Korean and Chinese governments.[59]

Against a backdrop of Western encroachment into China, including Russia's
"advance" (*shinshutsu*) into Manchuria, Japan is identified as the instigator
of the Russo-Japanese War, after diplomatic negotiations between the two
countries failed. The textbook pointedly remarks that "While many Japanese
supported this war, others like Kōtoku Shūsui and Sakai Toshihiko opposed
it, declaring, 'This war is not for the benefit the people!' The Christian
follower, Uchimura Kanzō, and the poet Yosano Akiko, also opposed the
war on religious and humanitarian grounds." The text also notes that Japan
suffered many casualties, and that the heavy financial cost of the war, which
was met through tax increases and loans from England and the United States,
placed great strains on Japan's finances and the livelihoods of her citizens.[60]

The story of Japan's annexation of Korea that appears in this textbook is
equally stark:

> Following the Russo-Japanese War, Japan established an office in Korea to
> guide political affairs there, and it disbanded the Korean military. Koreans
> staged protest movements in various parts of the country but Japan suppressed
> them, and in 1910, it completed a treaty of annexation that made Korea a colony.
> Once Korea became a Japanese colony, some Japanese bought land in Korea and
> became landlords, while some Koreans became tenant farmers, and many were
> forced to work in Japanese coal mines. Meanwhile, at school Korean children
> were obliged to study using textbooks written in Japanese. Thereafter, Koreans
> continued to stage resistance movements from time to time, and Itō Hirobumi,
> the architect of annexation, was assassinated by a supporter of the Korean
> independence movement.[61]

Whereas the 1968 edition of the *New Society* textbook made passing
reference to the Twenty-One Demands, the 1979 edition of *Primary School
Social Studies* devotes an entire page to this episode at the beginning of a
chapter entitled, "Advance into Asia" (*Ajia e no shinshutsu*). The authors
highlight the key demands that Japan issued to China in 1915; Chinese appeals to the international community to stand with her in resisting them; and
China's eventual capitulation to most of the demands. The textbook then
segues into a detailed, five-page account of the origins of the Great War; the
war's unprecedented cost in human lives, due to a new generation of lethal

weapons employed by both sides; the war's role as a catalyst for the Russian Revolution; the Siberian Intervention; and the economic boom and bust on the Japanese home front that culminated in the nationwide Rice Riots, factory closures, and rising unemployment. The Versailles Peace Treaty is also dealt with, of course, along with the League Nations:

> Countries that participated in the war convened a peace conference and signed the Versailles Treaty, which established a League of Nations for the purpose of resolving conflicts between countries through dialogue. Japan, along with countries like England and France, was selected for permanent membership in the League Secretariat. However, various factors, including the incessant pursuit of their own national interests by Secretariat members, prevented the League from fulfilling the role that it was expected to play.[62]

One of the most conspicuous features of this textbook's narrative of the Asia-Pacific War is its use of the term that provoked the aforementioned international outcry against MOE textbook "censorship" and historical revisionism in 1982: Japan's "invasion" (*shinryaku*) of Manchuria in 1931 and its creation of the puppet state of Manchukuo the following year:

> China appealed to the League of Nations to stop Japan's invasion. A League investigation concluded that Japan's occupation of Manchuria was unjust, and that the army should withdraw to its previous position. However, Japan was dissatisfied with this and withdrew from the League.[63]

Also conspicuous is the textbook's unsparing account of what previous textbooks obliquely labeled the "path to war" at home: the conscription of men for duty on the frontlines on the continent; the Young Officers' assassination campaigns against political and business leaders (Prime Minister Inukai Tsuyoshi in 1932; the attempted coup d'etat in February 1936); the appointment of military men to the post of prime minister; the arrest of anti-war protesters and critics of the military under the 1925 Peace Preservation Law; the abolition of labor and farmers' unions; the suspension of party government and the creation of the Imperial Rule Assistance Association in 1940; and efforts to suppress anti-war literature and art and harness these media to the war effort. The authors even describe the militarization of Japanese education: the insertion of martial anthems (*gunka*) into the curriculum; the insertion of patriotic themes into wartime textbooks; and the introduction of compulsory military training for boys attending middle school and higher school.[64]

The authors attribute the outbreak of hostilities between Japan and the Allied Forces (the United States, Britain, China) to Japan's decision to "advance" (*shinshutsu*) into Southeast Asia, in the hope of extricating itself from the China quagmire by procuring raw materials necessary to re-supply its troops. Like earlier postwar textbooks, the 1979 edition of *Primary School Social Studies* devotes considerable coverage to the wartime sufferings experienced by men, women and children. Yet, it differs from the typical "tragic narrative" in two ways. First, it does not dwell exclusively upon Japanese victims; noting, for example, that "Koreans and Chinese who were brought forcibly to the Japanese home islands were compelled to work relentlessly in factories and mines." Second, these personal tragedies are framed by a systematic condemnation of the decisions and actions taken by Japan's wartime leaders; noting, for example, that even when it was obvious to them that the cause had been lost, "the government and the military did not inform the people that Japan was losing the war, and they continued to proclaim victory. Ultimately, they made the people train for a final stand armed with bamboo spears."[65]

Turning to the concluding chapters of this 1979 textbook for sixth graders preparing to graduate to middle school, it is significant that in their account of Japanese and world history in the decades since the end of the Asia-Pacific War, the authors elected *not* to use the phrase "Japan in the world" (*sekai no naka no Nihon*) or its popular variant, "Japanese citizens in the world" (*sekai no naka no Nihonjin*). In fact, neither phrase appears anywhere in the sixth-grade text, in spite of their ubiquity in earlier postwar social studies textbooks, not to mention the MOE's 1977 Course of Study. I believe that in rejecting these phrases, the authors also rejected the nationalistic conviction of political conservatives that education which aspires to inculcate universally recognized humanitarian ideals and a transnational identity as global citizens somehow threatens the foundations of Japanese national identity and citizenship. Indeed, I believe that the authors rejected the conservatives' reified definition of Japaneseness, along with what Nakasone would soon trumpet as a "healthy nationalism" just a few years later.

The message which the authors seek to convey to the next generation of Japanese citizens is not that Japanese must be secure in a common national identity before they can employ the lessons of history to solve these problems. Rather, the message is that globalization means that local and national problems are now inextricably linked to global problems, and that solving these problems requires citizens who are secure in their *inter*-nationality. This is evident from their selection and treatment of "historic" issues deserving of the attention of sixth graders. At the top of their list is the Cold War between the United States and the Soviet Union, its various manifestations, and its threat to world peace: the Korean War, which not only jumpstarted the postwar Japanese economy but Japanese rearmament, as well; the continued presence of American military bases on Japanese soil, and Japan's subordination to American military policy under the terms of the Mutual Security

Treaty; massive public protests in the 1960s and early 1970s against renewal of the treaty and against the use of American bases in Japan to prosecute the Vietnam War; the Non-Aligned Movement spearheaded by newly independent countries in Asia and Africa; the spread of nuclear weapons, attendant anti-nuclear protests and diplomatic efforts to restrict weapons' testing; and the role of the United Nations in trying to prevent a Third World War.[66]

THE 1980S: ERA OF REFORM?[67]

Surveying the Japanese scene in the early 1980s, shortly before Prime Minister Nakasone established his Ad Hoc Council on Education, Harumi Befu observed, "The process Japanese call internationalization (*kokusaika*) is in fact not one but numerous and varied. . . . Since it is a popular term rather than a technical one, it never was properly 'introduced' with anything like a definition." Consequently, it and related terms like "internationality" (*kokusaisei*), "international sense" (*kokusaikan*), "internationalist" (*kokusaijin*) and "international exchange" (*kokusai kōryū*) have been used in a wide variety of contexts. Through his analysis of their usage in these contexts, Befu made several observations that are pertinent to the 1980s movement to internationalize Japanese education. One is that *kokusaika* had come to stand for many of the processes formerly subsumed under the labels "Westernization" (*seiōka*), "modernization" (*kindaika*) and "liberalization" (*jiyūka*). This suggests that, notwithstanding its reformist rhetoric, the internationalization movement as conceived by the Ad Hoc Council, and executed by the MOE, may have constituted less of a challenge to existing policies and practices than a reinforcement of them. A second is that while "noneconomic internationalization processes have their independent existence. . . it is difficult to deny the relative primacy of economic internationalization." Third, Befu concluded that "while internationalization proceeds on all fronts, each process reinforcing and interacting with others, the very processes of internationalization which are supposedly making Japanese more cosmopolitan have the unexpected effect of making Japanese more nationalistic."[68]

Befu's observations anticipated with considerable accuracy the ideological position that would be staked out by the Ad Hoc Council over the next several years. However, he did not anticipate the opposition that would be generated by the publication of the Council's reports between 1985 and 1987. Echoing throughout those reports is the urgent warning that Japan must prepare to cope with an increasingly interdependent community of nations that is openly critical of Japan's economic self-centeredness and cultural insularity and that expects all members—including Japan—to act responsibly for the welfare of the whole. To meet this challenge, education must nurture future generations of cosmopolitan "Japanese in the world" (*sekai no naka no Nihonjin*), who can help Japan assume a role in the new world order commensurate with its standing at the forefront of the most advanced nations and make positive contributions not only in the economic arena, but in education, science, and culture as well.[69]

As noted earlier, the Ad Hoc Council was oblivious to the fact that its prescription for reform, like its use of the phrase *sekai no naka no Nihonjin*, was not new at all, but was first debated and actively pursued by an earlier generation of reformers who wrestled with similar concerns in the 1920s. The same can be said for the Council's anthropomorphic portrait of tomorrow's cosmopolitan Japanese. Not surprisingly, it encompasses the ability to communicate in one or more foreign languages, a thorough knowledge of foreign countries and cultures, a capacity to appreciate cultural differences, and an "international consciousness" (*kokusaiteki ninshiki*). These qualities alone are not enough, however. In order to meet the challenges and achieve the goals outlined above, two other sets of qualities, skills, and values are required. On one hand, future generations should be encouraged to develop their individual character (*kosei*), creativity (*sōzōsei*), independence (*jiyū*), self-discipline (*jiritsu*), and personal responsibility (*jiko sekinin*): in short, the very same qualities touted by proponents of liberal education (*jiyū kyōiku*) in the 1920s. To accomplish this, of course, the existing system of Japanese education must be thoroughly reformed, which helps to explain the relationship between the issue of internationalizing education and the Ad Hoc Council's concurrent proposals to free the system from the grip of bureaucratic centralization, standardization, and credentialism.[70] On the other hand, in keeping with Nakasone's charge that they "contribute to the international community with a *Japanese* consciousness," tomorrow's cosmopolitan Japanese must also be imbued with a thorough knowledge of, and a deep respect for, Japanese tradition, culture, and society:

> In order for our country to continue living amid peace, international cooperation, and interdependent relations, it is necessary for the Japanese people to be sincerely trusted by the international community. To that end, firstly, the ability to assert the individual character (*kosei*) of Japanese society and culture within a broad international perspective, coupled with an ability to understand deeply the prominent individual character of many different cultures, is essential. Secondly, along with a love of country that comes with being Japanese (*Nihonjin to shite, kuni o aisuru kokoro o motsu to tomo ni*), it is necessary to stand on the principle of aiming to build human character not by judging things on the basis of narrow national interests, but within a broad international, global, and humanistic (*jinruiteki*) perspective.[71]

Here, the Ad Hoc Council fails to acknowledge the precedent set by its rival, the MOE, through its 1977 revised Course of Study.

The Ad Hoc Council attempts to defuse the potential contradiction between the qualities of individual character, creativity, and independence on one hand, and the virtues of patriotism and respect for Japanese tradition on the other, by expanding the meaning of individual character to refer not just to a person (*kojin*) but to a household (*katei*), a school, a region, an enterprise (*kigyō*), a nation-state (*kokka*), a culture, and an era, all of which are interrelated.[72] Hence, notwithstanding its criticism of the uniform, conformist, and insular nature of Japanese culture, society, and education, the Council's seemingly radical call to cultivate the individual character of tomorrow's cosmopolitan Japanese leaves no room for the development of an individual consciousness apart from a collective Japanese consciousness.

The most virulent criticism of the Ad Hoc Council and its proposals in the 1980s came from intellectuals identifying themselves with the political left. Yet, like the Council, these critics also stand in the shadow of that earlier generation of 1920s reformers, notably Shimonaka Yasaburō. For example, the comments of Morita Toshio—former director of the Citizens Institute for Educational Research (Kokumin Kyōiku Kenkyūjo), affiliated with the JTU—in his 1988 book, *The Ad Hoc Council on Education and Theories of the Japanese and Japanese Culture* (*Rinkyōshin to Nihonjin, Nihon bunkaron*), bring to mind those made by Shimonaka in his 1920 publication, *The Reconstruction of Education*, which was analyzed in chapter 2. Morita asserts that the Ad Hoc Council's proposals are really designed to rekindle Japanese militarism and imperialism. While professing support for American imperialistic, hegemonic "Pax Americana" impulses as a member of the so-called G5 group of nations, the Japanese ruling class endures Japan bashing in order to pursue its own hidden ambition for "Pax Japonica" hegemony over the Asian and Pacific regions, involving sharp confrontations and contradictions with workers in Japan, Asian and Pacific countries, and throughout the world.[73]

According to Morita, the Ad Hoc Council's proposals to internationalize Japanese education were not really prompted by a desire to "contribute to international society." On the contrary, they were calculated to expand the country's economic and political power in an international community that was becoming increasingly hostile to Japan. He concurs with Befu that the impetus for educational internationalization was a preexisting movement toward economic internationalization that commenced in the early 1980s and became a matter of official policy with the publication of the Maekawa Report in 1986, which advocated reducing Japan's conspicuous account surplus through such measures as deregulating financial and capital markets, encouraging domestic consumer spending, increasing agricultural imports, and increasing Japan's overseas development assistance. Together with education, Japan's economic internationalization was supposed to assuage foreign resentment and preempt foreign retaliation. In this scheme, the educational reforms put forward by the Ad Hoc Council to imbue a new generation with the attributes of cosmopolitanism, while instilling them with a culturally conservative and highly nationalistic consciousness, were meant to serve two purposes: one directed toward diminishing the external threat posed by continued foreign hostility; the other toward preventing the internal threat posed by domestic class conflict. Thus trained and indoctrinated, this new generation would be called upon not only to regain the trust and confidence of the international community by demonstrating Japan's openness and sensitivity toward foreign peoples and cultures, but also to propagate Japanese social values and even religious (Shintō) beliefs abroad, so as to command foreign respect for Japanese culture and traditions. At the same time, for the sake of the nation, they would be expected to endure the burden of increased taxes, lower wages, and higher unemployment that would likely ensue as Japanese enterprises turned increasingly to offshore manufacturing, employment of cheap foreign labor, and other policies designed to internationalize the Japanese economy.[74]

Morita's analysis and criticism of the Ad Hoc Council's alleged hidden agenda for educational reform are seconded by Horio Teruhisa, who charges that "internationalization here means nothing other than Japan's ambition to rise to a position of singular importance and power in the twenty-first century." It amounts to "a new, but no less dangerous, form of Japanese imperialism than that which led to Japan's militaristic adventurism in the 1930s and 1940s."[75]

INTERNATIONALIZATION AT CENTURY'S END

In light of the volatility of issues such as internationalizing Japanese education, it is no wonder that Nakasone sought to minimize interference from entrenched interest groups like the JTU and the MOE by securing parliamentary approval to establish the Ad Hoc Council on Education under his direct control. In the end, however, this ploy failed to achieve its objective. As noted in the Introduction to this study, throughout the 1990s both the national headquarters and various local branches of the JTU actively resisted government attempts to nurture a "Japanese consciousness" by forcing schools to display the Hinomaru flag and sing the Kimigayo anthem, although that campaign has, in turn, suffered its own setbacks due to Diet passage of a law granting official status to the flag and anthem, and to internal divisions among union members.

As for the MOE: with Nakasone's departure from office in November 1987, and the disbandment of his Ad Hoc Council on Education shortly thereafter, there was little to prevent MOE bureaucrats from reclaiming a large share of the responsibility for deciding when, whether, and how to act upon the Council's various proposals to internationalize Japanese education. Elsewhere I have reported on a variety of innovative, but problematic, initiatives that the MOE undertook in the 1990s. For example, in its hasty attempt to reach Nakasone's widely publicized goal of attracting 100,000 foreign students to Japan by the end of the century, the MOE failed to insure that Japanese colleges and universities were prepared to house and teach them once they arrived. Although the Ad Hoc Council recommended that Japanese children living abroad receive an education that would allow them to fully experience the region where they live, while also developing a Japanese consciousness, the MOE found that its real influence was limited to the 40 per cent of students who were enrolled in the 82 (in 1987) full-time, government-supported schools for Japanese (*Nihonjin gakkō*) in operation worldwide. Its remedy was to try and enlist the help of parents by emphasizing the role of home education (*katei kyōiku*) both for establishing their children's identity as Japanese and for shaping their view of the world beyond Japan. Its solution to the problem of reintegrating Japanese children into Japanese primary and secondary schools after lengthy residence abroad consisted of segregating them in a small number of new "international high schools" (*kokusai kōtō gakkō*) and an "international studies course" (*kokusai kyōyōka*) in other selected high schools.[76]

Accordingly, I will conclude this chapter by returning to the one issue that continues to impact virtually every student in Japanese schools, and that continues to generate the most debate and controversy: the compulsory curriculum, and the textbooks used to teach it. The question to be addressed is whether the Ad Hoc Council's very public pronouncements on the need to internationalize Japanese education had any appreciable effect on the official school curriculum and government-approved textbooks. As before, I will focus on the subject of social studies for grade six of primary school.

Following publication of the Ad Hoc Council's reports, the MOE revised its Course of Study for primary schools two more times before the end of the century: once in March 1989 (which took effect in 1992); and again in December 1998 (which took effect in 2002). According to Rose, the 1989 revisions coincided with a period when "textbook screening was once again relaxed," as the MOE was still smarting from diplomatic protests by Asian governments dating back to 1982, and was wary of the implications of Ienaga's third textbook trial, which began in 1984. However, the 1998 revisions coincided with the third major "textbook offensive" of the postwar period, which began in earnest in 1996 and centered mainly on middle school and high school history textbooks.[77]

In terms of the social studies curriculum in general, and the issue of internationalization in particular, neither of the MOE's late twentieth-century revisions to its Course of Study betray any fundamental shift in educational goals or pedagogy that could be credited to the work of Nakasone's Ad Hoc Council, save for a new provision to "help Japanese returnee children to become acclimated to school life, and to make the most of their experience living abroad."[78] Rather, like the Ad Hoc Council itself, they owe most of their inspiration to the CCE's 1970 report that was discussed earlier, and to the 1977 Course of Study, which was the first to act upon the CCE's findings. The authors of the 1998 Course of Study actually acknowledge the work of the CCE: not its 1970 report, but another study that the CCE conducted between 1996 and 1998 with the assistance of the MOE's Curriculum Council (Kyōiku Katei Shingikai).[79] Yet, even this later CCE study represents more of an extension of its own handiwork from 1970 than a new initiative.

The Ad Hoc Council's principal contribution to educational discourse after 1987 was a heightened sense of urgency about the challenges posed by economic, social and cultural internationalization, and about the need to "cope" with those challenges on the educational front. The following paragraph, written by the authors of the 1998 Course of Study, shows the unmistakable influence of the Ad Hoc Council's reports from the mid-1980s:

> Today, faced with the intensification of the entrance exam competition, problems like bullying and absenteeism, and a lack of social interaction outside of school, there are various issues pertaining to education for the enrichment of human nature. In order to respond appropriately to these issues, an examination has been undertaken with respect to the way that education is conducted. Furthermore, as we look toward the 21st century, our nation's society is experiencing a variety of major changes—internationalization, the growth of information (*jōhōka*), scientific and technological development, concern for environmental problems, aging and a declining birth rate—which raise questions about how education in this new age should be conducted.[80]

Henceforth, nearly every subject in the primary school curriculum was to be enlisted in the effort to increase pupils' "international understanding" (*kokusai rikai*) and "spirit of international cooperation" (*kokusai kyōchō no seishin*). The 1989 Course of Study advises sixth grade teachers of Japanese language (*kokugo*) to select teaching materials that "convey an understanding of the world's climate, natural features and cultures, and that contribute to the cultivation of a spirit of international cooperation." Moral education teachers are encouraged to cultivate a moral sensibility that will provide a foundation for "nurturing Japanese who possess the independence to contribute to a peaceful international society."[81]

Predictably, the Ad Hoc Council's reports also lent a new sense of urgency about arming tomorrow's cosmopolitan Japanese with a strong identity as patriotic citizens who love their country, respect their country's culture and traditions, and esteem (*keiai*) their emperor. Thus, the 1989 Course of Study for sixth grade social studies makes frequent use of phrases like "cultivate personal awareness of being Japanese in the world" (*sekai no naka no Nihonjin toshite no jikaku o sodateru*).[82] The 1998 revised Course of Study deliberately substitutes a new phrase—"personal awareness of the importance of living together with people of other countries around the world, as Japanese who desire peace" (*heiwa o negau Nihonjin toshite sekai no kuniguni no hitobito to tomo ni ikite iku koto ga taisetsu de aru koto o jikaku dekiru yō ni suru*)—but the message is the same.[83] This virtual obsession with producing self-consciously loyal and patriotic "Japanese in the world" creates a new problem for the teaching of history. Beginning with the 1998 Course of Study, the primary school social studies course would be expected to cultivate in pupils "an understanding and a *love of our country's history*," as well as of the land itself (*waga kuni no kokudo to rekishi ni taisuru rikai to aijō*), including the activities of the forebears of today's Japanese.[84] What would this new mandate to love Japan's history mean for coverage of topics that do not reflect well upon the country and its forebears, i.e., the colonization of Korea, government by assassination, or the Nanjing Massacre?

Another factor threatening the quality and degree of historical knowledge conveyed to sixth grade pupils has been a new push by the MOE, beginning in the 1990s, to reduce the volume of information that Japanese pupils (and their teachers) have traditionally been required to cover in class as part of their preparation for middle school, and ultimately, for the high school entrance exams. In addition to reducing the amount of weekly class time devoted to social studies, in order to make room for a new subject called "general studies" (*sōgō gakushū*)—for which the teacher decides which topics to take up and what activities to assign—the 1998 Course of Study stipulates that the teacher should *not* go into great detail when teaching Japanese history, lest pupils get bogged down in minutiae and lose interest altogether. Instead, the sixth-grade teacher is advised to concentrate on the activities of historical figures and representative cultural artifacts, and to guide pupils in a fulfilling study of history appropriate to primary school by limiting their study to representative events, and foregoing detailed study.[85]

Now, this goal of fostering a pupil-centered pedagogy—which seeks to make pupils active, engaged learners rather than passive recipients of encyclopedic information—is not only laudable, but consistent with earlier pupil-centered reform initiatives dating back to the Meiji period. However, beginning in the 1990s it has had an adverse effect on social studies textbooks, which have sacrificed historical detail and historiographical sophistication in favor of a glossy layout featuring a profusion of color photographs and drawings. The effects can be seen by comparing the 1992 edition of the sixth grade textbook, *Primary School Social Studies*, with the 1979 edition that was analyzed earlier. The effects are less pronounced in the chapters dealing with prehistoric and protohistoric Japan, and more pronounced in those covering developments following the Meiji Renovation. Put simply, the grim realities of modern Japanese history that were described in such candid detail by the authors in 1979 do not appear quite so grim in 1992, because candor has been replaced by euphemism and inference. For example, in its coverage of the Sino-Japanese War, the 1992 edition of *Primary School Social Studies* fails to explain the reciprocal nature of China's tributary relationship with Korea, leaving the reader to wonder why Korea sought Chinese help in quelling the 1894 domestic uprising against the Korean court, and why both countries viewed Japanese interference with alarm. The details of Japan's deliberate manipulation of events to justify sending its own troops have also been eliminated, along with any mention of the breakdown of Sino-Japanese negotiations to resolve the standoff, which the 1979 edition identified as the trigger that prompted Japan to commence the war. Consequently, the 1992 edition stops short of declaring that Japan precipitated the war, stating only that the presence of opposing forces from China and Japan on the peninsula resulted in war.[86] In the same manner, details of domestic opposition to the Russo-Japanese War are reduced to one phrase ("A small group opposed the war, but Japan fought with all of its strength"), as is Korean opposition to Japanese colonization, with no reference to Ito's assassination or to Japanese retaliation against protesters.[87] Ditto for the Manchurian Incident, and for the military's domestic campaign of political assassinations in the 1930s. However, thanks to the international scrutiny brought to bear on the MOE's textbook screening process in 1982, the 1992 edition of *Primary School Social Studies* does remark on the Japanese army's occupation of major Chinese cities in 1937, beginning with Nanjing, where "amid the confusion (*konran*) many residents were murdered by the Japanese army." Even so, the textbook avoids using the term "invasion," in favor of Japan's "occupation" (*senryō*) of China and Southeast Asia.[88]

One representative two-page spread in the 2002 edition of the *New Society* textbook for sixth graders encapsulates the MOE's new user-friendly approach to the study of history as the twentieth century was giving way to the new millennium. History here appears not as a single, linear narrative analyzing cause and effect, but as a busy collage of visual images. The actual text, describing the escalation of hostilities in the late 1930s to encompass both Europe and Asia, occupies less than a third of these pages. Surrounding the text are: seven photographs (showing the Pearl Harbor attack, Koreans paying their respects at a Shinto shrine, a Japanese draft notice, a Japanese solider bidding farewell to his family, Japanese students marching in formation with wooden guns, Japanese soldiers defending oil wells in Burma, and a monument in Singapore commemorating residents killed by the Japanese army); part of an eyewitness account from a Japanese nurse serving in the Philippines recounting American attacks on Japanese soldiers—and on the hospital where she worked—and the struggle to survive without adequate food; a modern poem of remembrance written by a sixth grader; a map showing the area occupied by the Japanese military during the war; and an inset describing the hardships suffered by Koreans and Chinese during the war.[89] Presumably, these visual aids are meant to serve as resources to provoke pupils to engage with the teacher, and each other, in thoughtful class discussions about the causes and consequences of the Asia-Pacific War. In that case, it falls to the teacher to avoid treating the topic in a superficial, episodic manner, akin to a television drama or an action movie.

It also falls to the teacher to supplement the textbook with outside resources in order to achieve more balanced coverage, since the images of war that appear in this textbook highlight the hardship and suffering experienced by Japanese civilians and soldiers, while presenting a softer picture of the hardship and suffering experienced by foreign victims of Japanese aggression and occupation. Japanese children are shown toiling in wartime factories, practicing military drills on a school playground, fleeing American bombs, and evacuating ruined Japanese cities. Korean children are shown paying their respects at a Shinto shrine and attending classes taught in Japanese.

The MOE's user-friendly approach is also applied to *New Society's* coverage of Japan's current relations with other countries and its role in creating a more peaceful world. To try and generate pupils' interest in these issues, the 1998 edition of the Course of Study includes the following advice to teachers:

> When taking up the topic of foreign countries with which Japan has close ties, choose a number of countries and have pupils each select one of them to investigate [on their own]; the goal being to gain a concrete understanding of various foreign cultures while nurturing an attitude of respect for the culture and traditions of our country and foreign countries.[90]

The authors of the 2002 edition of *New Society* decided to use this pedagogical model as the framework for a chapter entitled, "Japan and Countries
with which it has Close Relations," by creating fictionalized oral reports supposedly delivered by students based on their individual study of the United
States, China, Korea and Brazil. Once again, the text shares space with col-
lections of full-color photographs, as well as maps and graphs. For example,
the section on Brazil takes up the contemporary issue of Brazilian workers
of Japanese descent who began arriving in Japan in large numbers in the
1980s to help meet Japan's need for cheap labor. The fictionalized student
report appears beneath large photos of Japanese immigrant farmers and factory workers, a photo of the Amazon River, and a map of Brazil. The student
reports that

> [Fellow student] Sakata's family transferred from a school in Brazil when his
> father took a job at a Japanese factory. . . . Sakata's grandfather immigrated
> to Brazil during his youth and married a Brazilian woman, who gave birth to
> Sakata's father. There is a long history of Japanese immigrating to Brazil, where
> they work in agriculture and factories, so it is a country with which Japan has
> close ties.[91]

As with this textbook's treatment of Japan's wartime history, the calculated
paucity of factual information that is conveyed in this manner about foreign
countries, and their ties to Japan, places the onus on the classroom teacher to
ensure that this informational vacuum does not become an obstacle to "international understanding."

RECLAIMING A "NEW EDUCATION"

This new generation of user-friendly social studies textbooks is a testament to
the continued influence of the CCE upon educational policy. Consistent with
the recommendations contained in its 1970 report, *Basic Guidelines for the
Reform of Education*, the CCE in 1996 called for new teaching methods that
"put a high value on seeing that children become familiar with the processes
of feeling deep emotions, questioning and making decisions," in place of
methods which see "the be-all and end-all as getting children to memorize
vast quantities of knowledge or try to answer as many questions as they can
in a given time period." By the same token,

> It is from this kind of perspective too that, with a view to implementing a form
> of education that is responsive to social change, in every school sufficient
> care is taken to establish links connecting all of the regular subjects, moral

education, and special activities, and that educational activities are carried out with the entire curriculum in mind. For example, if we think of educational activities that make use of an international communications network like the Internet, they need not be seen only in terms of learning information; if these activities involve the English language, then they can also be seen as helping to raise a student's level of English competence, or . . . as contributing to a student's understanding of another country's culture and history. . . . In other words, it is important to develop activities of this kind within a framework that creates linkages between all school subjects, and between the teachers [who teach them].

If educational activities are developed within a framework of this kind of original thinking, then children will learn to study in a way that creates organic links between information, foreign languages, international understanding and other subjects; and this study can, in turn, become more multi-sided and effective.[92]

It is hard to miss the similarities between this late-twentieth century campaign for a new approach to education and movements during the first quarter-century calling for "new education" and "liberal education" that were examined in chapter 2. In both cases, reform centered on redefining the content of school knowledge, the relationship of the learner to that knowledge, the methods used to foster that relationship and, by extension, the relationship between teacher and learner. The biggest difference may lie in the relationship between "new" education and "international" education. Notwithstanding attempts by reformers like Sawayanagi, Noguchi, Shimonaka and Harada to convince fellow educators and the general public in Japan that the two were inseparably linked, the fact that Japanese historiography continues to offer little recognition of their efforts suggests that international education remained on the margins of public consciousness *and* the educational reform movement itself in the early twentieth century. Their cause received, at best, lukewarm support from the MOE, which did little more than convene an international education symposium in 1924, publish the symposium proceedings the following year, and allow textbook writers like Sawayanagi, Yumoto and Ikeoka a little room to introduce the doctrine of internationalism. By contrast, it is the MOE that seized the momentum in the 1980s to internationalize Japanese education from early advocates like the CCE and the Ad Hoc Council on Education, and placed it at the center of its own national agenda for educational reform.

This does not mean that teachers themselves have been content to play a passive role, however. For example, a number of primary school teachers and administrators have sought to help their brethren interpret MOE policies for internationalizing the curriculum and put them into practice by authoring commercially published handbooks and primers. One such handbook boldly declares that "education for international understanding means the creation of a new education" (*kokusai rikai kyōiku wa atarashii kyōiku no sōzō de aru*):

> When moral education classes were conducted as a part of education for international understanding, it became an issue whether or not the classes are for moral education or for education for international understanding. Although it is absurd that such a discussion arises, it may be a natural reaction for teachers who are accustomed to [the traditional division of the curriculum into academic] subjects and fields.
>
> Education for international understanding is education that encompasses the educational activities in the school as a whole, in contrast to teaching according to subjects. Consequently, it is more desirable to react flexibly, with creativity and techniques not confined to the parameters encompassing academic subjects and fields.
>
> In principle, education aims at forming well-rounded whole persons, and the policy of establishing academic subjects and fields was intended to make education more effective. However, in promoting education for international understanding, issues such as how to secure class time, what to do about academic subjects and fields, how to prepare educational materials, and how to have students learn it are becoming practical problems.
>
> While it is claimed that education for international understanding, human rights education (*jinken sonchō kyōiku*), environmental education, and information education (*jōhō kyōiku*) are important pending issues, creating educational opportunities [to act upon] such issues is difficult in reality, because the introduction of a five-day school week leaves less time for [the traditional] subjects. . . .
>
> In order to solve these problems, it is necessary to reevaluate the content of learning from new points of view, reorganize the curriculum, create inclusive units that encompass and transcend academic subjects, develop educational materials, and improve learning methods. All of these matters involve creating new educational perspectives and new learning methods, and only the steady accumulation of educational practice can achieve this.[93]

In keeping with this interdisciplinary approach, some of these handbooks offer practical advice on such topics as "understanding different cultures through the subject of music," "home economics and education for international understanding," "the connection between morals and education for international understanding," "the advancement of education for international understanding through club activities," and "utilizing the special characteristics of returnee children (*kikoku shijo*) for education for international understanding."

In one segment, Kobayashi Motoko, vice principal at a Tokyo elementary school, relates how a specialist in art education at her school discovered a way to bring education for international understanding into her art class.

Coming across a newspaper article that told of a local museum exhibition featuring pictures drawn by Sri Lankan children, she went to see it for herself. She was so impressed by their depictions of Japan, and their portraits of daily life in Sri Lanka, that she used the school newsletter to encourage students and their parents to visit the exhibition. After reading her students' enthusiastic accounts of their impressions of the exhibit, she decided to build upon this experience through her own teaching. But where to begin? What objectives should she strive for, and what kind of art project would be appropriate? Her solution was to have her students make a calendar using Japanese *washi* paper, depicting traditional seasonal activities in Japan. Through this exercise, writes Kobayashi, the students gained a new appreciation for their own cultural traditions while learning to appreciate the distinctive characteristics of foreign cultures. Their exposure to the artwork of Sri Lankan children was also valuable because it challenged their preconceived notions of Asian societies as less advanced than their Western counterparts.[94]

In another segment, Gotō Hirofumi, consultant for the Kusaka Municipal Board of Education, offers a less sanguine assessment of one teacher's attempt to internationalize his science course. The venue was an unnamed primary school that had been studying the issue of education for international understanding during the past year. To that end, one teacher, Noguchi sensei, had been appointed director of this project (*kokusai rikai kyōiku shunin*). As part of an in-service training seminar for teachers in her school, Noguchi first asked teachers in each subject area to prepare their own plans to internationalize courses taught in that subject, and to present the main points of their plans at a faculty meeting for evaluation. Once Noguchi was satisfied that each plan made adequate provisions to incorporate information about foreign countries and cultures, teachers were then called upon to demonstrate these plans in a classroom setting, for further evaluation by their peers. Tsukada sensei, the head science teacher, chose a lesson on the lifecycle of butterflies to have pupils study and compare butterflies in Japan with foreign species. First, students examined a real specimen of the domestic variety, observing the different stages of its development, its diet, and so forth. Later, they were shown pictures of foreign species and asked to comment on similarities and differences. Tsukada followed his lesson plan to the letter, to the satisfaction of Noguchi and the other faculty members in attendance, who agreed that Tsukada had successfully sparked the students' interest in foreign countries.

In Gotō's estimation, however, Noguchi, the project director, and Tsukada, the science teacher, both come in for criticism. Tsukada's demonstration class and the response it generated from fellow teachers reveal two shortcomings with the school's approach to education for international understanding, according to Gotō. First, the teachers at this school simplistically equated education for international understanding with teaching something—*any-thing*—about foreign countries, without stopping to consider what is the real purpose of this education. Second, the teachers were so preoccupied with the international component of Tsukada's lesson that they paid little attention to its scientific component. Education for international understanding, warns Gotō, should be a natural outgrowth of academic study in the different subject areas, not a substitute for sound academic content.[95]

In a rare departure from this multidisciplinary "catchall" approach, one handbook sets out to take primary school social studies teachers through each stage of planning and executing lesson plans in that subject for grades three through six. The book, *New Social Studies Instruction from a Human Per-spective: Learning how to Live in an Internationalized, Information-Oriented Society*, features chapters by twenty-two different contributors, all of whom are either primary school teachers or principals. The book takes as its start-ing point the MOE's 1989 Primary School Course of Study, which went into effect in 1992 and "aims to develop the personal qualities and abilities that will enable [Japanese] to cope individually with looming social change." The six essays in part 1 discuss the educational philosophy that underlies the new curriculum guidelines. Part 2 shifts the focus from principles to praxis, by presenting nine detailed social studies lesson plans (one for grade three, two for grade four, and three each for grades five and six). Part 3 presents twenty-six short question-and-answer segments that offer hints for teaching about such topics as: "What are the key points to be covered when learning about the livelihoods of people in countries sharing economic and cultural ties with Japan?" "When learning about international interchange, what are the key points to be covered regarding the importance of world peace?" "What are the key points to guide the development of Japanese who [will] live in international society?"[96]

A brief examination of one particular fourth-grade lesson in part 2 il-lustrates how the politics of educational policy can infiltrate the primary school classroom under the guise of internationalization. The topic of the lesson is the Northern Territories Dispute (*hoppō ryōdo mondai*), which has overshadowed Russian-Japanese relations ever since the former Soviet Union forcefully occupied four of the Kurile Islands claimed by the Japanese as the Asia-Pacific War came to an end in 1945. The objective of this lesson is to "identify the location of our country, understand that Japan is linked to other countries by the oceans separating them, and that there is a dispute over four northern islands. It is especially important [for pupils] to understand the im-portance of sovereign territory through their study of the Northern Territories Dispute." In association with this topic: (1) pupils should learn that return of these islands to Japan must be achieved through negotiations with the persistent Russians; (2) the teacher should introduce examples of people who wait hopefully for return of the islands to Japan. Teachers are advised not to bore pupils by treating the dispute as a complex historical and political problem, but to focus on humanizing this topic in order to bring the students to a sympathetic understanding of the dispute. This lesson plan leaves no doubt in the pupils' minds that Japan has a valid claim to these islands, and that failure to resolve the dispute is robbing Japanese fisherman of their livelihood, and the descendants of former Japanese residents of the islands of the chance to visit the graves of their ancestors.[97]

This brief sampling of teachers' handbooks cannot do justice to the variety of methodological approaches that individual teachers and groups of teachers, working in structured settings, are employing to transform an abstract concept, "education for international understanding," into a meaningful, purposeful reality for themselves and their students. But they do illustrate the complexity of the task facing Japanese primary and secondary school teachers and administrators. Accustomed to formulating lesson plans and teaching within the parameters demarcated for their specific subjects by a combination of MOE guidelines, textbooks and entrance exams based on those guidelines, the weight of precedent, and the advice of superiors, how should teachers go about navigating the uncharted waters of education for international understanding in an era when curricular integration and local innovation have become official policy? How much individual teacher initiative and diversity is acceptable, and who decides? How free are teachers to interpret the revised curriculum guidelines announced by the MOE? Where do they turn for inspiration, and for concrete ideas about how to proceed?

CONCLUSION

It is likely that few, if any, of the many educators who helped to author the CCE's reports in 1970 and 1996–1998, the Ad Hoc Council on Education's reports in the mid-1980s, the MOE Course of Study Guides dating back to the 1950s, and the successive editions of primary school textbooks that followed in the wake of each revision to the Course of Study, ever heard of Sawayanagi Masatarō. Yet, all of these publications share one characteristic with Sawayanagi's writings: a strong desire to demonstrate Japan's "contributions" to the pursuit of world peace and the advancement of human culture, and in the process, to vindicate its repeated claim to the title, "Japan in the world." Ironically, with the exception of Japan's membership in the League of Nations Secretariat, Sawayanagi and his contemporaries in the 1920s were hard pressed to point to any tangible evidence of Japan's contributions to humanity. Instead, they wrote about Japan's destiny to contribute to humanity in the future—thanks to its "unique" ability to assimilate, and perfect, the best attributes of Oriental and Occidental cultures—and they pleaded with their countrymen to make good on that promise to the world. A similar concern, and a similar outlook, have characterized official educational discourse since the 1950s and they have become more pronounced since the early 1980s. While the MOE Course of Study and attendant textbooks added the scientific discoveries of Kitasato Shibasaburō and Yukawa Hideki to the short list of prewar Japan's contributions, it is to postwar Japan, and to twenty-first century Japan, that they look to convince the rest of the world, and the Japanese themselves, that the century-old claim is deserved. Thus, recent editions of *New Society* and *Primary School Social Studies* always conclude with chapters bearing titles like, "World Peace and the Role of Japan" (*Sekai no heiwa to Nihon no yakuwari*), and "The World and Japan Building Peace" (*Heiwa o kizuku sekai to Nihon*).

Reading through their descriptions of Japan's undeniable "contributions" as an active member of the United Nations, the host of two Olympics, and a leading contributor of money and volunteers to various overseas development projects, it may seem curious that Japan's political and educational leaders still seem to treat this as a public relations campaign, needed to convince a skeptical audience—both at home and abroad—that Japan's national interests are inseparable from global interests. However, until they are prepared to acknowledge that Japanese history is, in turn, inseparable from world history—subject to the same historical laws, the same methods of historical analysis, and the same standards of historical truth—then public relations alone are unlikely to win the day in the court of public opinion.

NOTES

1. *Shimonaka Yasuburō jiten*, 275–80. According to Aspinall, 120,000 "right-wing" teachers and educators (22 percent of the entire teaching corps) were also purged and removed from their jobs. See *Teachers' Unions and the Politics of Education in Japan*, 31.

2. *Shimonaka Yasaburō jiten*, 219.

3. Jessamyn Reich Abel, "Warring Internationalisms: Multilateral Thinking in Japan, 1933-1964," PhD dissertation (Columbia University, 2004); Konrad M. Lawson, "The Persistence of Transnational Idealism in Early Postwar Japan, 1945–1949" unpublished manuscript.

4. *Shimonaka Yasaburō jiten*, 218–30; Hiroshima heiwa bunka sentā, ed., *Heiwa jiten* (Tokyo: Keisō Shobō, 1985, 1991), 59.

5. Quoted in Lawson, "The Persistence of Transnational Idealism," 30.

6. Ibid., 26.

7. *Shimonaka Yasaburō jiten*, 218–30, *Heiwa jiten*, 59.

8. *Shimonaka Yasaburō jiten*, 61–64.

9. Ibid., 198–200.

10. Ibid., 204–10; *Heiwa jiten*, 66–67.

11. Marshall, *Learning to be Modern*, 150.

12. Ibid., 153, 160; Aspinall, *Teachers' Unions and the Politics of Education in Japan*, 31–32.

13. Laura Hein and Mark Selden, "The Lessons of War, Global Power, and Social Change," in Laura Hein and Mark Selden, eds., *Censoring History: Citizenship and Memory in Japan, Germany, and the United States* (Armonk, NY: M. E. Sharpe, 2000), 8–10.

14. Mark Selden, "Remembering 'The Good War': The Atomic Bombing and the Internment of Japanese-Americans in U.S. History Textbooks," *Japan Focus*, May 8, 2005 (http://japanfocus.org/products/details/1943).

15. The Course of Study (*gakushū shidō yōryō*) is the basis for the MOE's guidelines for textbook writers (*kyōkasho kentei kijun*); see Caroline Rose, "The Battle for Hearts and Minds: Patriotic Education in Japan in the 1990s and Beyond," in Naoko Shimazu, ed., *Nationalisms in Japan* (London and New York: Routledge, 2006), 133–34. In 1958, the MOE made it mandatory for textbooks to conform to its guidelines: see Nozaki Yoshiko and Inokuchi Hiromitsu, "Japanese Education, Nationalism, and Ienaga Saburō's Textbook Lawsuits," in Hein and Selden, eds., *Censoring History*, 105.

16. Yoshiko Nozaki, "Educational Reform and History Textbooks in Occupied Japan," in Mark E. Caprio and Yoneyuki Sugita, eds., *Democracy in Occupied Japan: The U.S. Occupation and Japanese Politics and Society* (London and New York: Routledge, 2007), 134–37.

17. Marshall, *Learning to be Modern*, 157.

18. Nozaki and Inokuchi, "Japanese Education, Nationalism, and Ienaga Saburō's Textbook Lawsuits," 97–98.

19. Ibid., 98–102; Marshall, *Learning to be Modern*, 157–60.

20. Nozaki and Inokuchi, "Japanese Education, Nationalism, and Ienaga Saburō's Textbook Lawsuits," 104.

21. Rose, "The Battle for Hearts and Minds," 135–36.

22. Nozaki and Inokuchi, "Japanese Education, Nationalism, and Ienaga Saburō's Textbook Lawsuits," 104–05.

23. Monbushō, *Shōgakkō gakushū shidō yōryō* (Tokyo: Teikoku Chihō Gyōsei Gakkai, 1958), 6, 26.

24. Ibid., 44–45.

25. Ibid., 46

26. Ibid.

27. Ibid., 44.

28. Ibid., 44–45.

29. Ibid., 47.

30. Nozaki and Inokuchi, "Japanese Education, Nationalism, and Ienaga Saburō's Textbook Lawsuits," 105.

31. For an analysis of Japanese and American wrangling over trade policy with the PRC during and after the Occupation, see Sayuri Guthrie-Shimizu, "Occupation Policy and Postwar Sino-Japanese Relations: Severing Economic Ties," in Caprio and Sugita, eds., *Democracy in Occupied Japan*, 200–19.

32. Kaigo Tokiomi, ed., *Atarashii Shakai* 6:1 (Tokyo: Tokyo Shoseki Kabushiki-gaisha, 1958), 4–17.

33. Ibid., 38–63.

34. Ibid., 72–84.

35. Monbushō, *Shōgakkō gakushū shidō yōryō*, 44.

36. *Atarashii Shakai* 6:2, 66–67.

37. Ibid., 96.

38. Ibid.

39. Ibid., 97–98.

40. Ibid., 102–16.

41. John W. Dower, "Triumphal and Tragic Narratives of the War in Asia," in Laura Hein and Mark Selden, eds., *Living with the Bomb: American and Japanese Cultural Conflicts in the Nuclear Age* (Armonk, NY: M. E. Sharpe, 1997), 37–51.

42. *Atarashii shakai*, 108–10.

43. Monbushō, *Shōgakkō gakushū shidō yōryō* (Tokyo, 1968), 46, 48.

44. Ibid., 49.

45. Ibid.

46. Kaigo Tokiomi, ed., *Atarashii shakai* (Tokyo: Tokyo Shoseki Kabushikigaisha, 1968), 40–63.

47. Ibid., 121–39.

48. Ibid., 147.

49. Nozaki and Inokuchi, "Japanese Education, Nationalism, and Ienaga Saburō's Textbook Lawsuits," 107–22. See also: Rose, "The Battle for Hearts and Minds," 135–36; and Marshall, *Learning to be Modern*, 186–88.

50. Okuda Shinjo, "Jo: Hassō no tenkan o kitai suru," in Kobayashi Nobuo and Asakura Ryūtarō, general eds., *Kaisei shōgakkō gakushū shidō yōryō no tenkai: shakai hen* (Tokyo: Meiji Tosho Shuppan Kabushikigaisha, 1977), 3.

This shift in curriculum policy by the MOE in 1977, allowing individual schools and teachers more freedom to decide how to implement the Course of Study, was not unprecedented. Nozaki reports that the MOE's first postwar Course of Study guide, published in 1947, "criticized Japan's presurrender education and its policies over their having brought uniformity to schools. It argued, instead, that, within certain goals and frameworks, each school and teacher should creatively devise educational content and teaching methods appropriate to the needs of their students, school resources, and community environments. As such, the guidelines were 'tentative' rather than 'prescriptive.'" See Nozaki, "Educational Reform and History Textbooks in Occupied Japan," 133–34.

51. Ibid., 6.

52. Ibid., 3–8.

53. Ministry of Education Japan, *Basic Guidelines for the Reform of Education* (1970, 1972), 4.

54. Ibid.

55. "Maegaki," in Kobayashii and Asakura, general eds., *Kaisei shōgakkō gakushū shidō yōryō no tenkai: shakai hen*, 7.

56. Nagahara Keiji and Maruki Masaomi, general eds., *Shōgakkō shakai* 6:1 (Tokyo: Gakkō Tosho Kabushikigaisha, 1979), 4–5.

57. Ibid., 6–14.

58. Ibid., 108–09.

59. Ibid., 117–18.

60. Ibid., 119–21.

61. Ibid., 121.

62. Ibid., 6:2, 4–9. Besides providing more coverage of Chinese reaction to the Twenty-One Demands in its section on the Great War, the 1979 edition of *Primary School Social Studies* departs from the 1976 edition's explanation for the failure the League of Nations to "fulfill the role that it was expected to play." Whereas in 1979 the authors singled out the Secretariat members for blame, in 1976 they placed blame exclusively on the United States for failing to join the League. See Shiomi Toshitaka, Nagahara Keiji and Maruki Masaomi, general eds., *Shōgakkō shakai* 6:1 (Tokyo: Gakkō Tosho Kabushikigaisha, 1976), 122–23.

63. Ibid., 18–19. The 1976 edition of this textbook also uses the word "invasion" to describe Japan's actions in Manchuria: see *Shōgakkō shakai* 6:1 (1976), 133.

64. Ibid., 19–22. While the 1979 edition adheres closely to its predecessor's account of the rise of militarism in Japan following the Manchurian Incident, it drops any reference to the forced resignations of Professor Takigawa Yukitoki from his post at Kyoto University, and of Minobe Tatsukichi from the Upper House of the Diet on account of his "emperor organ theory," both of which are cited as examples of government coercion in the 1976 edition. See *Shōgakkō shakai* 6:1 (1976), 134–35.

65. Ibid., 23–26.

66. Ibid., 32–111.

67. Portions of this section were published previously in Lincicome, "Nationalism, Internationalization, and the Dilemma of Educational Reform in Japan."

68. Harumi Befu, "The Internationalization of Japan and Bunkaron," in Hiroshi Mannari and Harumi Befu, eds., *The Challenge of Japan's Internationalization: Organization and Culture* (Tokyo: Kwansei Gakuin University and Kodansha International, 1983), 232, 241.

69. *Kyōiku kaikaku ni kansuru tōshin* (Tokyo: Ōkurashō Insatsukyoku, 1988), 64, 129.

70. Ibid., 11–16, 129–38.

71. Ibid., 64–65.

72. Ibid., 12.

73. Morita Toshio, *Rinkyōshin to Nihonjin, Nihon bunkaron* (Tokyo: Shin Nihon Shuppansha, 1988), 12.

74. Ibid., 18-107.

75. Horio, *Educational Thought and Ideology in Modern Japan*, 378–79.

76. See Lincicome, "Nationalism, Internationalization, and the Dilemma of Educational Reform in Japan."

77. Rose, "The Battle for Hearts and Minds," 135–36.

78. Monbushō, *Shōgakkō gakushū shidō yōryō* (Tokyo: Ōkurasho Insatsu Kyoku, 1989), 3–4; Monbukagakushō, *Shōgakkō gakushū shidō yōryō* (Tokyo: Kokuristu Insatsu Kyoku, 1998; partially revised 2003), 6.

79. Monbukagakushō, *Shōgakkō gakushū shidō yōryō kaisetsu: sōsoku hen* (Tokyo: Tokyo Shoseki Kabushikigaisha, 1998; partially revised 2003), 1.

80. Ibid.

81. Monbushō, *Shōgakkō gakushū shidō yōryō* (1989), 23, 105.

82. Ibid., 33.

83. Monbushō, *Shōgakkō gakushū shidō yōryō kaisetsu: shakai hen* (Osaka: Nihon Bunkyō Shuppan Kabushikigaisha, 1999), 7.

84. Ibid., 13.

85. Ibid., 9.

86. Kato Ichirō et. al., *Shōgakkō shakai* 6:1 (Tokyo: Gakkō Tosho Kabushikigaisha, 1992), 98.

87. Ibid., 101.

88. Ibid., 6:2 (1992), 3–4. According to Rose, references to the Nanjing Massacre appeared in all middle school textbooks by 1984, and in all high school textbooks by 1985. See Rose, "The Battle for Hearts and Minds," 136.

89. *Atarashii shakai* 6:1 (Tokyo: Tokyo Shoseki Kabushikigaisha, 2002), 96–97.

90. Monbushō, *Shōgakkō gakushū shidō yōryō* (1998, 2003), 31.

91. *Atarashii shakai* 6:2 (Tokyo: Tokyo Shoseki Kabushikigaisha, 2002), 38–39.

92. Central Council on Education, "The Model for Japanese Education in the Perspective of the 21st Century." (Tokyo: Ministry of Education, Sports and Culture, July 1996).

93. Maki Masami, Itō Kazuhiko, and Takeda Shinichi, eds., *"Kokusai rikai kyōiku" mondai kaiketsu shirīzu 4: gakushū o meguru mondai ni dō kotaeru ka* (Tokyo: Tōyōkan Shuppansha, 1997), 18–19. Other handbooks in this genre include: Saitō Gunbei, ed., *"Sōgōteki na gakushū" no jissen" No. 3: Kokusai rikai kyōiku no kangaekata, susumekata* (Tokyo: Kyōiku Kaihatsu Kenkyūjo, 1997); Tada Takashi, *Gakkō ni okeru kokusai rikai kyōiku: gurōbaru maindo o sodateru* (Tokyo: Tōyōkan Shuppansha, 1997); Zenkoku kaigai shijo kyōiku, kokusai rikai kyōiku kenkyū kyōgikai, ed., *Chiiki ni nezashita kokusai rikai kyōiku jissen jirei shū* (Tokyo: Daiichi Hōki Shuppan Kabushikigaisha, 1993); Ōyamada Jō, Watabe Yaeko, Kobayashi Kenji, and Komatsuzawa Masato, eds., *Ningen o kangaeru atarashii shakaika no jugyō 5: "Kokusaika, jōhōka shakai de no ikikata" o manabu* (Tokyo: Tōyōkan Shuppansha, 1994); Okuda Shinjo and Nagaoka Jun, eds., *Shin gakkō kyōiku zenshū 6: Kokusaika to gakkō kyōiku* (Tokyo: Gyōsei, 1995); Miura Kenji, ed., *Shōgakkō kokusai rikai kyōiku no susumekata: atarashii gakuryokukan o fumaete* (Tokyo: Kyōiku Shuppan, Kabushikigaisha, 1994).

94. Kobayashi Motoko, "Zuga kōsakuka o tōshite kokusai rikai," in *"Kokusai rikai kyōiku" mondai kaiketsu shirīzu 4: gakushū o meguru mondai ni dō kotaeru ka*, 64–68.

95. Gotō Hirofumi, "Rika de kokusai rikai kyōiku ga dekiru no ka," in Ibid., 53–60.

96. Ōyamada et al., *Ningen o kangaeru atarashii shakaika no jugyō 5*, i–iv.

97. Ibid., 46–58.

Epilogue

What lessons are we supposed to learn from Japan's repeated attempts throughout the twentieth century to navigate between the shoals of nationalism, imperialism and internationalism aboard the vessel known as educational reform? What does "Japan's struggle with internationalism"—as historian Ian Nish terms the period between the two world wars—through a self-proclaimed "international education movement" teach us about Japan's struggle after 1970 to "cope with internationalization," culminating in the Nakasone administration's highly touted movement to "internationalize Japanese education?" And what is the legacy of this late-twentieth struggle for Japanese education, society and politics in the twenty-first century, when the term "internationalization" has given way to "globalization?"

It is not difficult to muster historical evidence that seems to prove that the late-twentieth century campaign to integrate "Japan in the world" by internationalizing Japanese education has succeeded where the early twentieth-century campaign failed. Consider, for example, Japan's record since the 1970s of implementing the recommendations that emerged from the 1923 World Conference on Education in San Francisco, which were identified in chapter 2. To promote international cooperation, Sawayanagi and the other delegates who gathered in San Francisco advocated the appointment of an educational attaché for each embassy or legation. Today, Japanese embassies and consulates around the world employ staff members who serve as cultural liaisons to their host communities. Their duties include making presentations at local schools, distributing films and other materials on Japan for educational purposes, and sponsoring cultural programs for the general public. In 1923 the conference delegates also proposed the creation of graduate scholarships for students in international civics, economics and comparative education. These, too, have become a reality through grant programs sponsored by agencies like the MOE and the Japan Foundation that fund scholarship in various branches of the humanities and social sciences. A third recommendation called for research on the feasibility of establishing a world university. Today Japan is home to the United Nations University. Contemporary Japan also has an undisputed record of following through on the delegates' recommendations to aid the dissemination of education information by exchanging educational periodicals, creating a universal library service, and conducting exchanges of school teachers and university professors with those from abroad.

Japanese education officials and politicians today can even claim to abide by the 1923 conference's recommendations pertaining to the controversial issue of textbooks. "With a view to correcting misrepresentations about any country and to furnishing material that will foster international friendship," the delegates proposed that countries exchange textbooks. In the early 1980s, scholars from Japan and the United States participated in a bi-national comparative study of textbooks used in the two countries. A similar project was launched in 2002 by the Committee on History Research, which is jointly sponsored by the Japanese and Korean governments, and the Japanese and Chinese governments agreed in November 2006 to form a similar committee.[1] Finally, as noted in chapter 4, contemporary Japan has implemented two other conference proposals from 1923: (1) "that especially history, civics, and geography textbooks (including international law) emphasize the interdependence of all members of the human family, and the necessity of peace as an essential condition of the highest human development"; (2) that instruction in world civics and ethics permeate all subjects in the school curriculum, at all age levels.

At the same time, however, recent events also betray a legacy of continuing ideological and political conflict over the question of Japanese national identity and Japan's relationship to the international community. Seen from this perspective, it can be debated whether the New Millennium has really delivered anything new. Witness the third textbook offensive, which has straddled the not-so-great divide separating the twentieth and twenty-first centuries.

As Rose explains, the principal conservative groups who made common cause in the third offensive were products of the 1990s. Over one hundred Liberal Democractic Party (LDP) politicians, including future prime minister Abe Shinzō, joined forces in 1993 to establish the Committee to Investigate History (Rekishi Kentō Iinkai), which contends that the Greater East Asia War was one of self-defense and liberation; that the Nanjing Massacre and the "comfort women" system were fabrications; and that a new textbook battle was necessary to counter the invasion narrative. In 1996, over one hundred LDP members formed another group, the Diet Members' Alliance for a Bright Japan (Akarui Nihon Kokkai Giin Renmei) to press for a more positive narrative of Japanese history. Abe has also been a prominent figure in a third LDP group, the Young Diet Members Committee to Consider the Future of Japan and History Education (Nihon no Zento to Rekishi Kyōiku o Kangaeru Wakate Giin no Kai), which formed in 1997. The last-named group is especially significant for two reasons. First, its tactics in the third textbook offensive include putting pressure on the Textbook Bureau in the MOE and on textbook publishing companies, as well as collaborating with a private advocacy group, the Society to Produce New Textbooks (Atarashii Kyōkasho o Tsukuru Kai).[2] Second, as the group's name implies, its activities have not been confined to the reform of textbooks.

The third textbook offensive reached a crescendo in 2000 when the Society to Produce New Textbooks published its *New History Textbook* (*Atarashii rekishi kyōkasho*) for middle school students. Based upon the MOE's 1998 Course of Study, the *New History Textbook* received authorization from the MOE in 2001. After the MOE updated the Course of Study in 2003 the textbook was revised, reauthorized by the MOE and republished in 2005, including a "commercial edition" (*shihanbon*) marketed to the general public that sold over one million copies. The revised commercial edition carries a postscript in which lead author Fujioka Nobukatsu, a professor at Shokutaku University, praises a recent change in MOE regulations that permits commercial editions of textbooks to be sold to the public during the time period when local boards of education deliberate on which textbooks to adopt for their schools. This new policy, he writes, invests citizens with both the right and the responsibility to scrutinize textbooks and voice their concerns as part of the adoption process. Alluding to the outcry from foreign critics of the first edition of the *New History Textbook*, Fujioka accuses the foreign minister of the People's Republic of China of condemning the book without ever reading it. "For countries like China, criticism of textbooks is nothing more than a tool with which to bash Japan. Those who read the textbook will surely realize that foreign countries' criticisms have absolutely no foundation. My hope is for the broad dissemination of a history textbook with which Japanese children grow up soundly." Fujioka's postscript also highlights the ideological underpinnings of the *New History Textbook* and of the Society to Produce New Textbooks itself:

> The MOE Course of Study clearly states that the objectives of middle school history education are "to deepen [pupils'] love for our nation's history and to cultivate their awareness of themselves as citizens." The most unique feature of this textbook is that it was compiled so as to fully achieve these Course of Study objectives. If one reads and compares it to other publishers' textbooks, this feature is obvious. Many people who have toured textbook exhibits around the country have echoed the refrain that this is a textbook that instills fondness for Japan and pride in having been born in Japan.[3]

Fujioka's statement begs the question: What happens to historical narrative when "love of country" replaces "search for truth" and "quest for objectivity" as the principal aim? In the case of the revised commercial edition of his *New History Textbook*, the answer to that question depends, to some extent, upon the particular historical time period and topic under consideration.

For example, the opening section of the first chapter, narrating "The Dawn of Japan," makes no allusion to the divine origins of the Japanese islands or the Japanese ethnic nation. Instead, it is content to present the widely accepted hypothesis that *homo sapiens* emerged in Africa and then migrated north to Europe and east throughout Asia, eventually reaching Japan by crossing northern land bridges during the last Ice Age. Other groups arrived on Japan's shores in dugout canoes from islands to the south. It combines archaeological evidence and descriptions found in the early Chinese dynastic histories to describe the origins and customs of the Jōmon and Yayoi peoples and the continental origins of rice agriculture.[4]

It is in the next section, "Formation of the Ancient State," that the authors take up the related topics of the imperial court, divinity, myth and history in a special one-page "feature column" (*yomimono koramu*) on "The Legend of Emperor Jinmu's Subjugation of the East." This is accompanied by a subtle shift in narrative technique that recurs throughout the textbook, whenever the authors broach a controversial subject and shape it to conform to their objective ("love of country") under the guise of historical balance and objectivity. Empirical evidence and analysis that place Japanese history in a favorable light are highlighted, while those that cast a critical light on the past are ignored outright, criticized as inconclusive, or dismissed as politically motivated. In this instance, the authors acknowledge that the story of Jinmu's conquest and consolidation of control over rival clans and barbarians is a "legend" or "folktale" (*denshō, monogatari*) recorded in "Japan's oldest historical texts, the *Kojiki* and the *Nihon shoki*." They state explicitly that Jinmu was not an actual historical figure, but an idealized representation of an outstanding leader who must have founded the imperial court. "Thus, even though [the legend of Jinmu] is not a historical fact, it is a valuable clue to understand what ideas people in ancient times held about the state (*kokka*) and the emperor (*tennō*)."[5]

The problem with this analysis is twofold. First, it generalizes about "the people in ancient times" by treating legends like Jinmu's conquest as innocuous, apolitical folktales that were widely accepted among a population which, in reality, was still marked by regional ethnic, linguistic and cultural differences, intense clan rivalries, and extreme social stratification. Second, it treats the *Kojiki* and the *Nihon shoki* in similar fashion, as unproblematic and uncontroversial. The former is described as "a tale that coherently weaves together myths and history of the ethnic nation (*minzoku no shinwa to rekishi ga sujimichidatta monogatari*)," while the latter is described as "an official history of the state, which records in detail the genealogy of successive generations of emperors and their deeds."[6] No mention is made of compelling historical research that identifies these texts as tools of political control and expressions of power. According to this widely accepted interpretation, the court-sponsored *Kojiki* and the *Nihon shoki*, like the early Chinese dynastic histories on which they were modeled, creatively combined myth and fact to invent an "official history" of conquest and political consolidation that would help to legitimize the government of the Yamato court.

The authors also seek to emphasize the contemporary importance of the Jinmu myth to Japan's national identity by noting that Jinmu's enthronement is still celebrated each year on National Founding Day (February 11). Mindful of their youthful audience of soccer-crazy middle school children, they even point out that the logo of the Japanese Soccer Federation proudly displays the image of an auspicious three-legged crow that, according to legend, was sent by the Sun Goddess Amaterasu to guide Jinmu and his army to the land of Yamato.[7]

This strategy becomes more blatant in chapters 4 and 5, covering "The Construction of Modern Japan" and "The Age of World Wars and Japan." The authors are at pains to defend Japanese imperialism at every turn. While rightly noting important features that it shared with British, French, Dutch and American imperialism, they leap to the conclusion that Japanese imperialism was both benign and necessary. Taking a page from purveyors of Japanese imperial internationalism in the 1930s, the authors characterize Japanese imperialism as a beneficent counterweight to Western imperialism and credit it with catalyzing Asian liberation from centuries of Western subjugation. Japanese military and police actions against non-Japanese are noted occasionally, but only to minimize their severity, while the death tolls for Asian peoples from Japanese aggression go unmentioned.

The passage that attracted the sharpest criticism from both Japanese and non-Japanese observers following publication of the first edition of the *New History Textbook* was its account of the Nanjing Massacre. It remains controversial in the 2005 revised edition. The only reference to the incident in the main body of the text reads: "Thinking that Chiang Kai-shek would surrender if it conquered the seat of the Nationalist Party Government in Nanjing, the Japanese army occupied Nanjing in December. However, Chiang Kai-shek transferred his capital to Chungking, so the fighting continued." It is only in a footnote positioned in the margins of the page that the reader discovers the following additional statement: "During this time [of the Nanjing Incident] many deaths occurred among Chinese soldiers and people (*gunmin*) because of the Japanese army. Even so, on the basis of the available evidence, questions remain about the actual number of victims and other matters, which has fueled an ongoing debate marked by various opinions." The authors' deliberate obfuscation here is not limited to the well-worn tactic of questioning the credibility of the historical evidence, but extends to the introduction of a new word into the Japanese lexicon—*gunmin*, composed of the characters for "soldiers" and "people"—in place of the standard word for "soldiers" (*gunjin*). *Gunmin* alludes to the possibility that the Japanese army targeted both those who surrendered and those who fled, while taking refuge in the disclaimer that the evidence is inconclusive.[8]

Elsewhere, in another "feature column" entitled, "Wars of the Twentieth Century and the Victims of Totalitarianism," the authors admit that the Japanese military, like its counterparts in other countries, violated internationally accepted rules of warfare by killing and torturing soldiers and civilians in territories it occupied. But this single sentence offers no specific examples of Japanese misconduct, and is overshadowed by numerous examples that portray the Japanese as victims rather than victimizers. They include the American bombing of Tokyo and the nuclear bombings of Hiroshima and Nagasaki, as well as the Soviet invasion of Manchuria in August 1945 that resulted in the capture of some 600,000 Japanese civilians and soldiers, ten percent of whom died as a result of forced labor, starvation, and murder. (Accompanying photographs of the A-Bomb Dome in Hiroshima and a painting depicting the burial of prisoners in Siberia add to the sense of Japanese victimization.) The main point conveyed by this feature column is that totalitarian states like Hitler's Germany and Stalin's Soviet Union—Japan is pointedly excluded from the totalitarian camp—engaged in the wanton murder, torture and starvation of their own people and of foreigners during the Second World War, which are far more heinous crimes than the regrettable but inevitable casualties of war.[9]

In another "feature column" on the facing page, the authors tackle the controversial topic, "Considering the Tokyo Trials." Thanks to widely read books by Richard Minear and John Dower,[10] the politically motivated irregularities and illegal courtroom tactics that SCAP resorted to in these show trials are now widely recognized by English-language readers. For Fujioka and his team of authors, the trial presents an opportunity to question the verdict that the Greater East Asian War itself was unjust, and to decry the trials' impact on the Japanese psyche and the public's understanding of history:

> When the occupation commenced, GHQ strictly censored all newspapers, magazines, radio broadcasts and movies. It also used the mass media to proclaim that Japan's war was unjust. This kind of propaganda, together with the Tokyo Trials, fostered a sense of guilt among Japanese about their country's war and has affected how postwar Japanese view history.[11]

The *New History Textbook* concludes its survey of Japanese history with the death of Hirohito, which brought the long and eventful Shōwa period to an end. It devotes only three paragraphs to an enigmatic description of "Japan's Role in International Society" during the succeeding Heisei period. Whereas the Shōwa period ended on a series of high notes—the collapse of the Berlin Wall, the end of the Cold War and the disappearance of communism in Eastern Europe—the Heisei period has ushered in new challenges to Japanese security and to world peace and prosperity. Prevented by the postwar Constitution from sending troops to fight against Iraq in the first Gulf War, Japan was criticized for failing to participate militarily, in spite of its generous financial contribution to the war effort. And while the collapse of communism has eliminated the danger of global warfare, the survival of a small number of communist states and the persistence of ethnic and religious rivalries mean that regional conflicts will not disappear. In this environment, Japan, holding fast to its own culture and traditions, must firmly preserve its national security while contemplating how to contribute to global peace and prosperity in the future.[12]

It is fitting that the revised commercial edition of the *New History Textbook* closes with a hagiography of the Shōwa Emperor, along with an essay on "Studying History." Together they resurrect the same personification of national identity and xenophobic sense of nationalism as that which inspired the late Tokugawa slogan, "Revere the Emperor, Expel the Barbarian!" Observing that Hirohito took the throne at a time when Japan was in peril, the hagiography remarks that his heartfelt desire for friendship and goodwill between all nations ran counter to the trend of the time. However, even when his opinions diverged from those of Japan's government and military leaders, his position as a constitutional monarch obligated him to abide by their decisions. Shortly after the Japanese surrender, Hirohito demonstrated his courage and earned the respect of Douglas MacArthur by presenting himself to the general and offering to take responsibility for the wartime conduct of all Japanese. After the war, "the Emperor toured the regions of Japan, conversing with those who devoted themselves to rebuilding [the nation] and offering encouragement. Throughout his life he strode together with the people through the tumultuous era known as Shōwa."[13] Needless to say, no mention is made of the emperor as the inspiration for wartime propaganda at home, or of allegations made since his death in 1989 that Hirohito was not the innocent pawn of Japan's military leaders that his handlers, and MacArthur himself, made him out to be.[14]

Complementing this hagiographic attempt at "imperial restoration," the accompanying remarks on "Studying History" admonish yet another generation of Japanese to preserve their distinctive tradition and culture from the latest wave of foreign influence, or risk the disappearance of Japanese identity alto-gether. After proudly recalling how earlier generations of Japanese managed to cherish their own unique culture even as they risked life and limb to travel abroad and learn about foreign cultures, the authors lament that over the past half-century Japanese have gradually lost this perspective on their past. This sad state of affairs is due, in part, to the very success of postwar Japan in achieving its original goal of catching up to the advanced countries of Europe and America, which has left Japan with no other countries to try and surpass. However, another reason is that the destruction and defeat that Japan experi-enced in the Greater East Asian War, followed by foreign occupation, stripped the Japanese of self-confidence and left behind scars that have yet to heal. The cure for this ailment is twofold. First, take a measured approach to for-eign learning and resist the temptation to zealously imitate foreign standards and models. Second, and most importantly, Japanese must be certain of their own identity by thoroughly studying their own history and traditions.[15] Or, as Nakasone phrased it some two decades earlier, what Japanese need most is a "healthy" or "justifiable nationalism."

As noted above, the third textbook offensive was not confined to private sector groups like Fujioka's Society to Produce New Textbooks, but also attracted the support of conservative politicians like Abe Shinzō and other members of groups like the Young Diet Members Committee to Consider the Future of Japan and History Education, whose revisionist agenda reached far beyond textbooks. In fact, the first major legislative initiative undertaken by Abe during his short-lived (September 2006–September 2007) tenure as prime minister was to revise the 1947 Fundamental Law of Education.[16]

The revised law, which was passed by the Diet in November 2006, is significantly longer and more detailed than its predecessor. Whereas the individual figured prominently in the 1947 law, many of the new articles stress the national character and collective purpose of education, while em-phasizing the authority of government to plan and oversee the education of its citizens. Article 10 goes a step further, breaching the sanctity of the home with statements defining the aims of education in the home (*katei kyōiku*). Since parents bear primary responsibility for their children's education, they should instill habits necessary in daily life, cultivate a spirit of self-reliance, and develop both their children's minds and bodies in equal measure.

Even more important than the insertion of statements that privilege the state over the individual, according to Adam Lebowitz and David McNeill, is the "language of mystique and belief" that "makes the amended version of the law appear less a legal document than an expression of authoritarian will," and that "makes the very notion of individual rights seem anachronistic at best." As one example, they cite Article Nine which addresses professional teachers using the same rhetoric that the MOE has used against JTU activists for decades: admonishing them to be mindful of their "noble mission" (*sūkō na shimei*) and to devote themselves tirelessly to further study and professional improvement. Lebowitz and McNeill explain that "'noble' is not a legal term and whether or not an individual teacher's behavior is sufficiently 'noble' can only be a matter of personal interpretation." They liken such language to that used in wartime educational edicts.[17]

Another throwback to wartime educational discourse in the amended law is its reference to "homeland" (*gyōdo*); a term once used by political leaders to foster a populist nationalism. According to Lebowitz and McNeill, "the ideology of 'homeland' itself was as authoritarian as it was uncritical. This suggests that the amended education law views students as future subjects rather than citizens. It shows that the Law itself is less based on 'law' — 'homeland' does not appear in any Japanese legal dictionary — than on a narrow and subjective vision of society."[18]

And what about internationalism? The original Fundamental Law of Education set forth lofty international aspirations for postwar Japan as early as 1947, expressed in language that resonates with that used by Sawayanagi, Noguchi, Harada and Shimonaka in their prewar writings. The 1947 Preamble begins, "Having established the Constitution of Japan, we have shown our resolution to contribute to the peace of the world and welfare of humanity by building a democratic and cultural state." The very next sentence echoes their commitment to "liberal education" that respects the individual: "We shall esteem individual dignity and endeavor to bring up people who love truth and peace, while education which aims at the creation of culture, general and rich in individuality, shall be spread far and wide."

It may be said that parts of the 2006 amended law not only retain the emphasis on peace, internationality, and respect for the individual that marks the original, but even strengthens that emphasis. For example, chapter 1, "The Aims and Principles of Education," now includes new phrases such as "develop [the individual's] faculties, cultivate creativity, foster a spirit of independence and self-determination" as well as "cultivate an attitude of respecting other countries [and of] contributing to international peace and development."

However, these new phrases are carefully juxtaposed to others that channel the individual's creativity and spirit of independence to the advancement of the nation and to goals of the state, as in "cultivate an attitude of asserting oneself in shaping society and contributing to its advancement, based on a spirit of community." Similarly, the aforementioned aim of fostering respect for other countries is juxtaposed to a more nationalistic one. The full sentence reads, "Respect tradition and culture, and love our country and one's birthplace which they fostered, as well as cultivate an attitude of respecting other countries [and of] contributing to international peace and development." In short, the longstanding tensions between the individual, society and state, and between the national and international self that first appeared in the Imperial Charter Oath of 1868, continue to permeate official policy 140 years later.

Does this mean that nothing has changed? Rose, for one, disagrees. She notes that in contrast to its predecessors, the third textbook offensive inspired an unprecedented "counter-offensive" mounted by individuals and citizens groups "such as Children and Textbooks Japan Network 21, academics, journalists and writers, PTA groups and so on, seeking to raise awareness of, and protest against, the activities of the LDP, MOE, the Tsukuru kai and other groups. Support has also come from overseas groups and academics." As with the JTU's protests against mandatory displays of the Hinomaru Rising Sun flag and singing of the Kimigayo anthem during the 1990s, this counter-offensive was informed by a similar sense of history, as when sixty Japanese historians appealed to the MOE to refrain from authorizing the *New History Textbook* because "the certification of such a textbook by the Japanese government and its adoption for use in history education will pave the way for the revival of chauvinistic history education of pre-war and wartime Japan."[19]

Apart from the issue of history education and textbooks, Yōko Motani also finds that "progressive educators" have recently experienced greater success than before in addressing "the issues of citizenship, democracy, and justice to prepare Japanese children for an increasingly interdependent, global, and multicultural world through public education."[20] Even so, she concludes her analysis on a cautionary note:

> The evidence does not suggest progressive educators can now exercise their power to influence the educational policy. It is difficult for progressive educators to impact on educational policies directly, since as a quite recent and diversified group of educators, establishing a channel of communication with the Ministry of Education can be a challenge. . . . However, in the context of a society where a civil movement has taken off since the mid-1990s, progressive educators cannot be ignored as a significant element in influencing educational practices and discourse.[21]

Ironically, the same might be said of an earlier generation of "progressive educators" nearly a century earlier, which found inspiration in a fleeting era of Taishō Imperial Democracy to dedicate themselves to ill-fated movements for "liberal education" and "international education."

NOTES

1. Kondō Takahiro, "Historical Issues in East Asian International Order from an Educational Perspective," *Educational Studies in Japan: International Yearbook*, No. 1 (December 2006), pp. 37–48. Kondō rejects the common argument that cultural differences between Japan and Germany account for the latter's greater willingness to admit Nazi Germany's responsibility for World War II and to include information about Germany's conduct during the war in German textbooks. Rather, Kondō believes that Germany's candor and its commitment to learn from the past is due to pressure from the international community, which made this a condition of Germany's readmission into the international community. Japan, before the 1980s, was not held similarly accountable, since its principal ally throughout the Cold War period was the United States, which showed "a fundamental lack of interest in the Japanese people's historical perceptions," and whose "occupation policies laid a groundwork making it difficult for the Japanese to overcome [sic] its past in the early post-war years by providing immunity to the emperor, whose war responsibility was called into question by some in Japan."

2. Rose, "The Battle for Hearts and Minds," pp. 136–38.

3. Fujioka Nobukatsu, "*Kaiteiban atarashii rekishi kyōkasho* no shihan ni atatte," in Fujioka Nobukatsu et. al., *Atarashii rekishi kyōkasho*, revised commercial edition (Tokyo: Fusōsha, 2005), p. I. To further highlight the badge of legitimacy that the MOE bestowed upon this textbook's version of Japanese history when the MOE authorized it for publication and distribution to middle schools, Fujioka also appends excerpts from the 2003 MOE revised Course of Study for the subject of middle school history. See pp. II–IV.

4. Ibid., pp. 16–25.

5. Ibid., p. 30.

6. Ibid., p. 44.

7. Ibid.

8. Ibid., p. 199.

9. Ibid., p. 214.

10. Richard H. Minear, *Victors' Justice: The Tokyo War Crimes Trial* (Princeton, NJ: Princeton University Press, 1971); John W. Dower, *Embracing Defeat: Japan in the Wake of World War II* (New York: W. W. Norton and Company, 2000), especially chapter 15.

11. Fujioka et. al.., *Atarashii rekishi kyōkasho*, p. 215.

12. Ibid., p. 223.

13. Ibid., p. 225.

14. See Herbert P. Bix, *Hirohito and the Making of Modern Japan* (New York: Harper Perennial, 2001).

15. Ibid., p. 227.

16. Abe's early preoccupation as prime minister with revising the Fundamental Law was presaged in his book, *Toward a Beautiful Country* (*Utsukushii kuni e*), which devotes an entire chapter to "The Rebirth of Education." Abe's book was first published in July 2006, two months before he was named to that post. See Abe Shinzō, *Utsukushii kuni e* (Tokyo: Bunshun Shinsho, 2006).

17. Adam Lebowitz and David McNeill, "Hammering Down the Educational Nail: Abe Revises the Fundamental Law of Education," in *Japan Focus* (July 9, 2007).

18. Ibid.

19. Rose, "The Battle for Hearts and Minds," pp. 141–42. Rose notes that within a few months after these historians issued their appeal, it had attracted more than 800 other signatories.

20. Yōko Motani, "Hopes and Challenges for Progressive Educators in Japan: an Assessment of the 'Progressive Turn' in the 2002 Educational Reform," in *Comparative Education* 14:3 (August 2005), p. 310.

21. Ibid., p. 323.

Bibliography

SOURCES IN JAPANESE

Abe Shinzō, *Utsukushii kuni e*. Tokyo: Bunshun Shinsho, 2006.

Asada Kyōji. *Nihon shokuminchi kenkyū shiron*. Tokyo: Miraisha, 1990.

Asada Kyōji, ed., *"Teikoku Nihon" to Ajia*. Yoshikawa Hirofumi Kan, 1994.

Atarashii shakai. Tokyo: Tokyo Shoseki Kabushikigaisha, 2002.

Dai Nihon Gakujutsu Kyōkai, ed. *Nihon gendai kyōikugaku taikei*. Tokyo: Monasu, 1927.

Fujii Yūsuke. "Tōji no hihō: bunka kensetsu wa nanika?" Pp. 11-73 in *Dai Tōa kyōeiken no bunka kensetsu*, edited by Ikeda Hiroshi. Tokyo: Jimbun Shoin, 2007.

Fujioka Nobukatsu et. al. *Atarashii rekishi kyōkasho*. Revised commercial edition. Tokyo: Fusōsha, 2005.

Gotō Hirofumi, "Rika de kokusai rikai kyōiku ga dekiru no ka." Pp. 53–60 in *"Kokusai rikai kyōiku" mondai kaiketsu shirīzu 4: gakushū o meguru mondai ni dō kotaeru ka*, edited by Maki Masami, Itō Kazuhiko, and Takeda Shinichi. Tokyo: Tōyōkan Shuppansha, 1997.

Harada Minoru, "Kyōiku sekaika no genri." Pp. 141–48 in *Kokusai kyōiku no riron oyobi jissai*. Tokyo: Kokusai Kyōiku Kyōkai, 1923.

———. *Nihon no kyōiku o kangaeru*. Tokyo: Jinbun Shobō, 1929.

———. *Nihon kyōiku no shiteki shin shiya*. Tokyo: Meiji Tosho Kabushikigaisha, 1937.

———. *Shin taiseika no kyōshi*. Tokyo: Shōgakkan, 1941.

———. "Dai Tōa Kyōeiken no kyōiku seisaku." Pp. 211–36 in *Dai Tōa sensō to sekai*, edited by Sekai Seiji Kenkyūkai. Tokyo: Chūō Kōronsha, 1944.

Hiroshima heiwa bunka sentā, ed., *Heiwa jiten*. Tokyo: Keisō Shobo, 1985, 1991.

Hiroshima ken kyōshokuin kumiai kyōgikai, ed. *Dare no tame no "Hinomaru, Kimigayo"? Sono uso to oshitsuke*. Tokyo: Meiseki Tosho, 1999.

Hiroshima Kōtō Shihan Gakkō Fuzoku Shōgakkō, Gakkō Kyōiku Kenkyūkai, ed. *Kōa Nihon no kyōiku*. Tokyo: Kabushikigaisha Jitsubunkan, 1940.

Horinouchi Tsuneo. "Kōa Nihon no shūshin kyōiku." Pp. 179–89 in *Kōa Nihon no kyōiku*, edited by Hiroshima Kōtō Shihan Gakkō Fuzoku Shōgakkō, Gakkō Kyōiku Kenkyūkai. Tokyo: Kabushikigaisha Jitsubunkan, 1940.

Ikeda Hiroshi, ed. *Dai Tōa kyōeiken no bunka kensetsu.* Tokyo: Jimbun Shoin, 2007.

Ikeda Susumu and Motoyama Yukihiko, eds. *Taishō no Kyōiku.* Tokyo: Dai Ippō Ki Shuppan Kabushikigaisha, 1978.

Ikeoka Naotaka. *Chūtō kōmin kyōkasho.* Tokyo: Kōdōkan, 1926.

Inoue Tetsujirō. "Kokumin dōtoku to kokusai kyōiku." Pp. 53–73 in *Kokusai kyōiku no riron oyobi jissai.* Tokyo: Kokusai Kyōiku Kyōkai, 1923.

Ishizuki Minoru. "Kokuminshugi to jiyūshugi," in *Meiji kyōiku yoron no kenkyū*, Vol. 1, edited by Motoyama Yukihiko. Tokyo: Fukumura Shuppan Kabushikigaisha, 1972.

Itō Akihiro, Kitamura Kazuyuki and Ebuchi Kazuhiro. "Nihon ni okeru kokusaika shisō to sono keifu." Pp. 9–74 in *Nihonjin no kokusaika: 'chikyū shimin' no jōken o saguru*, edited by Sawada Akio and Kadowaki Kōji. Tokyo: Nihon Keizai Shinbunsha, 1990.

Izumi Tetsu, "Rikken kokumin to kokusai kyōiku." Pp. 37–47 in *Kokusai kyōiku no riron oyobi jissai.* Tokyo: Kokusai Kyōiku Kyōkai, 1923.

Kaigo Tokiomi, ed. *Atarashii Shakai.* Tokyo: Tokyo Shoseki Kabushikigaisha, 1958, 1968.

Kato Ichirō et. al., *Shōgakkō shakai.* Tokyo: Gakkō Tosho Kabushikigaisha, 1992.

Kindai Nihon Kyōiku Seidō Shiryō Hensankai, ed. *Kindai Nihon kyōiku seido shiryō.* Tokyo: Dai Nihon Yūbenkai Kōdansha, 1956.

Kobayashi Motoko. "Zuga kosakuka o toshite kokusai rikai." Pp. 64–68 in *"Kokusai rikai kyōiku" mondai kaiketsu shirīzu 4: gakushū o meguru mondai ni dō kotaeru ka*, edited by Maki Masami, Itō Kazuhiko, and Takeda Shinichi. Tokyo: Tōyōkan Shuppansha, 1997.

Kobayashi Nobuo and Asakura Ryūtarō, eds. *Kaisei shōgakkō gakushū shidō yōryō no tenkai: shakai hen.* Tokyo: Meiji Tosho Shuppan Kabushikigaisha, 1977.

Kōdansha no ehon (February 1, 1940–June 5, 1941). Tokyo: Kōdansha.

Kokutai no hongi. Reprinted in *Kindai Nihon kyōiku seido shiryō*, Vol. 7, edited by Kindai Nihon Kyōiku Seido Shiryō Hensankai. Tokyo: Dai Nihon Yūbenkai Kōdansha, 1956.

Komine Kazuo. "Kaikokuki ni okeru kaigai shokuminron." Pp. 34–53 in *"Teikoku Nihon" to Ajia*, edited by Asada Kyōji. Yoshikawa Hirofumi Kan, 1994.

Koyama Kenzō. "Jitsugyō kyōiku zōkan." *Jitsugyō sekai Taiheiyō* 2:1 (January 1, 1904), 8–9.

Kyōiku kaikaku ni kansuru tōshin. Tokyo: Ōkurashō Insatsukyoku, 1988.

Kyōiku no seiki 1, no. 1 (October 1923).

Maki Masami, Itō Kazuhiko, and Takeda Shinichi, eds. *"Kokusai rikai kyōiku" mondai kaiketsu shirīzu 4: gakushū o meguru mondai ni dō kotaeru ka.* Tokyo: Tōyōkan Shuppansha, 1997.

Miura Kenji, ed. *Shōgakkō kokusai rikai kyōiku no susumekata: atarashii gakuryokukan o fumaete.* Tokyo: Kyōiku Shuppan, Kabushikigaisha, 1994.

Miyata Setsuko, "Tennōsei kyōiku to kōminka seisaku." Pp. 152–72 in *"Teikoku Nihon" to Ajia*, edited by Asada Kyōji. Yoshikawa Hirofumi Kan, 1994.

Monbukagakushō. *Shōgakkō gakushū shidō yōryō*. Tokyo: Kokuristu Insatsu Kyoku, 1998; partially revised 2003.

———. *Shōgakkō gakushū shidō yōryō kaisetsu: sōsoku hen* (Tokyo: Tokyo Shoseki Kabushikigaisha, 1999; partially revised 2004.

———. *Nijūisseiki no kyōiku kaikaku: Monbukagaku hakusho*. Tokyo: Zaimushō, 2001.

Monbushō. *Jinjō Shōgaku Shūshinsho*. Tokyo: 1922.

———. *Yoi kodomo*. Tokyo: Nihon Shoseki Kabushikigaisha, 1941.

———. *Shotōka rekishi*. Tokyo: Tokyo Shoseki Kabushikigaisha, 1943.

———. *Shotōka shūshin*. Tokyo: Nihon Shoseki Kabushikigaisha, 1943.

———. *Shōgakkō gakushū shidō yōryō*. Tokyo: Teikoku Chihō Gyōsei Gakkai, 1958, 1968, 1989.

———. *Shōgakkō gakushū shidō yōryō kaisetsu: shakai hen*. Osaka: Nihon Bunkyō Shuppan Kabushikigaisha, 1999.

Monbushō Futsugakumukyoku, ed. *Kokusai kyōiku*. Tokyo: 1925.

Monbushō Jitsugyō Gakumukyoku, ed. *Ishokumin kyōiku*. Tokyo: Monbushō, 1929.

Morita Toshio. *Rinkyōshin to Nihonjin, Nihon bunkaron*. Tokyo: Shin Nihon Shuppansha, 1988.

Motoyama Yukihiko. *Kindai Nihon no seiji to kyōiku*. Kyoto: Mineruba Shobō, 1972.

———. ed. *Meiji kyōiku yoron no kenkyū*, Vol. 1. Tokyo: Fukumura Shuppan Kabushikigaisha, 1972.

———. "Meiji kokka no kyōiku shisō: Taishō kyōiku to no kanren o chūshin ni." Pp. 39–162 in *Taishō no Kyōiku*, edited by Ikeda Susumu and Motoyama Yukihiko. Tokyo: Dai Ippō Ki Shuppan Kabushikigaisha, 1978.

Nagahara Keiji and Maruki Masaomi, eds. *Shōgakkō shakai*. Tokyo: Gakkō Tosho Kabushikigaisha, 1979.

Nakano Akira. *Kyōiku kenkyū chosaku senshū 3: Senkanki kyōiku e no shiteki sekkin*. Tokyo: EXP, 2000.

———. *Taishō demokurashi to kyōiku: 1920 nendai no kyōiku*. Tokyo: Shin Hyōron, 1977, 1990.

Nakauchi Toshio, Tajima Hajime and Hashimoto Noriko, eds. *Kyōiku no Seikisha no sōgōteki kenkyū*. Tokyo: Ikkōsha, 1984.

Nitta Takayo. *Sawayanagi Masatarō: sono shōgai to gyōseki*. Tokyo: Seijō Gakuen Sawayanagi Kenkyū kai, 1971.

Noguchi Entarō. "Jo." In *Kokusai kyōiku no riron oyobi jissai*. Tokyo: Kokusai Kyōiku Kyōkai, 1923.

———. "Kokusai kyōiku kaigi oyobi sono mokuteki." Pp. 309–27 in *Kokusai kyōiku no riron oyobi jissai*. Tokyo: Kokusai Kyōiku Kyōkai, 1923.

———. *Mazu kyōiku o kakushin seyo: Nihon kokumin ni tsugu*. Tokyo: Heibonsha, 1938.

Nozawa Masako, "Sekaishugi." Pp. 175–217 in *Meiji kyōiku yoron no kenkyū*, Vol. 1, edited by Motoyama Yukihiko. Tokyo: Fukumura Shuppan Kabushikigaisha, 1972.

Obara Kunio and Kobayashi Kenzō. *Sawayanagi kyōiku: sono shōgai to shisō.* Tamagawa Daigaku, 1963.

Ōi Yoshio. *Nihon no "shin kyōiku" shisō: Noguchi Entarō o chūshin ni.* Tokyo: Keisō Shobō, 1984.

Okuda Shinjo. "Jo: Hassō no tenkan o kitai suru." P. 3 in *Kaisei shōgakkō gakushū shidō yōryō no tenkai: shakai hen*, edited by Kobayashi Nobuo and Asakura Ryūtarō. Tokyo: Meiji Tosho Shuppan Kabushikigaisha, 1977.

——— and Nagaoka Jun, eds. *Shin gakkō kyōiku zenshū 6: Kokusaika to gakkō kyōiku.* Tokyo: Gyōsei, 1995.

Ōta T. and Nakauchi Toshio, eds. *Minkan kyōiku shi kenkyū jiten.* Tokyo: Hyōronsha, 1975.

Ōtsuki Takeshi and Matsumura Kenichi. *Aikokushin kyōiku no shiteki kyūmei.* Tokyo: Aoki Shoten, 1970.

Ōyamada Jō, Watabe Yaeko, Kobayashi Kenji, and Komatsuzawa Masato, eds. *Ningen o kangaeru atarashii shakaika no jugyō 5: "Kokusaika, jōhōka shakai de no ikikata" o manabu.* Tokyo: Toyokan Shuppansha, 1994.

Ozawa Yūsaku. "Sawayanagi Masatarō no shokuminchi kyōiku kan." Pp. 192–233 in *Sawayanagi Masatarō zenshū bekkan.* Tokyo: Kokudosha, 1979.

Saitō Gunbei, ed. *"Sōgōteki na gakushū" no jissen" No. 3: Kokusai rikai kyōiku no kangaekata, susumekata.* Tokyo: Kyōiku Kaihatsu Kenkyūjo, 1997.

Satō Shigeki. "Nēshon, nashonarizumu, esunishitei." *Shisō* 854 (1995): 103–27.

Satō Tokuichi. "Kōa Nihon no kokugo kyōiku," Pp. 190–97 in *Kōa Nihon no kyōiku*, edited by Hiroshima Kōtō Shihan Gakkō Fuzoku Shōgakkō, Gakkō Kyōiku Kenkyūkai. Tokyo: Kabushikigaisha Jitsubunkan, 1940.

Sawada Akio and Kadowaki Kōji, eds. *Nihonjin no kokusaika: 'chikyū shimin' no jōken o saguru.* Tokyo: Nihon Keizai Shinbunsha, 1990.

Sawayanagi Masatarō. *Chūgaku shūshinsho.* Tokyo: Dobunkan, 1909.

———. *Kaitei chūgaku shūshinsho.* Tokyo: Dobunkan, 1923.

———. *Ajia shugi.* Tokyo: Daitōkaku, 1919.

———. "Sekai no taisei to kokusai kyōiku." Pp. 5–8 in *Kokusai kyōiku no riron oyobi jissai.* Tokyo: Kokusai Kyōiku Kyōkai, 1923.

Sawayanagi Masatarō zenshū. Vols. 8–9. Tokyo: Kokudosha, 1976–1977.

Sekai Seiji Kenkyūkai, ed. *Dai Tōa sensō to sekai.* Tokyo: Chūō Kōronsha, 1944.

Sekai no Nihon 1:1–15 (July 25, 1896–May 1, 1897).

Shimomura Tetsuo, ed. *Kokumin gakkō sōgō zasshi "Nihon kyōiku."* Tokyo: Emutei Shuppan, 1991.

Shimonaka Yasaburō. *Kyōiku saizō.* Tokyo: Keimeikai, 1920.

———. "Zenjinrui ai ni tettei seyo: hirakaruru kokusai kyōiku kaigi no sho mondai." Pp. 173–88 in *Kokusai kyōiku no riron oyobi jissai.* Tokyo: Kokusai Kyōiku Kyōkai, 1923.

———. "Dai Tōa kyōeiken seiji taiseiron." In *Nihon kyōiku.* Kokumin Kyōiku Tosho Kabushikigaisha (July 1942). Reprinted in Shimomura Tetsuo, ed. *Kokumin gakkō sōgō zasshi "Nihon kyōiku,"* Vol. 2, 22–32. Tokyo: Emutei Shuppan, 1991.

———. "Ajia minzoku no sho mondai." In *Nihon kyōiku.* Kokumin Kyōiku Tosho Kabushikigaisha (February 1943). Reprinted in Shimomura Tetsuo, ed. *Kokumin gakkō sōgō zasshi "Nihon kyōiku,"* Vol. 4, 16–21. Tokyo: Emutei Shuppan, 1991.

———. *Shisōsen o kataru.* Tokyo: Izumi Shobō, 1944.

Shimonaka Yasaburō Den Kankōkai, ed. *Shimonaka Yasaburō jiten.* Tokyo: Heibonsha, 1965.

Shinmi Yoshiharu. "Kokka, kokumin, minzoku to kyōiku." Pp. 20–23 in *Kōa Nihon no kyōiku*, edited by Hiroshima Kōtō Shihan Gakkō Fuzoku Shōgakkō, Gakkō Kyōiku Kenkyūkai. Tokyo: Kabushikigaisha Jitsubunkan, 1940.

Shinmin no michi. Reprinted in *Kindai Nihon kyōiku seidō shiryō*, Vol. 7, edited by Kindai Nihon Kyōiku Seidō Shiryō Hensankai. Tokyo: Dai Nihon Yūbenkai Kōdansha, 1956.

Shiomi Toshitaka, Nagahara Keiji and Maruki Masaomi, eds. *Shōgakkō shakai.* Tokyo: Gakkō Tosho Kabushikigaisha, 1976.

Tada Takashi. *Gakkō ni okeru kokusai rikai kyōiku: gurōbaru maindo o sodateru.* Tokyo: Tōyōkan Shuppansha, 1997.

Teikoku Kyōiku 68–77 (August 1920-February 1922).

Toda Teizō. *Shinsei chūgaku kōmin kyōkasho.* Tokyo: Chūtō Gakkō Kyōkasho Kabushikigaisha, 1937, 1943.

Tsubouchi Hirokiyo. *Kokumin gakkō no kodomotachi: senjika no 'kami no kuni' kyōiku.* Tokyo: Sairyūsha, 2003.

Yamagata Tōkon. "Shinajin zakkyo mondai." Pp. 9–16 in *Chūō Kōron* (July 1899).

Yamashina Saburō. *21 seiki o ikiru Nihonjin to wa: shin gakushū shidō yōryō o yomu.* Tokyo: Gakushū no Tomo Sha, 1989.

Yamazaki Yūji. "Dai ichiji taisengo ni okeru 'kokusai kyōiku undō' no seiritsu to tenkai: Taishōki kyōiku kaizō undō no kokusaishugiteki sokumen." Pp. 71–97 in *Kyōiku kenkyū* 30 (March 1986). Tokyo: Aoyama Gakuin Daigaku Kyōiku Gakkai.

Yumoto Genichi. *Shinsei kōmin kyōhon, toshi yō.* Tokyo: Tokyo Kaiseikan, 1926.

Zenkoku kaigai shijo kyōiku, kokusai rikai kyōiku kenkyū kyōgikai, ed. *Chiiki ni nezashita kokusai rikai kyōiku jissen jirei shū.* Tokyo: Daiichi Hōki Shuppan Kabushikigaisha, 1993.

www.aim25.ac.uk/cgi-bin/search2?coll_id=2282&inst_id=5 (7 August 2008).

www.yasukuni.or.jp/english/ (6 August 2008).

SOURCES IN ENGLISH

Abel, Jessamyn Reich. "Warring Internationalisms: Multilateral Thinking in Japan, 1933–1964." PhD dissertation. Columbia University, 2004.

Akami, Tomoko. *Internationalizing the Pacific: The United States, Japan and the Institute of Pacific Relations in War and Peace, 1919–1945.* London and New York: Routledge, 2002.

Anderson, Benedict. *Imagined Communities: Reflections on the Origin and Spread of Nationalism.* London: Verso, 1983, 1991.

Annals of America, Vol. 12: *1895-1904, Populism, Imperialism, and Reform.* Chicago: Encyclopaedia Britannica, Inc., 1968.

Apple, Michael W. *Education and Power.* Boston: Ark Paperbacks, 1982, 1985.

Aspinall, Robert W. *Teachers' Unions and the Politics of Education in Japan*. Albany: State University of New York Press, 2001.

Bamba, Nobuya and John F. Howes, eds. *Pacifism in Japan: The Christian and Socialist Tradition*. Kyoto: Mineruba Shobō, 1978.

Bauman, Zygmunt. "Modernity and Ambivalence." Pp. 143–69 in *Global Culture: Nationalism, Globalization and Modernity*, edited by Mike Featherstone. London: Sage Publications, 1990.

Beasley, W. G. *Japan Encounters the Barbarian: Japanese Travellers in America and Europe*. New Haven, CT: Yale University Press, 1995.

Beauchamp, Edward R. "Education." Pp. 225–51 in *Democracy in Japan*, edited by Takeshi Ishida and Ellis S. Krauss. Pittsburgh, PA: University of Pittsburgh Press, 1988.

———. "The Development of Japanese Educational Policy, 1945–1985." Pp. 27–50 in *Windows on Japanese Education*, edited by Edward R. Beauchamp. Westport, CT: Greenwood Press, 1991.

Befu, Harumi. "The Internationalization of Japan and Bunkaron." Pp. ?? in *The Challenge of Japan's Internationalization: Organization and Culture*, edited by Hiroshi Mannari and Harumi Befu. Tokyo: Kwansei Gakuin University and Kodansha International, 1983.

———. ed. *Windows on Japanese Education*. Westport, CT: Greenwood Press, 1991.

Betts, Raymond F. *Uncertain Dimensions: Western Overseas Empires in the Twentieth Century*. Minneapolis: University of Minnesota Press, 1985.

Bix, Herbert P. *Hirohito and the Making of Modern Japan*. New York: Harper Perennial, 2001.

Borg, Dorothy and Shumpei Okamoto, eds. *Pearl Harbor as History: Japanese-American Relations, 1931–1941*. New York: Columbia University Press, 1973.

Brooks, Barbara J. *Japan's Imperial Diplomacy: Consuls, Treaty Ports, and War in China*. Honolulu: University of Hawai'i Press, 2000.

Burkman, Thomas W. "Nationalist Actors in the Internationalist Theatre: Nitobe Inazō and Ishii Kikujirō and the League of Nations." Pp. 89–113 in *Nationalism and Internationalism in Imperial Japan: Autonomy, Asian Brotherhood, or World Citizenship?* edited by Dick Stegewerns. London and New York: Routledge Curzon, 2003.

Caprio, Mark E. and Yoneyuki Sugita, eds., *Democracy in Occupied Japan: The U.S. Occupation and Japanese Politics and Society*. London and New York: Routledge, 2007.

Central Council on Education. "The Model for Japanese Education in the Perspective of the 21st Century." Tokyo: Ministry of Education, Sports and Culture, July 1996.

Ching, Leo T. S. *Becoming "Japanese": Colonial Taiwan and the Politics of Identity Formation*. Berkeley: University of California Press, 2001.

Condliffe, J. B., ed. *Problems of the Pacific: Proceedings of the Second Conference of the Institute of Pacific Relations, Honolulu, Hawaii, July 15 to 29, 1927*. Chicago: The University of Chicago Press, 1928.

Cummings, William. *Education and Equality in Japan*. Princeton, NJ: Princeton University Press, 1980.

Daniels, Roger. *Coming to America: A History of Immigration and Ethnicity in American Life*. New York: Harper Collins Publishers, 1990.

Danly, Robert Lyons. *In the Shade of Spring Leaves: The Life and Writings of Higuchi Ichiyō, a Woman of Letters in Meiji Japan*. W. W. Norton & Company, 1981.

Dean, Arthur L. "Assimilation in Hawaii." Pp. 118–19 in *Institute of Pacific Relations: Honolulu Session*. Honolulu: Institute of Pacific Relations, 1925.

Dickinson, Frederick R. *War and National Reinvention: Japan and the Great War, 1914–1919*. Cambridge, MA: Harvard University Asia Center, 1999.

Doak, Kevin M. "Colonialism and Ethnic Nationalism in the Political Thought of Yanaihara Tadao (1893–1961)." *East Asian History* 10 (1995): 79–98.

———. "Nationalism as Dialectics: Ethnicity, Moralism, and the State in Early Twentieth-Century Japan." Pp. 174–96 in *Rude Awakenings: Zen, the Kyoto School & the Question of Nationalism*, edited by James W. Heisig and John C. Maraldo. Honolulu: University of Hawai'i Press, 1994–1995.

———. "Culture, Ethnicity, and the State in Early 20th Century Japan." Pp. 181–205 in *Japan's Competing Modernities: Issues in Culture and Democracy, 1900–1930*, edited by Sharon A. Minichiello. Honolulu: University of Hawai'i Press, 1998.

———. "Narrating China, Ordering East Asia: The Discourse on Nation and Ethnicity in Imperial Japan." Pp. 85–113 in *Constructing Nationhood in Modern East Asia*, edited by Kai-wing Chow, Kevin M. Doak, and Poshek Fu. Ann Arbor: The University of Michigan Press, 2001.

———. "Liberal Nationalism in Imperial Japan: The Dilemma of Nationalism and Internationalism." Pp. 17–41 in *Nationalism and Internationalism in Imperial Japan: Autonomy, Asian Brotherhood, or World Citizenship?* edited by Dick Stegewerns. London and New York: Routledge Curzon, 2003.

———. *A History of Nationalism in Modern Japan*. Leiden: Brill, 2007.

Dower, John W. "Triumphal and Tragic Narratives of the War in Asia." Pp. 37–51 in *Living with the Bomb: American and Japanese Cultural Conflicts in the Nuclear Age*, edited by Laura Hein and Mark Selden. Armonk, NY: M. E. Sharpe, 1997.

———. *Embracing Defeat: Japan in the Wake of World War II*: New York: W. W. Norton and Company, 2000.

Duke, Benjamin C. *Japan's Militant Teachers: A History of the Left-Wing Teachers Movement*. Honolulu: University Press of Hawaii, 1973.

———. ed. *Ten Great Educators of Modern Japan*. Tokyo: University of Tokyo Press, 1990.

Eskildsen, Robert. "'Leading the Natives to Civilization': The Colonial Dimension of the Taiwan Expedition." Harvard University, Edwin O. Reischauer Institute of Japanese Studies, *Occasional Papers in Japanese Studies*, Number 2003-01 (March 2003).

Fujitani, Takashi. *Splendid Monarchy: Power and Pageantry in Modern Japan*. Berkeley: University of California Press, 1998.

Gauntlett, John Owen, trans. *Kokutai no Hongi: Cardinal Principles of the National Entity of Japan*, edited by Robert King Hall. Cambridge, MA: Harvard University Press, 1949.

———. trans. *Kokutai no Hongi: Cardinal Principles of the National Entity of Japan*, reprint edition. Newton, MA: Crofton Publishing Company, 1974.

Gellner, Ernest. *Nations and Nationalism*. Oxford: Basil Blackwell, 1983.

Gluck, Carol. *Japan's Modern Myths: Ideology in the Late Meiji Period*. Princeton, NJ: Princeton University Press, 1985.

Goodman, Grant K. *Japan: The Dutch Experience*. London and Dover, NH: The Athlone Press, 1986.

Gordon, Andrew. *Labor and Imperial Democracy in Prewar Japan*. Berkeley: University of California Press, 1991.

Guthrie-Shimizu, Sayuri. "Occupation Policy and Postwar Sino-Japanese Relations: Severing Economic Ties." Pp. 200–219 in *Democracy in Occupied Japan: The U.S. Occupation and Japanese Politics and Society*, edited by Mark E. Caprio and Yoneyuki Sugita. London and New York: Routledge, 2007.

Hardacre, Helen. *Shintō and the State, 1868–1988*. Princeton, NJ: Princeton University Press, 1992.

———. ed. *New Directions in the Study of Meiji Japan*. Leiden: Brill, 1997.

Harootunian, Harry. "Memory, Mourning, and National Morality: Yasukuni Shrine and the Reunion of State and Religion in Postwar Japan." Pp. 144–60 in *Nation and Religion*, edited by Peter van der Veer and Hartmut Lehmann. Princeton, NJ: Princeton University Press, 1999.

Hein, Laura and Mark Selden. "The Lessons of War, Global Power, and Social Change." Pp. 3–51 in *Censoring History: Citizenship and Memory in Japan, Germany, and the United States*, edited by Laura Hein and Mark Selden. Armonk, NY: M. E. Sharpe, 2000.

———, eds. *Living with the Bomb: American and Japanese Cultural Conflicts in the Nuclear Age*. Armonk, NY: M. E. Sharpe, 1997.

———, eds. *Censoring History: Citizenship and Memory in Japan, Germany, and the United States*. Armonk, NY: M. E. Sharpe, 2000.

Heisig, James W. and John C. Maraldo, eds. *Rude Awakenings: Zen, the Kyoto School & the Question of Nationalism*. Honolulu: University of Hawai'i Press, 1994–1995.

Hobsbawm, E. J. *Nations and Nationalism Since 1780: Programme, Myth, Reality*. Cambridge: Cambridge University Press, 1990.

Hood, Christopher P. *Japanese Education Reform: Nakasone's Legacy*. London and New York: Routledge, 2001.

Horio, Teruhisa. *Educational Thought and Ideology in Modern Japan: State Authority and Intellectual Freedom*, edited and translated by Steven Platzer. Tokyo: University of Tokyo Press, 1988.

Hoshino, Aiko. "How Japan is Trying to Develop the International Mind in Her Young People." Typewritten text of speech delivered at the Institute of Pacific Relations Conference, Second Session, July 20, 1927. Seijō Gakuen Kyōiku Kenkyūjo, Item Number 110-006.

Hunter, Janet. *The Emergence of Modern Japan: An Introductory History Since 1853.* London: Longman, 1989.

Ienaga, Saburō. *The Pacific War, 1931–1945.* New York: Random House, 1978.

Inoue, Kyoko. *Individual Dignity in Modern Japanese Thought: The Evolution of the Concept of Jinkaku in Moral and Educational Discourse.* Ann Arbor: Center for Japanese Studies, University of Michigan, 2001.

Institute of Pacific Relations: Honolulu Session. Honolulu: Institute of Pacific Relations, 1925.

International Conciliation: Documents for the Year 1930. New York: Carnegie Endowment for International Peace, 1930.

Iriye, Akira. *Cultural Internationalism and World Order.* Baltimore: Johns Hopkins University Press, 1997.

Ishida, Takeshi and Ellis S. Krauss, eds. *Democracy in Japan.* Pittsburgh: University of Pittsburgh Press, 1988.

Jansen, Marius B. and Gilbert Rozman, eds. *Japan in Transition: From Tokugawa to Meiji.* Princeton: Princeton University Press, 1986.

Kai-wing Chow, Kevin M. Doak, and Poshek Fu, eds. *Constructing Nationhood in Modern East Asia.* Ann Arbor: The University of Michigan Press, 2001.

Keene, Donald. *The Japanese Discovery of Europe, 1720–1830.* Stanford: Stanford University Press, 1952, 1969.

Kinmonth, Earl H. *The Self-Made Man in Meiji Japanese Thought.* Berkeley: University of California Press, 1981.

Kondō, Takahiro. "Historical Issues in East Asian International Order from an Educational Perspective." *Educational Studies in Japan: International Yearbook,* No. 1 (December 2006), 37–48.

Kushner, Barak. *The Thought War: Japanese Imperial Propaganda.* Honolulu: The University of Hawai'i Press, 2006.

Lammers, D. N. "Taking Japan Seriously." Pp. 195–214 in *Asia in Western Fiction,* edited by Robin Winks and James Rush. Honolulu: University of Hawai'i Press, 1990.

Lawson, Konrad M. "The Persistence of Transnational Idealism in Early Postwar Japan, 1945–1949." Unpublished manucript.

LaFeber, Walter. *The Clash: U.S.-Japanese Relations Throughout History.* New York: W. W. Norton and Company, 1997.

Lebowitz, Adam and David McNeill. "Hammering Down the Educational Nail: Abe Revises the Fundamental Law of Education." *Japan Focus* (July 9, 2007).

Lee, Robert. "Service to Christ and Country: Uchimura's Search for Meaning." Pp. 71–99 in *Culture and Religion in Japanese-American Relations: Essays on Uchimura Kanzō, 1861–1930,* edited by Ray A. Moore. Ann Arbor: Center for Japanese Studies, University of Michigan, 1981.

Lincicome, Mark E. "Nationalism, Internationalization, and the Dilemma of Educational Reform in Japan." *Comparative Education Review* 37, no. 2 (May 1993): 123–51.

———. *Principle, Praxis, and the Politics of Educational Reform in Meiji Japan.* Honolulu: University of Hawai'i Press, 1995.

————. "Local Citizens or Loyal Subjects? Enlightenment Discourse and Educational Reform." Pp. 451–65 in *New Directions in the Study of Meiji Japan*, edited by Helen Hardacre. Leiden: Brill, 1997.

————. "Nationalism, Imperialism, and the International Education Movement in Early Twentieth-Century Japan." *Journal of Asian Studies* 58, no. 2 (May 1999), 338–60.

————. Review of *Moving Mountains: Japanese Education Reform. Journal of Asian Studies* 58, no. 4 (November 1999): 1153–154.

————. "Meiji Period." Pp. 129–35 in *Encyclopedia of Modern Asia*, vol. 4, edited by David Levinson and Karen Christensen. New York: Charles Scribner's Sons, 2002.

Lu, David, ed. *Japan: A Documentary History*. Armonk, New York: M. E. Sharpe, 1997.

McVeigh, Brian J. *Japanese Higher Education as Myth*. Armonk, NY: M. E. Sharpe, 2002.

Mannari, Hiroshi and Harumi Befu, eds. *The Challenge of Japan's Internationalization: Organization and Culture*. Tokyo: Kwansei Gakuin University and Kodansha International, 1983.

Marshall, Byron K. *Learning to be Modern: Japanese Political Discourse on Education*. Boulder, CO: Westview Press, 1994.

Masaoka, Naoichi, ed. *Japan's Message to America: A Symposium of Representative Japanese on Japan and American-Japanese Relations*. New York: G. P. Putnam's Sons, 1914.

Minear, Richard H. *Victors' Justice: The Tokyo War Crimes Trial*. Princeton, NJ: Princeton University Press, 1971.

Minichiello, Sharon A., ed. *Japan's Competing Modernities: Issues in Culture and Democracy, 1900–1930*. Honolulu: University of Hawai'i Press, 1998.

Ministry of Education Japan. *Basic Guidelines for the Reform of Education*. 1970, 1972.

Mizuuchi, Hiroshi. "Sawayanagi Masatarō." Pp. 149–65 in *Ten Great Educators of Modern Japan*, edited by Benjamin C. Duke. Tokyo: University of Tokyo Press, 1990.

Moore, Ray A., ed. *Culture and Religion in Japanese-American Relations: Essays on Uchimura Kanzō, 1861–1930*. Ann Arbor: Center for Japanese Studies, University of Michigan, 1981.

Motani, Yoko. "Hopes and Challenges for Progressive Educators in Japan: an Assessment of the 'Progressive Turn' in the 2002 Educational Reform." *Comparative Education* 14:3 (August 2005).

Motoyama, Yukihiko. *Proliferating Talent: Essays on Politics, Thought, and Education in the Meiji Era*, edited by J. S. A. Elisonas and Richard Rubinger. Honolulu: University of Hawai'i Press, 1997.

Munro, Paul. "Educational Deflation and Inflation. Pp. 43–50 in *Pacific Regional Conference of the World Federation of Education Associations*. Honolulu, 1932.

Nairn, Tom. "Internationalism and the Second Coming." *Daedalus* 22, no. 3 (1993): 155–70.

Nakano, Akira. "Shimonaka Yasaburō." Pp. 167–89 in *Ten Great Educators of Modern Japan*, edited by Benjamin C. Duke. Tokyo: University of Tokyo Press, 1990.

Nish, Ian. *Japan's Struggle with Internationalism: Japan, China and the League of Nations, 1931–1933*. London: Kegan Paul International, 1993.

Nozaki, Yoshiko. "Educational Reform and History Textbooks in Occupied Japan." Pp. 120–46 in *Democracy in Occupied Japan: The U.S. Occupation and Japanese Politics and Society*, edited by Mark E. Caprio and Yoneyuki Sugita. London and New York: Routledge, 2007.

Nozaki, Yoshiko and Inokuchi Hiromitsu. "Japanese Education, Nationalism, and Ienaga Saburō's Textbook Lawsuits." Pp. 99–126 in *Censoring History: Citizenship and Memory in Japan, Germany, and the United States*, edited by Laura Hein and Mark Selden, eds. Armonk, NY: M. E. Sharpe, 2000.

Ogata, Sadako. "The Role of Liberal Nongovernmental Organizations in Japan." Pp. 459–86 in *Pearl Harbor as History: Japanese-American Relations, 1931–1941*, edited by Daniel Borg and Shumpei Okamoto. New York: Columbia University Press, 1973.

Oka, Yoshitake. *Five Political Leaders of Modern Japan*, translated by Andrew Fraser and Patricia Murray. Tokyo: University of Tokyo Press, 1986.

Okano, Kaori and Motonori Tsuchiya. *Education in Contemporary Japan: Inequality and Diversity*. Cambridge, UK: Cambridge University Press, 1999.

Ōkuma, Shigenobu. "Our National Mission." Pp. 1–5 in *Japan's Message to America: A Symposium of Representative Japanese on Japan and American-Japanese Relations*, edited by Naoichi Masaoka. New York: G. P. Putnam's Sons, 1914.

Ōkuni Takamasa. "Bankoku Kōhō." Translated by John Breen. Pp. 233–47 in *Readings in Tokugawa Thought*, Second Edition, Select Papers, Vol. 9. Chicago: The Center for East Asian Studies, The University of Chicago, 1994.

Pacific Regional Conference of the World Federation of Education Associations. Honolulu, 1932.

Paine, S.C.M. *The Sino-Japanese War of 1894–1895: Perceptions, Power and Primacy*. Cambridge: Cambridge University Press, 2003.

Parkhurst, Helen. *Education on the Dalton Plan*. New York: E. P. Dutton & Company, 1922.

Passin, Herbert. *Society and Education in Japan*. New York: Teachers College, Columbia University, 1965.

Pierson, John D. *Tokutomi Sohō, 1863–1957: A Journalist for Modern Japan*. Princeton, NJ: Princeton University Press, 1980.

Platt, Brian. *Burning and Building: Schooling and State Formation in Japan, 1750–1890*. Cambridge, MA: Harvard University Asia Center, 2004.

Plomer, William. *Paper Houses*. New York: Coward-McCann, Inc., 1929.

Proceedings of the Second Biennial Conference. Augusta, ME: The World Federation of Education Associations, 1927.

Pyle, Kenneth B. *The New Generation in Meiji Japan: Problems of Cultural Identity, 1885–1895*. Stanford, CA: Stanford University Press, 1969.

———. "Meiji Conservatism." Pp. 674–720 in *Cambridge History of Japan*, Vol. 5. Cambridge: Cambridge University Press, 1989.

———. *The Making of Modern Japan*, 2nd ed. Lexington: D. C. Heath and Company, 1996.

Roesgaard, Marie H. *Moving Mountains: Japanese Education Reform*. Aarhus, Denmark: Aarhus University Press, 1998.

Rose, Caroline. "The Battle for Hearts and Minds: Patriotic Education in Japan in the 1990s and Beyond." Pp. 131–54 in *Nationalisms in Japan*, edited by Naoko Shimazu. London and New York: Routledge, 2006.

Rowell, Chester H. "The Kyoto Conference of the Institute of Pacific Relations." Pp. 233–80 in *International Conciliation: Documents for the Year 1930*. New York: Carnegie Endowment for International Peace, 1930.

Rubinger, Richard. "Education: From One Room to One System." Pp. 195–230 in *Japan in Transition: From Tokugawa to Meiji*, edited by Marius B. Jansen and Gilbert Rozman. Princeton, NJ: Princeton University Press, 1986.

Sawayanagi, Masatarō. "Some Suggestions for Internationalizing Education." Typewritten draft of speech dated July 7, 1925. Seijō Gakuen Kyōiku Kenkyūjo.

Schoppa, Leonard James. *Education Reform in Japan: A Case of Immobilist Politics*. London and New York: Routledge, 1991.

Selden, Mark. "Remembering 'The Good War': The Atomic Bombing and the Internment of Japanese-Americans in U.S. History Textbooks." *Japan Focus* (May 8, 2005). http://japanfocus.org/products/details/1943.

Shields, James J. Jr., ed. *Japanese Schooling: Patterns of Socialization, Equality, and Political Control*. University Park: Pennsylvania State University, 1990, 1993.

Shimahara, Nobuo. "Japanese Education Reforms in the 1980s: A Political Commitment." Pp. 270–81 in *Japanese Schooling: Patterns of Socialization, Equality, and Political Control*, edited by James J. Shields, Jr. University Park: Pennsylvania State University, 1990, 1993.

Shimazu, Naoko. *Japan, Race and Equality: The Racial Equality Proposal of 1919*. London: Routledge, 1998.

———, ed. *Nationalisms in Japan*. London and New York: Routledge, 2006.

Smith, Anthony. *National Identity*. Reno: University of Nevada Press, 1991.

Stegewerns, Dick. *Nationalism and Internationalism in Imperial Japan: Autonomy, Asian Brotherhood, or World Citizenship?* edited by Dick Stegewerns. London and New York: Routledge Curzon, 2003.

Stegewerns, Dick. "The Dilemma of Nationalism and Internationalism in Modern Japan: National Interest, Asian Brotherhood, International Cooperation or World Citizenship?" Pp. 3–16 in *Nationalism and Internationalism in Imperial Japan: Autonomy, Asian Brotherhood, or World Citizenship?* edited by Dick Stegewerns. London and New York: Routledge Curzon, 2003.

Stephanson, Anders. *Manifest Destiny: American Expansion and the Empire of Right*. New York: Hill and Wang, 1995.

Swale, Alistair. "Tokutomi Sohō and the Problem of the Nation-State in an Imperialist World." Pp. 68–88 in *Nationalism and Internationalism in Imperial Japan: Autonomy, Asian Brotherhood, or World Citizenship?* edited by Dick Stegewerns. London and New York: Routledge Curzon, 2003.

Takekoshi, Yosaburō. *Prince Saionji*, translated by Kozaki Nariaki. Kyoto: Ritsumei-kan University, 1932.

Tanaka, Stefan. *Japan's Orient: Rendering Pasts into History*. Berkeley: University of California Press, 1993.

Thomas, J. E. *Modern Japan: A Social History Since 1868*. London: Longman, 1996.

Thurston, Donald R. *Teachers and Politics in Japan*. Princeton, NJ: Princeton University Press, 1973.

Tsunoda, Ryūsaku, Wm. Theodore deBary and Donald Keene, eds. *Sources of Japanese Tradition*, Vol. 2. New York: Columbia University Press, 1958.

Tsurumi, E. Patricia. *Japanese Colonial Education in Taiwan, 1895–1945*. Cambridge, MA: Harvard University Press, 1977.

van der Veer, Peter, and Hartmut Lehmann, eds. *Nation and Religion*. Princeton, NJ: Princeton University Press, 1999.

Verdery, Katherine. "Whither 'Nation' and 'Nationalism'?" *Daedalus* 22, no. 3 (Summer 1993): 37–46.

Vlastos, Stephen, ed. *Mirror of Modernity: Invented Traditions of Modern Japan*. Berkeley: University of California Press, 1998.

Wilbur, Ray Lyman. "An Interpretation of America in Pacific Relations." Pp. 55–61 in *Problems of the Pacific: Proceedings of the Second Conference of the Institute of Pacific Relations, Honolulu, Hawaii, July 15 to 29, 1927*, edited by J. B. Condliffe. Chicago: The University of Chicago Press, 1928.

Wiley, Peter Booth. *Yankees in the Land of the Gods: Commodore Perry and the Opening of Japan*. New York: Penguin Books, 1990.

Winks, Robin and James Rush, eds. *Asia in Western Fiction*. Honolulu: University of Hawai'i Press, 1990.

World-Wide Education for Peace: Report of the World Conference on Education, Held in San Francisco, June 28–July 5, 1923. Educational Series, Pamphlet III. Washington, DC: National Council for the Prevention of War.

Index

liberal internationalism, xxv–xxvii, 95, 98, 102, 110, 115, 119
liberalism (*jiyūshugi*), 12, 65, 91, 111

MacArthur, Douglas, 165
Maekawa Report (1986), 141
Mamiya, Rinzō, 107
Manchukuo. *See* Manchuria
Manchuria, 89, 103–04, 108, 136, 164; Japanese occupation of, 9, 92, 106, 131, 137
Manchurian Incident (1931), xix, xxvi, 6, 95, 97–98, 101, 104, 110–11, 131, 137, 146, 157n64
Marshall, Byron, 119
Matsuoka, Yōsuke, 95
McNeill, David, 166–67
Meiji Renovation (*Meiji ishin*), xxi, 6–7, 25n18, 82, 98, 103, 124, 127, 130–31, 146
Meiji Restoration. *See* Meiji Renovation
militarism (*gunkokushugi*), 38, 131
military-style physical training (*heishiki taisō*), 4, 137
Minear, Richard, 164
Ministry of Education (MOE), xxii–xxiii, 22–23, 34–37, 85, 119, 160, 167–68; and Ad Hoc Council on Education (Rinji Kyōiku Shingikai), xvi, 139, 142–43, 149; Committee to Investigate the Problem of Student Thought (Gakusei Shisō Mondai Chōsa Iinkai), 101; Course of Study Guide (*gakushū shidō yōryō*), xxvii, 120–21, 153–54; Course of Study Guide 1958 edition, 123–30; Course of Study Guide 1968 edition, 129–30, 133; Course of Study Guide 1977–78 edition, 129, 132–34, 138, 141; Course of Study Guide 1989 edition, 143–45, 152; Course of Study Guide 1998 edition, 143–45, 147, 161; Course of Study Guide 2003 edition, 161, 169n3; Course of Study Outline

(Kyōsoku Taikō), 18; emigration education symposium (1929), 88–91, 101; international education symposium (1924), 87–88, 149; policy on national anthem and national flag, xiii–xiv; Sawayanagi Masatarō and, 35–36; and textbook production, 87, 105–06, 110, 120–22, 129, 132, 134–35, 137, 143, 146, 155n15, 161
Ministry of Foreign Affairs, 89
Minobe, Tatsukichi, 31, 157n64
minzoku (ethnic nation), 14, 49, 51, 61, 76n48, 84, 94, 96, 102–03, 117, 163
minzokushugi (ethnic nationalism), 38–39, 46, 102
Miura, Tōsaku, 36
Miyake, Setsurei, 17–18, 21
Monbushō. *See* Ministry of Education
Montessori, Maria, 24n3, 34, 75n42
Morioka, Tsunezō, 87
Morita, Tatsuo, 141–42
Moriya, Shigeo, 89
Morse, Edward S., 135
Motani, Yōko, 168
Motoyama, Yukihiko, 17–18
movement for freedom and popular rights, 11, 17, 32
Munro, Paul, 99–100

Nabeyama, Sadachika, 96
Nagasaki, 129, 164
Nagata, Chū, 90–91
Nairn, Tom, 5
Nakamura, Yoshinori, 89
Nakano, Akira, 23
Nakasone, Yasuhiro, 122, 143, 159; and Ad Hoc Council on Education, xiv, 115, 120, 123, 129, 133, 139–40, 142, 144; and "healthy nationalism," xiv–xx, xxiii, 138, 166
Nanjing massacre, xxiii, 120, 145–46, 160, 163–64
Nanyō. *See* South Seas
national polity. *See kokutai*

About the Author

Mark Lincicome is Associate Professor of History and Director of the Study Abroad Program at the College of the Holy Cross in Worcester, Massachusetts. Previously he served as Associate Director of the Asian Studies Program at the University of Pittsburgh, and as Executive Director of the Japan America Society of Chicago. A graduate of Bowdoin College (BA) and the University of Chicago (MA, PhD), he has conducted funded research at various Japanese universities and worked in the Japanese public school system during more than eight years of residence in Japan. He is the author of *Principle, Praxis, and the Politics of Educational Reform in Meiji Japan* (University of Hawai'i Press, 1995) along with articles on modern Japanese history, Japanese education, and globalization in the Asia-Pacific. Presently he is conducting research that compares Japanese and Australian perceptions of themselves as nations situated on Asia's geographical and cultural periphery.